BALTIC
PHRASEBOOK

Eva Aras, Inna Feldbach
Jana Teteris & Alan Trei

Baltic phrasebook
2nd edition – June 2001

Published by
Lonely Planet Publications Pty Ltd ABN 36 005 607 983
90 Maribyrnong St, Footscray, Victoria 3011, Australia

Lonely Planet Offices
Australia Locked Bag 1, Footscray, Victoria 3011
USA 150 Linden St, Oakland CA 94607
UK 10a Spring Place, London NW5 3BH
France 1 rue du Dahomey, 75011 Paris

Cover illustration
Leggy Lavinia Loves to Lope around Latvia by Patrick Marris

ISBN 1 86450 369 6

text © Lonely Planet Publications 2001
cover illustration © Lonely Planet 2001

Printed by Colorcraft Ltd, Hong Kong

About the Authors

This revised edition of the Estonian chapter with transliterations was prepared by Alan Trei, a marketing consultant and literary translator of Estonian origin living in Northampton, Massachusetts, working with Inna Feldbach. The Estonian section in the first edition was written by Lisa Trei, then a correspondent for the Wall Street Journal and a Fulbright Scholar at Tartu University in Estonia, assisted by Inna Feldbach, a governmental and literary translator.

Jana Teteris, author of the Latvian chapter, was born and brought up as a Latvian in the UK. She lived and worked in Latvia from the late 1980s to 1992 and then again from 1994 to 1998, when she returned to London. She now works at the Institute of Linguists and continues to do some translating and interpreting on a freelance basis.

Eva Aras updated the Lithuanian section based on the the first edition written by Paul Jokubaitis. Originally a teacher of French and German, then a university librarian, Eva now teaches Lithuanian at the Victorian School of Languages in Melbourne. She also translates between Lithuanian and English and does on-site and telephone interpreting for various agencies and government bodies. All these activities help to keep her well in touch with the language of her birth, despite spending most of her life in an English-speaking environment.

From the Authors

Jana Teteris would like to thank her mother and friends in Latvia for their assistance in re-writing the Latvian chapter. She is especially indebted to Judith Gill who managed to find the time in the run-up to her wedding to proofread the transliterations.

Eva Aras would like to thank her son Danielius for his technical assistance and also for some helpful language suggestions.

From the Publisher

This book was coordinated by Peter D'Onghia and Ingrid Seebus. Karin Vidstrup Monk and Karina Coates supervised. The book was edited with flair by Emma Koch and meticulously proofread by Lou Callan. The splendiferous illustrations were done by Patrick Marris, who also laid out the book, and Fabrice Rocher supervised layout. Natasha Velleley drew the map.

CONTENTS

LITHUANIAN 185

INTRODUCTION

The three Baltic countries, Latvia, Lithuania and Estonia, have been occupied by various powers throughout the centuries. During this time, and especially during Soviet occupation after World War II, when Russian was the official language of each of the three countries, language played a key role in maintaining national identity.

After their successful and remarkably peaceful individual bids for independence in 1991, Latvia, Lithuania and Estonia have become inextricably linked in many people's minds. However, you may be surprised to learn that the Latvian, Lithuanian and Estonian languages are not all related to one other. Estonian is a Finno-Ugric language, closely related to Finnish and more distantly to Hungarian. Estonian and Finnish are mutually intelligible and share a large proportion of their respective vocabularies. Latvian and Lithuanian belong to the Baltic branch of the Indo-European language tree and are the only surviving spoken Baltic languages. However, in spite of their close relationship, the two are not mutually intelligible.

This book will enable you to make the most of these exciting and dynamic countries. English is spoken in the cities, but if you learn at least a few phrases in the local language you'll find that you're more than rewarded for your efforts.

TRANSLITERATIONS
Simplified transliterations have been provided in pink throughout this book. Italic is used to indicate where to place stress in a word.

INTRODUCTION

POLITE FORMS

When a language has polite and informal forms of the singular pronoun 'you', the polite form has been used in most cases. However, you will come across the informal form of 'you' in some phrases, such as those for talking with children.

ARTHUR OR MARTHA?

When there are both feminine and masculine forms of a word, it's indicated in either of two ways, with the feminine form always appearing first:

- with a slash separating the feminine and masculine endings of a word:

  eg, hungry   **ish-*ahl-k*-usi/-as**   *išalkusi/ęs* (f/m)

- when the distinction between masculine and feminine is more complex, each word is given in full, separated with a slash:

  eg, married   **ish-tak-*eh*-yu-si/*vad*-as**   *ištekėjus/vedęs* (f/m)

ABBREVIATIONS USED IN THIS BOOK

f	feminine	n	noun
inf	informal	pl	plural
lit	literally	pol	polite
m	masculine	sg	singular

Map 9

INTRODUCTION

ESTONIAN, LATVIAN & LITHUANIAN

FINLAND

Gulf of Finland

TALLINN

Narva

Kohtla-Järve

ESTONIA

Hiiumaa

RUSSIAN FEDERATION

Lake Peipus

Saaremaa

Pärnu

Tartu

Baltic Sea

Gulf of Riga

Ventspils

Sigulda

RĪGA

LATVIA

Rēzekne

Daugava

Liepāja

Daugavpils

Palanga

Šiauliai

Panevėžys

Klaipēda

LITHUANIA

Nemunas

Kaunas

BELARUS

VILNIUS

RUSSIAN FEDERATION

Alytus

Estonian
Latvian
Lithuanian

PO AND

0   50   100 km
0   30   60 mi

HOW TO USE THIS PHRASEBOOK
You *Can* Speak Another Language

Anyone can speak another language. Don't worry if you haven't studied languages before, or that you studied a language at school for years and can't remember any of it. It doesn't even matter if you failed English grammar. After all, that's never affected your ability to speak English! And this is the key to picking up a language in another country. You don't need to sit down and memorise endless grammatical details and you don't need to memorise long lists of vocabulary. You just need to start speaking.

Once you start, you'll be amazed how many prompts you'll get to help you build on those first words. You'll hear people speaking, pick up sounds from TV, catch a word or two that you think you know from the local radio, see something on a billboard – all these things help to build your understanding.

Plunge In

There's just one thing you need to start speaking another language – courage. Your biggest hurdle is overcoming the fear of saying aloud what may seem to you to be just a bunch of sounds. There are a number of ways to do this.

The best way to start overcoming your fear is to memorise a few key words. These are the words you know you'll be saying again and again, such as 'hello', 'thank you' and 'How much?'. Here's an important hint though: right from the beginning, learn at least one phrase that will be useful but not essential. Such as 'See you later' or even a conversational piece like 'It's nice today, isn't it?' (people everywhere love to talk about the weather). Having this extra phrase (just start with one, if you like, and learn to say it really well) will enable you to move away from the basics, and when you get a reply and a smile, it'll also boost your confidence. You'll find that people you speak to will like it too, as they'll understand that at least you've tried to learn more of the language than just the usual essential words.

INTRODUCTION

Ways to Remember

There are several ways to learn a language. Most people find they
learn from a variety of these, although people usually have a preferred way to remember. Some like to see the written word and
remember the sound from what they see. Some like to just hear it
spoken in context (if this is you, try talking to yourself in the
foreign language, but do it at home or somewhere private, to give
yourself confidence, and so others don't wonder about your san-
ity!). Others, especially the more mathematically inclined, like to
analyse the grammar of a language, and piece together words according to the rules of grammar. The very visually inclined like to
associate the written word and even sounds with some visual
stimulus such as illustrations, TV and general things they see in
the street. As you learn, you'll discover what works best for you
– be aware of what made you really remember a particular word,
and if it sticks in your mind, keep using that method.

Kicking Off

Chances are you'll want to learn some of the language before you
go. The first thing to do is to memorise those essential phrases
and words. Check out the basics and don't forget that extra phrase.
Try the sections on making conversation or greeting people for a
phrase you'd like to use. Write some of these words and phrases
down on a piece of paper and stick them up around the place: on
the fridge, by the bed, on your computer, as a bookmark –
somewhere where you'll see them often. Try putting some
words in context – the 'How much is it?' note, for instance, could
go in your wallet.

Any Questions?

Try to learn the main question words. Each language chapter con-
tains a box with the most common ones. As you read through
different situations, you'll see these words used in the example
sentences, and this will help you remember them. So if you want
to take a bus, turn to the Bus section in each chapter (use the
Index pages to find it quickly). You've already tried to memorise

INTRODUCTION

the word for 'which' and you'll see the word for 'bus'. When you
come across the sentence 'Which bus goes to ...?', you'll recognise
the key words and this will help you remember the whole phrase.

I Have a Flat Tyre

Doesn't seem like the phrase you're going to need? Well, in fact it
could be very useful. As are all the phrases in this book, provided
you have the courage to mix and match them. We have given
specific examples within each section. But the key words remain
the same even when the situation changes. So while you may not
be planning on any driving during your trip, the first part of the
phrase 'I have ...' could refer to anything else, and there are plenty
of words in the other phrases that, we hope, will fit your needs.
So whether it's 'a ticket' or 'a visa', you'll be able to put the words
together to convey your meaning.

Finally

Don't be concerned if you feel you can't memorise words. You'll
find the most essential words and phrases on the Quick Reference
page at the start of each chapter. You could also try tagging a few
pages for other key phrases, or use the notes pages at the back of
the book to write your own reminders.

ESTONIAN

ESTONIAN

QUICK REFERENCE

ESTONIAN

Hello.	*te*-rre	*Tere.* (inf/pol)
Goodbye.	head *ae*-gah	*Head aega.* (inf/pol)
Yes./No.	yah/ay	*Jah./Ei.*
Excuse me/ Sorry.	*vah*-bahn-dah-ge	*Vabandage.*
Thank you.	*ta*-nahn	*Tänan.*
You're welcome.	*pah*-lun	*Palun.*

Please give me a ... ticket.	*pah*-lun ... *pi*-let	*Palun ... pilet.*
one-way	üks	*üks*
return	e-dah-si-tah-gah-si	*edasi-tagasi*

I don't understand.
   mah ay saah ah-rru   *Ma ei saa aru.*

Do you speak English?
   kahs te *rraa*-gi-te
   ing-li-se kehlt?   *Kas te räägite inglise keelt?*

Where is ...?
   kus on ...?   *Kus on ...?*

Go straight ahead.
   ot-se   *Otse.*

Turn left/right.
   vah-sah-ku-le/
   pah-rre-mah-le.   *Vasakule/ Paremale.*

Where's the toilet?
   kus on tua-lett?   *Kus on tualett?*

Help!
   ahp-pi!   *Appi!*

1	üks	*üks*	6	koos	*kuus*
2	kahks	*kaks*	7	*sayt*-se	*seitse*
3	kolm	*kolm*	8	*kah*-hek-sah	*kaheksa*
4	*ne*-li	*neli*	9	*üh*-hek-sah	*üheksa*
5	vees	*viis*	10	*küm*-me	*kümme*

ESTONIAN

INTRODUCTION

Estonian, a Finno-Ugric tongue, is the official language of the Republic of Estonia and is spoken by about one million people. Closely related to Finnish, Estonian belongs to the Uralic language family and not to the Indo-European language family to which Latvian, Lithuanian, English and Russian belong.

Apart from a few names, words and phrases in earlier chronicles, the oldest surviving Estonian text dates from the 16th century. Estonian was regarded by the Germans, Danes, Swedes and Russians who ruled the land as a simple peasants' tongue and was not honoured as a language in its own right until the period of national awakening in the latter 19th century. An Estonian-German dictionary was published in 1869 and an Estonian grammar guide in 1875. In the early 20th century, language reformers de-Germanised the sentence structure, helped develop new vocabulary and made Estonian the language of instruction at Tartu University. During the first period of independence from 1920 to 1940, many people Estonianised their German surnames.

Through 800 years of occupation, Estonians kept their language alive as a means of maintaining their national identity. Although many foreign words and expressions crept into the language during the various occupations, Estonian has survived as a distinct and mellifluous tongue.

You'll find that Estonians are much more welcoming of visitors who make an effort to speak their language. So don't be shy!

BALKANS OR BALTICS?

Don't make the mistake of confusing the Balkans with the Baltics because the two are totally unrelated.

ESTONIAN

Help!

It's a good idea to take the time to learn a few basic words of Estonian to help you get by and to make your stay more enjoyable. 'Hello' is *Tere* (**te-rre**) and 'Goodbye' is *Head aega* (**head ae-gah**). *Palun* (**pah-lun**) is the word for 'Please' and is also used to mean 'You're welcome' and 'Here you are'. *Tänan* (**ta-nahn**) means 'Thank you'. The word for 'Yes' is *Jah* (**yah**) and 'No' is *Ei* (**ay**). If you find yourself stuck just say *Ma ei räägi eesti keelt.* (**mah ay rraa-gi ehs-ti kehlt**) which translates as 'I don't speak Estonian'. Pages 30-35 are crammed with handy phrases to help you make small talk with the locals.

PRONUNCIATION

You'll discover that Estonian words are not difficult to pronounce once you have learned the basics set out in this chapter. Unlike English, Estonian letters have only one pronunciation. The alphabet consists of 23 letters – *a, b, d, e, g, h, i, j, k, l, m, n, o, p, r, s, t, u, v, õ, ä, ö* and *ü*. The letters *c, č, f, q, š, z, ž, w, x* and *y* are used only in words of foreign origin.

Vowel combinations (diphthongs) don't form completely new sounds as they often do in English; each vowel is still pronounced individually. Estonian also uses many double vowels, which indicate that the vowel sound is extended.

FIRST IN, BEST STRESSED

In Estonian, stress is almost always on the first syllable with the exception of a few words such as *aitäh*, 'thanks', where it's on the second syllable, and some foreign words.

Vowels, Diphthongs & Double Vowels

Estonian	Translit	Sounds
a	ah	as the 'a' in 'father'
ä	a	as the 'a' in 'act'
e	e	as the 'e' in 'ten'
i	i	as the 'i' in 'in'
o	o	as the 'o' in British English 'hot'
ö	er	as the 'ir' in 'girl' (rounding the lips)
õ	y	roughly as the 'i' in 'girl' (without rounding the lips)
u	u	as the 'u' in 'put'
ü	ü	as the 'oo' in 'too' said with a small, round opening of the lips

ae	ae	as the 'ie' in 'diet' (two sounds)
ai	ai	as the 'ai' in 'aisle'
ää	aa	as the 'a' in 'Aaron'
äe	aeh	as the 'ae' in 'aesthetic'
ee	eh	as the 'e' in 'ten' but longer
ea	ea	as the 'ea' in 'bear'
ei	ay	as the 'ai' in 'paid'
ii	ee	as the 'ee' in 'see'
oo	aw	as the 'aw' in 'dawn'
oi	oy	as the 'oi' in 'loiter'
öö	err	as the 'yrr' in 'myrrh' (rounding the lips)
uu	oo	as the 'oo' in 'zoo'
ui	uy	as the 'oui' in 'Louie', but shorter and clipped
õi	yi	roughly as the word 'curly' leaving out the 'c', 'r' and 'l'

ESTONIAN

ESTONIAN

Consonants

Consonants are pronounced as in English, with the exception of the following:

Estonian	Translit	Sounds
p	p	halfway between English 'p' and 'b'
t	t	halfway between English 't' and 'd'
g	g	always as in 'good', never as in 'page'
k	k	softer than in English
j	y	as the 'y' in 'yes'
r	rr	always trilled, as the Italian 'r'
č	ch	as the 'ch' in 'change'
š	sh	as the 'sh' in 'shampoo'
ž	zh	as the 's' in 'treasure'

Stress

Stress is on the first syllable. There are very few exceptions to this rule but there's one that's very conspicuous – the word for 'thanks' *aitäh* (ai-*tahh*) stresses the second syllable.

Pronunciation Practice

Here are a few phrases. Practise these and you'll pick up Estonian pronunciation in no time. Stress is indicated by italics.

What are the Estonian flag's colours?
    mis on *ehs*-ti *li*-pu *varr*-vid?   *Mis on Eesti lipu värvid?*

They are blue, black and white.
    nehd on *si*-ni-ne must yah vahl-ge   *Need on sinine, must ja valge.*

Do you speak English?
    kahs te *rraa*-gi-te *ing*-li-se kehlt?   *Kas te räägite inglise keelt?*

I like this performance.
    mul-le *mehl*-dib seh e-ten-dus   *Mulle meeldib see etendus.*

Where do you come from?
kust te *pa*-rrit *o*-le-te?   *Kust te pärit olete?*

Happy birthday!
pahl-yu *yn*-ne   *Palju õnne sünnipäevaks!*
sün-ni-*paeh*-vahks!

GRAMMAR
Word Order
There are no articles or grammatical genders in Estonian. Sentences don't have a strict word order. Parts of speech, such as the subject and object, are identified by their different endings, called case endings. Even if your sentence structure is slightly awkward, you'll be understood if you use the endings correctly.

- What?/Who? (nominative case – no specific ending)

  plane   *lennuk*
  boy   *poiss*

- Of what?/Whose? (genitive or possessive case)

  plane's   *lennuk-i*
  The plane's size.   *Lennuki suurus.*

  boy's   *pois-i*
  The boy's size.   *Poisi suurus.*

- What?/Whom? (accusative or objective case)

  plane   *lennuk-it*
  I see the plane.   *Ma näen lennukit.*

  boy   *pois-si*
  I see the boy.   *Ma näen poissi.*

ESTONIAN

ESTONIAN

ON THE CASE

In English, we're able to recognise the 'role' of a noun in a sentence – who is performing an action, to whom, with what and so on – by its position in a sentence and/or by the use of prepositions.

However, like Latin, German and many other languages, Estonian uses what is known as 'case' to make these distinctions. Different suffixes known as case endings act like labels on nouns to indicate their relationship to other words in a sentence.

The case endings of other words in a sentence, such as adjectives and pronouns, must agree in number and gender with the case ending of the noun they refer to.

Estonian has fourteen cases, but you don't need to know them all. Here's a brief explanation of the three cases which are most important:

1. The nominative case refers to the subject of a verb in a sentence and is also the form you'll find in a dictionary. It indicates what or who is performing an action:

The audience threw flowers to the dancer, stomped the ground with their feet and yelled 'Encore!'.

2. The accusative is the direct object of a sentence. It indicates what or whom the verb refers to. Here it indicates what was given:

The audience threw *flowers* to the dancer, stomped the ground with their feet and yelled 'Encore!'.

3. The genitive case refers to possession, a bit like English 'of' or the possessive 's' ('s). It indicates whose or of what/of whom:

The audience threw flowers to the dancer, stomped the ground with *their feet* and yelled 'Encore!'.

Adjectives

Adjectives are placed before nouns and usually take the same case endings as the nouns they modify:

in a big city *suures linnas*
(lit: big city-in)

Both comparative and superlative adjectives add *-m* to the genitive case. Superlative adjectives also begin with the word *kõige* which translates as 'most'.

big	*suur*
bigger	*suurem*
biggest	*kõige suurem*
	(lit: most bigger)
beautiful	*ilus*
more beautiful	*ilusam*
	(lit: beautiful-er)
most beautiful	*kõige ilusam*
	(lit: most beautiful-er)

Adverbs

To form adverbs from adjectives, add the endings *-lt* or *-sti* to their genitive (second form given in the dictionary) forms:

slow	*aeglase*
slowly	*aeglaselt*
quick	*kiire*
quickly	*kiiresti*

ESTONIAN

Pronouns

Personal and possessive pronouns have two forms. Short forms are common in speech; long forms are used to stress a point.

Verbs

All Estonian verbs have either *-ma* or *-da* as an ending. The ending is dropped when the verb is conjugated. The following shows the present tense endings which are the same for most verbs:

to come	*tulema*
I come	*ma tulen*
you come (sg & inf)	*sa tuled*
she/he comes	*ta tuleb*
we come	*me tuleme*
you come (pl & pol)	*te tulete*
they come	*nad tulevad*

PRONOUNS		
PERSONAL		
I	mah/*mi*-nah	*ma/mina*
you (sg & inf)	sah/*si*-nah	*sa/sina*
she/he	tah/*te*-mah	*ta/tema*
we	me/*may*-e	*me/meie*
you (pl & pol)	te/*tay*-e	*te/teie*
they	nahd/*ne*-mahd	*nad/nemad*
POSSESSIVE		
my	mu/*mi*-nu	*mu/minu*
your (sg & inf)	su/*si*-nu	*su/sinu*
her/his	tah/*te*-mah	*ta/tema*
our	me/*may*-e	*me/meie*
your (pl & pol)	te/*tay*-e	*te/teie*
their	*nen*-de	*nende*

Present

In Estonian grammar, there's no distinction between a continuous activity and one that happens only once. Actions are expressed through context:

He comes here every day.	*Ta tuleb siia iga päev.*
	(lit: she/he comes to-here every day)
He is coming this way.	*Ta tuleb siiapoole.*
	(lit: she/he comes to-here-towards)

Future

The future tense is also expressed through context:

He will come tomorrow.	*Ta tuleb homme.*
	(lit: she/he comes tomorrow)

Past

Most verbs take a form of the suffix *-si* to create the simple past. To make the verb agree with the subject add, *-sin* for the subject 'I', *-sid* for 'you' (inf), *-s* for 'she/he', *-sime* for 'we', *-site* for 'you' (pl & pol) or *-sid* for 'they':

We asked for the menu.	*Me palusime menüüd.*
	(lit: we asked menu-for)
They went to the cinema.	*Nad läksid kinno.*
	(lit: they went cinema-to)

The verb 'to be' is an exception to this rule:

I was ill.	*Ma olin haige.*
	(lit: I was ill)

ESTONIAN

ESTONIAN

Imperatives

To make formal imperatives (commands), drop the *-ma* or *-da* ending of a verb and add *-ge*.

Infinitive	Imperative	
sööma	*Sööge!*	Eat!
kirjutama	*Kirjutage!*	Write!
vabandama	*Vabandage!*	Excuse me!
tulema	*Tulge siia!*	Come here!
	Ärge tulge!	Don't come!

TO BE

The bracketed form of the pronoun is used for emphasis.

I am	*(mina) ma olen*
you are (sg & inf)	*(sina) sa oled*
she/he is	*(tema) ta on*
we are	*(meie) me oleme*
you are (pl & pol)	*(teie) te olete*
they are	*(nemad) nad on*

TO HAVE

The verb 'to have' (*omama*) is rarely used in Estonian. Possession is expressed by using the third person of the verb 'to be'. Once again, the bracketed form is used for emphasis:

I have a car.	*(Minul) Mul on auto.*
	(lit: on-me is car)
We have two tickets.	*(Meil) Meil on kaks piletit.*
	(lit: on-us are two tickets)
She has a cat.	*(Temal) Tal on kass.*
	(lit: on-him/her is cat)

Questions

Who are you?	*Kes te olete?*
	(lit: who you are?)
Why are they shouting?	*Miks nad karjuvad?*
	(lit: why they shout?)
How do I get there?	*Kuidas ma sinna saan?*
	(lit: how I to-there get?)
What's your name?	*Mis te nimi on?*
	(lit: what your name is?)

Another way to turn a sentence into a question is to place the word *kas* (**kahs**) at the beginning of a sentence. This roughly translates as 'do':

You speak English.	*Te räägite inglise keelt.*
	(lit: you speak
	English language)
Do you speak English?	*Kas te räägite inglise keelt?*
	(lit: do you speak
	English language?)

QUESTION WORDS

who?	kes?	*kes?*
what?	mis?	*mis?*
where?	kus?	*kus?*
when?	*mil*-lahl?	*millal?*
why?	miks?	*miks?*
how?	*kuy*-dahs?	*kuidas?*

ESTONIAN

Negatives

To make a sentence negative, place the word *ei* ('no') in front of the verb:

I am not.	*Ma ei ole.*
	(lit: I no am)
She/He doesn't drink.	*Ta ei joo.*
	(lit: she/he no drink)

Modals

A modal is a word or phrase placed in front of the verb that changes the mood of that verb by expressing ability, necessity, desire or need. Estonian modals denoting ability are more specific in meaning than their English counterparts. For example, the English modal verb 'can' translates into four different modals, with four different meanings, in Estonian:

I can dance.	
(I can because I have learned)	*Ma oskan tantsida.*
(I may if I choose to)	*Ma võin tantsida.*
(I can because I will be invited)	*Ma saan tantsida.*
(I am able to, I am not too tired)	*Ma suudan tantsida.*

Prepositions

above	*ko*-hahl	*kohal*
at	*joo*-rres	*juures*
next to	*kyr*-vahl	*kõrval*
on	peal	*peal*
under	ahll	*all*
with	kaws	*koos*
without	*il*-mah	*ilma*

Conjunctions

and	yah	*ja*
because	sest	*sest*
but	*ah*-gah	*aga*
or	vyi	*või*

GREETINGS & CIVILITIES

Most Estonians, especially younger people, understand some English and Finnish. Many speak some Russian, although they are often sensitive about using it.

Estonians are a reserved and polite people and are generally rather shy with strangers. If you're lucky enough to be invited to someone's home, it's customary to bring flowers as a gift. When entering a household, it's considered unlucky to shake hands across the threshold. You should take off your shoes. Your host will usually give you slippers to wear instead.

ESTONIAN

Greetings & Goodbyes

| Hello. | te-rre | *Tere.* |
| Welcome. | te-rre tu-le-mahst | *Tere tulemast.* |

Good ...	te-rre ...	*Tere ...*
morning	hom-mi-kust	*hommikust*
afternoon	paeh-vahst	*päevast*
evening	yh-tust	*õhtust*

Good night.	head errd	*Head ööd.*
Goodbye.	head ae-gah	*Head aega.*
See you later.	na-ge-mi-sc-ni	*Nägemiseni.*

Civilities

In Estonia, it's considered awkward to ask a stranger, 'How are you?'. Such a question is often taken literally and not as a courtesy question, but if you do ask, it will be understood.

How are you? (How's it going?)
   kuy-dahs la-heb?   *Kuidas läheb?*

Very nice (to meet you).
   va-gah *mehl*-div   *Väga meeldiv.*

Fine.
   has-ti   *Hästi.*

Okay (Nothing wrong).
   po-le *vi*-gah   *Pole viga.*

Please./You're welcome.
   pah-lun   *Palun.*

Thank you (very much).
   ta-nahn (*va*-gah)   *Tänan (väga).*

Thanks.
   ai-*tahh*   *Aitäh.*

Okay. (agreed)
   hea küll   *Hea küll.*

No, thank you.
   ta-nahn ay   *Tänan, ei.*

Forms of Address

Miss	*prray*-li	*preili*
Mrs	*prrou*-ah	*proua*
Mr	har-rah	*härra*

COME ON STRONG

When greeting someone who is working, it's customary to say *Jõudu!* (lit: strength-to-you!). The reply is *Tarvis!* (lit: it's-needed!).

Use the formal 'you', *te* (**te**) or *teie* (**tay-e**), when addressing strangers or people you just met. The informal *sa* (**sah**) or *sina* (**si-nah**) is reserved for children, family and friends. Except with children, don't use it until you are invited to.

Do you speak English?
    kahs te *rraa*-gi-te
    ing-li-se kehlt?   *Kas te räägite*
                   inglise keelt?
You're a good child.
    sah *o*-led *tub*-li lahps   *Sa oled tubli laps.*

Useful Words & Phrases

Yes.	yah	*Jah.*
No.	ay	*Ei.*
Pardon?	*kuy*-dahs?	*Kuidas?*
Certainly.	*kind*-lahs-ti	*Kindlasti.*
Of course.	*muy*-du-gi	*Muidugi.*
Just a moment.	üks hetk	*Üks hetk.*
Never mind.	*po*-le *vi*-gah	*Pole viga.*
Wait!	*aw*-dah-ke!	*Oodake!*
Excuse me/	*vah*-bahn-dah-ge	*Vabandage.*
I'm sorry.		
What a pity!	*kah*-yu!	*Kahju!*

Can I help you? (How can I be of service?)
    kuy-das mah saahn   *Kuidas ma saan*
    kah-su-lik *ol*-lah?   *kasulik olla?*

Where's the ...?	kus on ...?	*Kus on ...?*
hotel	ho-*tell*	*hotell*
telephone	te-le-fon	*telefon*
toilet	tuah-*lett*	*tualett*

ESTONIAN

SMALL TALK
Meeting People

What's your name?	mis te *ni*-mi on?	*Mis te nimi on?*
My name is ...	mu *ni*-mi on ...	*Minu nimi on ...*
I like Estonians.	*mul*-le *mehl*-di-vahd	*Mulle meeldivad*
	ehst-lah-sed	*eestlased.*

This is my ...	seh on *mi*-nu ...	*See on minu ...*
friend	*sy*-berr	*sõber*
husband	mehs	*mees*
spouse	*ah*-bi-kaah-sah	*abikaasa*
wife	*nai*-ne	*naine*

ESTONIAN

Nationalities

When Estonians ask visitors about their nationality, it doesn't always mean their citizenship. An ethnic Russian, even though born in Estonia and holding an Estonian passport, will still be called a Russian.

I'm ...	mah *o*-len ...	*Ma olen ...*
American	ah-*meh*-rik-lah-ne	*ameeriklane*
Australian	aust-*rrahl*-lah-ne	*austraallane*
British	*ing*-lah-ne	*inglane*
Canadian	*kah*-nah-dah-lah-ne	*kanadalane*
Danish	*taahn*-lah-ne	*taanlane*
Estonian	*ehst*-lah-ne	*eestlane*
Finnish	*sawm*-lah-ne	*soomlane*
French	*prrahnts*-lah-ne	*prantslane*
German	*sahks*-lah-ne	*sakslane*
Latvian	*lat*-lah-ne	*lätlane*
Lithuanian	*leh*-du-lah-ne	*leedulane*
Norwegian	*nor*-rrah-lah-ne	*norralane*
Russian	*ve*-ne-lah-ne	*venelane*
Swedish	*rrawts*-lah-ne	*rootslane*

Age

How old are you?

    kuy *vah*-nah te *o*-le-te?   *Kui vana te olete?*

I'm ...

    mah *o*-len ...   *Ma olen ...*

WHEN IN ROME

Remember, in keeping with the polite and formal character of the Estonians, it's considered impolite to ask strangers their age.

ESTONIAN

Occupations

What's your line of work?

    mis terrd te *teh*-te?   *Mis tööd te teete?*

I'm (a) ...	mah *o*-len ...	*Ma olen ...*
business person	a-rri-nai-ne	*ärinaine* (f)
	a-rri-meehs	*ärimees* (m)
doctor	ahrrst	*arst*
farmer	*tah*-lu-nik	*talunik*
journalist	a-yah-kirr-yah-nik	*ajakirjanik*
labourer	terr-line	*tööline*
lawyer	*yu*-rrist	*jurist*
nurse	*y*-de	*õde*
retired	*pen*-sio-narr	*pensionär*
sailor/mariner	*me*-rre-mehs	*meremees*
state official	*rree*-gi-ah-met-nik	*riigiametnik*
student	*tu*-deng	*tudeng*
teacher	*y*-pe-ta-ya	*õpetaja*
tour guide	geed	*giid*
unemployed	*terr*-tu	*töötu*
waiter	*et*-te-kahnd-yah	*ettekandja* (f)
	kel-nerr	*kelner* (m)
writer	*kirr*-yah-nik	*kirjanik*

Religion

Most ethnic Estonians are Lutheran but only about 10% of them actively practise it. Russian Orthodoxy is more common on the islands and among the Russian population. On the island of Saaremaa off the west coast (a popular holiday destination for Estonians) you'll hear Orthodox services delivered entirely in Estonian.

What's your religion?
    mis *us*-**ku te** *o*-**le-te?**   *Mis usku te olete?*

I'm ...	**mah** *o*-**len ...**	*Ma olen ...*
Buddhist	*bu*-**dist**	*budist*
Catholic	*kah*-**to-leek-lah-ne**	*katoliiklane*
Christian	*krrist*-**lah-ne**	*kristlane*
Hindu	*in*-**du-ist**	*induist*
Jewish	*yu*-**dah-ist**	*judaist*
Lutheran	*lu*-**terr-lah-ne**	*luterlane*
Muslim	*mu*-**sul-mahn**	*musulman*
Russian Orthodox	*ve*-**ne** *yi*-**ge-usk-lik**	*vene õigeusklik*

I'm not religious.   **mah ay** *o*-**le** *usk*-**lik**   *Ma ei ole usklik.*

Family

Are you married?
    kahs te *o*-**le-te**   *Kas te olete*
    ah-**bi-e-lus?**   *abielus?*

I'm ...	**mah** *o*-**len ...**	*Ma olen ...*
divorced	*lah*-**hu-tah-tud**	*lahutatud*
gay	*les*-**bi/gay**	*lesbi/gei* (f/m)
married	*ah*-**bi-e-lus**	*abielus*
single	*vahl*-**lah-li-ne**	*vallaline*
widowed	**lesk**	*lesk*

Do you have any ...? **kahs tayl on ...?** *Kas teil on ...?*
   children ***lahp*-si** *lapsi*
   sisters/brothers **y-de-sid/ven-di** *õdesid/vendi*

I have a daughter/son.
   mul on *tü*-tahrr/poeg *Mul on tütar/poeg.*
I don't have any children.
   mul ei *o*-le *lahp*-si *Mul ei ole lapsi.*

Is your ... here **kahs *tay*-e ... on** *Kas teie ... on*
as well? **kah seen?** *ka siin?*
   boyfriend ***sy*-berr** *sõber*
   girlfriend ***syb*-rrah-tarr** *sõbratar*
   wife/husband ***ah*-bi-kaah-sah** *abikaasa*

aunt ***ta*-di** *tädi*
family ***pe*-rre** *pere*
father ***i*-sah** *isa*
mother **e-mah** *ema*
uncle ***o*-nu** *onu*

ESTONIAN

Kids' Talk

How old are you?
   kuy *vah*-nah sah *o*-led? *Kui vana sa oled?*
When's your birthday?
   ***mil*-lahl su *sün*-ni-paehv on?** *Millal su sünnipäev on?*
What do you do after school?
   ***mi*-dah sah *parr*-ahst** *Mida sa pärast*
   ***kaw*-li tehd?** *kooli teed?*
Do you have a pet at home?
   kahss sul on *ko*-dus *Kas sul on kodus*
   ***lem*-mik-law-mah?** *lemmiklooma?*

ESTONIAN

I have a ...	mul on ...	Mul on ...
bird	lind	lind
budgerigar	veerr-pah-pah-goy	viirpapagoi
canary	kah-nah-rri-lind	kanaarilind
cat	kahss	kass
dog	koerr	koer
duck	pahrrt	part
fish	kah-lah	kala
frog	konn	konn
guinea pig	me-rri-si-gah	merisiga
hamster	hahms-terr	hamster
horse	ho-bu-ne	hobune
tortoise	kilp-konn	kilpkonn

Expressing Feelings

I'm ...	mul on ...	Mul on ...
cold	külm	külm
hot	pah-lahv	palav
happy	hea tu-yu	hea tuju
in a hurry	kee-rre	kiire
scared	hirrm	hirm
sorry	kah-yu	kahju

I'm ...	mah o-len ...	Ma olen ...
angry	vi-hah-ne	vihane
grateful	ta-nu-lik	tänulik
sad	kurrb	kurb
sick	hai-ge	haige
tired	va-si-nud	väsinud

I feel ...	mul on ...	Mul on ...
bad	hahlb	halb
good	hea	hea

Expressing Opinions

What do you think?	mis te *ahr*-vah-te?	*Mis te arvate?*
I like this ...	*mul*-le *mehl*-dib seh ...	*Mulle meeldib see ...*
I don't like this ...	*mul*-le ay *mehl*-di seh ...	*Mulle ei meeldi see ...*
city	**linn**	*linn*
country	**maah**	*maa*
hotel	ho-***tell***	*hotell*
performance	**e-ten-dus**	*etendus*
restaurant	***rres***-to-rran	*restoran*

I like her/him.
   ta *mehl*-dib *mul*-le   *Ta meeldib mulle.*
I don't like this/that.
   seh ay *mehl*-di *mul*-le   *See ei meeldi mulle.*

BODY LANGUAGE

Estonians tend to be reserved and formal with strangers. Friends shake hands rather than embrace when they greet each other. Shouting, arm gestures and standing too close are considered uncouth. The old-fashioned customs of men helping women on with their coats and holding doors open are commonplace.

ESTONIAN

BREAKING THE LANGUAGE BARRIER

I don't speak Estonian.
   mah ay rraa-gi ehs-ti kehlt   *Ma ei räägi eesti keelt.*

Estonian is difficult.
   ehs-ti kehl on rrahs-ke   *Eesti keel on raske.*

I don't understand.
   mah ay saah ah-rru   *Ma ei saa aru.*

Do you understand?
   kahs te saah-te ah-rru?   *Kas te saate aru?*

ESTONIAN

SIGNS

PARKIMINE KEELATUD	NO PARKING
SISSESÕIT KEELATUD	NO ENTRY
STOPP	STOP
TEE REMONT	ROADWORKS
ÜLEKÄIK	PEDESTRIAN CROSSING
VALUUTAVAHETUS	CURRENCY EXCHANGE
AVARII	ACCIDENT/DANGER
AVATUD/LAHTI	OPEN
KASSA	CASHIER/TICKETS
KURI KOER	VICIOUS DOG
LÕUNA	AT LUNCH
MEESTELE	MEN'S TOILET
MITTE SUITSETADA	NO SMOKING
NAISTELE	WOMEN'S TOILET
RESERVEERITUD	RESERVED
SISSEPÄÄS	ENTRANCE
SULETUD/KINNI	CLOSED
VÄLJAPÄÄS	EXIT
WC	PUBLIC TOILET

Please repeat it.
  pah-lun kor-rrah-ke   *Palun korrake.*
Please write it down here.
  pah-lun kirr-yu-tah-ge   *Palun kirjutage*
  seh see-ah   *see siia.*

Do you speak ...?	**kahs te rraa-gi-te ...**	*Kas te räägite ...*
	kehlt?	*keelt?*
English	**ing-li-se**	*inglise*
Finnish	**saw-me**	*soome*
French	**prrahnt-su-se**	*prantsuse*
German	**sahk-sah**	*saksa*
Russian	**ve-ne**	*vene*

ESTONIAN

Sports & Interests

What do you do with your free time?
  mi-dah te vah-bahl   *Mida te vabal*
  ah-yahl teh-te?   *ajal teete?*

I like (to) ...	**mul-le mehl-dib ...**	*Mulle meeldib ...*
art	**kunst**	*kunst*
ballet	**bahl-lett**	*ballett*
the cinema	**fil-mi-kunst**	*filmikunst*
(classical) music	**(klahs-si-kah-li-ne)**	*(klassikaline)*
	moo-si-kah	*muusika*
opera	**aw-perr**	*ooper*
reading	**lu-ge-dah**	*lugeda*
the theatre	**teah-terr**	*teater*
travelling	**rray-si-dah**	*reisida*
visit exhibitions	**kai-ah nai-tus-tel**	*käia näitustel*
visit museums	**kai-ah**	*käia*
	moo-se-u-mi-des	*muuseumides*
visit national parks	**kai-ah rrah-vus-**	*käia*
	pahrr-ki-des	*rahvusparkides*

ESTONIAN

I want to go ...	ma *tah*-han *min*-nah ...	*Ma tahan minna ...*
bird watching	*lin*-de *vaaht*-le-mah	*linde vaatlema*
bobsledding	*saah*-ni-gah *syit*-mah	*saaniga sõitma*
camping	*tel*-gi-gah	*telgiga*
	maht-kah-mah	*matkama*
canoeing	*süs*-tah-maht-kah-le	*süstamatkale*
cycling	*yahlg*-rraht-tah-gah *syit*-mah	*jalgrattaga sõitma*
(ice) fishing	(*yaa*-le) *kah*-lahs-tah-mah	*(jääle) kalastama*
gliding	*pu*-rri-len-nu-ki-gah *syit*-mah	*purilennukiga sõitma*
hiking	*maht*-kah-mah	*matkama*
horse riding	*rrat*-su-tah-mah	*ratsutama*
jogging	*yawks*-mah	*jooksma*
sailing	*purr*-ye-tah-mah	*purjetama*
skiing	*soo*-sah-tah-mah	*suusatama*
swimming	*u*-yu-mah	*ujuma*
tobogganing	*kel*-gu-tah-mah	*kelgutama*

I play ...	mah *man*-gin ...	*Ma mängin ...*
basketball	*korrv*-pahl-li	*korvpalli*
cards	*kaahrr*-te	*kaarte*
chess	*mah*-let	*malet*
guitar	ki-*tahr*-rri	*kitarri*
soccer	*yahlg*-pahl-li	*jalgpalli*
tennis	*ten*-nist	*tennist*
winter sports	tah-li-*sporr*-di-ah-lahd	*talispordialad*

Useful Words & Phrases

Well done!	*tub*-li!	*Tubli!*
Let's go.	*lah*-me	*Lähme.*
Let's start.	*hak*-kah-me *pih*-tah	*Hakkame pihta.*
Let's try.	*prraw*-vi-me	*Proovime.*
Just joking!	mah *te*-gin *nahl*-yah!	*Ma tegin nalja!*
Congratulations!	*pal*-yu *yn*-ne!	*Palju õnne!*

GETTING AROUND

You'll find many travel agencies in Tallinn that can help you with
bookings and queries about travel within and out of Estonia. They
also organise city tours, guided trips to other parts of the country
and provincial accommodation.

Directions

Excuse me.	**vah**-bahn-dah-ge	*Vabandage.*

Where's the ...?	**kus on ...?**	*Kus on ...?*
airport	**len**-nu-yaahm	*lennujaam*
bus station	**bus**-si-yaahm	*bussijaam*
ferry terminal	**sah**-dahm	*sadam*
taxi rank	**tahk**-so-pea-tus	*taksopeatus*
train station	**rron**-gi-yaahm	*rongijaam*

Is it far?
  kahs seh on *kau*-gel?   *Kas see on kaugel?*
Please show me on the map.
  pah-lun *nai*-dah-ke *mul*-le   *Palun näidake mulle*
  se-dah *kaahrr*-dil   *seda kaardil.*

Buying Tickets

I'd like a ticket to ... please.	*pah*-lun üks *pi*-let ...	*Palun üks pilet ...*
Tartu	**tahrr**-tus-se	*Tartusse*
Pärnu	**par**-nus-se	*Pärnusse*
Riga	**rree**-gah	*Riiga*
Vilnius	**vil**-nius-se	*Vilniusse*
Moscow	**mosk**-vahs-se	*Moskvasse*
St Petersburg	**pe**-terr-bu-rri	*Peterburi*
Helsinki	**hel**-sin-gis-se	*Helsingisse*
Stockholm	**stock**-hol-mi	*Stockholmi*

ESTONIAN

ESTONIAN

Air

Tallinn is served by several European airlines. The national airline is Estonian Air, but there are no domestic flights. Tallinn Airport is close to the city and easily reached by bus or taxi. It uses English as its international language so it's not difficult to ask for help there.

Is there a flight to ...?
kahs tayl on *len*-nu-rray-si ...?   *Kas teil on lennureisi ...?*

Where's the ticket office?
kus on *pi*-le-ti-kahs-sah?   *Kus on piletikassa?*

Where's the left luggage?
kus-on *pah*-gah-si *hoy*-u-rroom?   *Kus on pagasi hoiuruum?*

ON THE STREETS

TÄNAV	STREET
VÄLJAK/PLATS	SQUARE
PUIESTEE	AVENUE/BOULEVARD
TEE	ROAD
MAANTEE	HIGHWAY
SILD	BRIDGE

Bus & Train

Bus travel is comfortable and domestic routes are inexpensive. Links to Europe are good. Domestic trains go to many Estonian towns and there's only one class. Some trains continue to foreign destinations and they offer several classes of service.

It's advisable to buy tickets in advance, especially for holiday and weekend travel. Many trains have restaurant cars and facilities to carry bikes. Bus and train tickets are one-way. A return ticket is twice the one-way fare.

Please give me a ... ticket.	*pah*-lun ... *pi*-let	*Palun ... pilet.*
one-way	üks	*üks*
return	e-dah-si–*tah*-gah-si	*edasi-tagasi*

A student/child ticket, please.
   pah-lun *y*-pi-lah-se/   *Palun õpilase/*
   lahp-se *pi*-let   *lapse pilet.*

ESTONIAN

City Public Transport

Tickets for all city public transport are sold in kiosks and on board vehicles at a slightly higher cost. A ticket must be punched for every ride and failure to do this can result in a fine. You can buy tickets for unlimited rides for 10, 20 and 30 days. There are discounts if you can show an International Student ID Card.

Which ... do I take to get there?	mis ... mah *sin*-nah saahn?	*Mis ... ma sinna saan?*
bus	*bus*-si-gah	*bussiga*
tram	*trrahm*-mi-gah	*trammiga*
trolleybus	*trrol*-li-gah	*trolliga*

What time is the next ...?	mis kell on *yarrg*-mi-ne ...?	*Mis kell on järgmine ...?*
bus	buss	*buss*
train	rrong	*rong*

What time does the train depart?
    mis kell *la*-heb rrong?   *Mis kell läheb rong?*
Which platform?
    mis *plaht*-vorrm?   *Mis platvorm?*
What time does the bus arrive?
    mis kell *saah*-bub buss?   *Mis kell saabub buss?*
What bus stop?
    mis *peah*-tus?   *Mis peatus?*
This train is cancelled.
    seh rrong yaab *a*-rrah   *See rong jääb ära.*
How long will it be delayed?
    kui *pahl*-yu seh *hi*-li-neb?   *Kui palju see hilineb?*
I want to get off.
    mah *ta*-hahn *mah*-hah *min*-nah   *Ma tahan maha minna.*
Excuse me, you're sitting in my seat.
    vah-bahn-dah-ge te *is*-tu-te   *Vabandage, te istute*
    ***mi*-nu *ko*-hah peal**   *minu koha peal.*

Ferry

Many ferries and hydrofoils ply the Gulf of Finland between Tallinn and Helsinki, and there's also ferry services to Sweden and Germany. Baltic travellers continue to use ferries because they're inexpensive and convenient. There are also ferries between the mainland and the large Estonian islands.

boat	**paaht**	*paat*
ferry	**prraahm**	*praam*
harbour	***sah*-dahm**	*sadam*
hydrofoil	***tee*-burr**	*tiibur*

Where does the ferry leave from?
   kust prraahm *val*-yub?   *Kust praam väljub?*
What time does the ferry arrive?
   mis kell prraahm *saah*-bub?   *Mis kell praam saabub?*
Which ferry goes to ...?
   ***mil*-li-ne prraahm *la*-heb ...?**   *Milline praam läheb ...?*
Is this the ferry for ...?
   kahs seeh on ... prraahm?   *Kas see on ... praam?*

DID YOU KNOW ...	Estonia is only slightly bigger than Denmark or the Netherlands, and is the smallest of the three Baltic countries.

ESTONIAN

Taxi

I want to go to ...
   mah *tah*-han *min*-nah ...   *Ma tahan minna ...*
How much will it cost?
   mis seh *mahk*-sab?   *Mis see maksab?*
Please drive to ...
   ***pah*-lun *syit*-ke ...**   *Palun sõitke ...*
Go left.
   ***vah*-sah-ku-le**   *Vasakule.*
Go right.
   ***pah*-rre-mah-le**   *Paremale.*
Go straight ahead.
   ***ot*-se**   *Otse.*
Please stop here.
   ***pah*-lun *pea*-tu-ge seen**   *Palun peatuge siin.*
Please wait.
   ***pah*-lun *aw*-dah-ke**   *Palun oodake.*
How much does it cost?
   kuy *pahl*-yu seh *mahk* sahb?   *Kui palju see maksab?*

Car

Where can I rent a car?
kus mah saahn	*Kus ma saan*
rren-ti-dah au-to?	*rentida auto?*

What is the daily/weekly rate?
mis on paeh-vah/	*Mis on päeva/*
na-dah-lah rrent?	*nädala rent?*

Does that	**kahs seh on**	*Kas see on*
include ...?	**kaws ...?**	*koos ...?*
insurance	**kind-lus-tu-se-gah**	*kindlustusega*
mileage	**ki-lo-met-rraah-zhi-gah**	*kilometraažiga*

Where can I buy a parking card?
kus saahb os-tah	*Kus saab osta*
pahrr-ki-mis-kaahrr-te?	*parkimiskaarte?*

Where does this road go?
ku-hu seh teh veeb?	*Kuhu see tee viib?*

Where's a petrol station?
kus on ben-see-ni-yaahm?	*Kus on bensiinijaam?*

air (for tyres)	**yhk**	*õhk*
battery	**ah-ku**	*aku*
driving licence	**yu-hi-lu-bah**	*juhiluba*
engine	**maw-torr**	*mootor*
lights	**tu-led**	*tuled*
oil	**y-li**	*õli*
radiator	**rrah-di-aah-torr**	*radiaator*
road map	**maahn-tee-de kaahrrt**	*maanteede kaart*
windscreen	**too-le-klaahs**	*tuuleklaas*

My ... isn't/aren't working. **mu au-to ... ay terr-tah** *Mu auto ... ei tööta.*
brakes	**pi-du-rrid**	*pidurid*
clutch	**si-durr**	*sidur*
gears	**kai-gu-kahst**	*käigukast*

ESTONIAN

My tyre is flat.
    mu *au*-**to kumm on** *tü*-**hi**   *Mu auto kumm on tühi.*
Where's a garage?
    kus on *au*-**to-teh-nin-dus?**   *Kus on autoteenindus?*
How much will repairs cost?
    kuy *kahl*-**lis on** *rre*-**mont?**   *Kui kallis on remont?*
When will the car be ready?
    mil-**lahl** *au*-**to** *vahl*-**mis saahb?**   *Millal auto valmis saab?*
My car has been stolen.
    mu *au*-**to on** *vah*-**rrahs-tah-tud**   *Mu auto on varastatud.*
Is your car insured?
    kahs *tay*-**e** *au*-**to on** *kind*-**lus-tah-tud?**   *Kas teie auto on kindlustatud?*

ESTONIAN

ACCOMMODATION

There are hotels to suit all budgets in Estonia. Bed and breakfast accommodation is becoming increasingly common in the countryside. Camp sites can also be found.

Finding Accommodation

Where can I find a ...?	**kus** *ah*-**sub** ...?	*Kus asub ...?*
hotel	ho-***tell***	*hotell*
pension	*vyy*-**rrahs-te-mah-yah**	*võõrastemaja*
camp site	*kam*-**ping**	*kämping*

Is it far?	**kahs seh on** *kau*-**gel?**	*Kas see on kaugel?*
Is it expensive?	**kahs seh on** *kahl*-**lis?**	*Kas see on kallis?*

At the Hotel

I'd like a ...	**mah** *tah*-**hak-sin** ... *tu*-**bah**	*Ma tahaksin ... tuba.*
single room	*ü*-**he** *vaw*-**di-gah**	*ühe voodiga*
double room	*kah*-**he** *vaw*-**di-gah**	*kahe voodiga*
room with a bathroom	*vahn*-**ni-toa-gah**	*vannitoaga*

ESTONIAN

I'm staying ...	mah yaan ...	*Ma jään ...*
one day	*ü*-heks *paeh*-vahks	*üheks päevaks*
two days	*kah*-heks *paeh*-vahks	*kaheks päevaks*
one week	*ü*-heks *na*-dah-lahks	*üheks nädalaks*

Is there (a) ...?	kahs seal on ...?	*Kas seal on ...?*
hot water	soe *ve*-si	*soe vesi*
bathroom	*vahn*-ni-tu-bah	*vannituba*
sauna	saun	*saun*
shower	*du*-shi-rroom	*duširuum*
telephone	*te*-le-fon	*telefon*
television	*te*-le-vee-sorr	*televiisor*

How much is it per person/per night?
  kui *pahl*-yu *mahk*-sab   *Kui palju maksab*
  vaw-di-koht/*err*-paehv?   *voodikoht/ööpäev?*
Please write down the price.
  pah-lun *kirr*-yu-tah-ge   *Palun kirjutage siia*
  see-ah hind   *hind.*
Does it include breakfast?
  kahs *hom*-mi-ku-serrk on   *Kas hommikusöök on*
  hin-nah sehs?   *hinna sees?*

THEY MAY SAY ...

kahs tayl on pahss?
   Do you have a passport?
kah-yuks ay *o*-le mayl *vah*-bu *koh*-ti
   Sorry, we're full.
kuy *kau*-ahks te *yaa*-te?
   How long will you be staying?
vaw-di-koht/*err*-paehv *mahk*-sab ...
krraw-ni
   It's ... kroons per person/per day.

Can I see it?
   kahs mah vyin se-dah
   na-hah?
                                   Kas ma võin seda
                                     näha?
Can I see the bathroom?
   kahs mah vyin vaah-dah-tah
   vahn-ni-tu-bah?
           Kas ma võin vaadata
           vannituba?
Are there any cheaper rooms?
   kahs tayl on o-dah-vah-maid
   tu-be?
           Kas teil on odavamaid
           tube?
Fine, I'll take it.
   ke-nah mah vy-tahn sel-le
           Kena, ma võtan selle.
I'd like to pay the bill.
   mah tah-hahks mahks-tah
   ahrr-ve
           Ma tahaks maksta arve.

Requests & Complaints

Please order a taxi for me.
   pah-lun tel-li-ge
   mul-le tahk-so
           Palun tellige
           mulle takso.
Please wake me up at ...
   pah-lun a-rrah-tah-ge
   mind kell ...
           Palun äratage
           mind kell ...
My room needs to be cleaned.
   mu tu-bah vah-yahb
   ko-rris-tah-mist
           Mu tuba vajab
           koristamist.
Please change the sheets.
   pah-lun vah-he-tah-ge
   vaw-di-pe-su
           Palun vahetage
           voodipesu.
I can't open the window.
   mah ay saah
   ah-vah-dah ah-kent
           Ma ei saa
           avada akent.
I can't get into my room.
   mah ay paa-se o-mah tup-pah
           Ma ei pääse oma tuppa.
The toilet won't flush.
   tuah-le-tis po-le vett
           Tualetis pole vett.

ESTONIAN

My room is very cold.
    mu *tu*-bah on *va*-gah külm   *Mu tuba on väga külm.*
My telephone/television
isn't working.
    mu *te*-le-fon/*te*-le-vee-sorr   *Mu telefon/televiisor*
    ay *terr*-tah   *ei tööta.*
I don't like this room.
    mul-le ay *mehl*-di seh *tu*-bah   *Mulle ei meeldi see tuba.*

It's too ...	seh on *lee*-gah ...	*See on liiga ...*
expensive	*kahl*-lis	*kallis*
noisy	*ka*-rrah-rri-kahs	*kärarikas*
small	*vai*-ke	*väike*

Laundry

Can I have my clothes cleaned?
    kahs mah vyin *lahs*-tah *pe*-su   *Kas ma võin lasta pesu*
    pes-tah?   *pesta?*
How long will it take?
    kuy *kau*-ah seh *ae*-gah *vy*-tab?   *Kui kaua see aega võtab?*

Useful Words

bed	*vaw*-di	*voodi*
bill	*ahrr*-ve	*arve*
blanket	tekk	*tekk*
chair	tawl	*tool*
clean	*pu*-hahs	*puhas*
dark	*pi*-me	*pime*
dirty	must	*must*
double bed	*kah*-he-i-ni-me-se-vaw-di	*kaheinimesevoodi*
electricity	e-*lek*-terr	*elekter*
key	*vy*-ti	*võti*
lift (elevator)	lift	*lift*
light bulb	pirrn	*pirn*

ESTONIAN

lock (n)	**lukk**	*lukk*
mattress	**mahd-rrahts**	*madrats*
pillow	**pah-di**	*padi*
quiet	**vaik-ne**	*vaikne*
room (in hotel)	**ho-tel-li-tu-bah**	*hotellituba*
sheet	**li-nah**	*lina*
shower	**dush**	*duš*
soap	**sehp**	*seep*
suitcase	**koh-verr**	*kohver*
toilet	**tua-lett**	*tualett*
towel	**ka-te-rra-tik**	*käterätik*
hot/cold water	**soe/külm ve-si**	*soe/külm vesi*
window	**ah-ken**	*aken*

ESTONIAN

AROUND TOWN

Many Estonian towns have tourist information offices that offer visitors multilingual help. If you are planning a visit during the winter months, check in advance to ensure attractions and accommodations are open.

Where's (a/an/the) ...?	**kus on ...?**	*Kus on ...?*
art gallery	**kuns-ti-gah-le-rri**	*kunstigalerii*
bank	**pahnk**	*pank*
church	**ki-rrik**	*kirik*
city centre	**kesk-linn**	*kesklinn*
... embassy	**... saaht-kond**	*... saatkond*
my hotel	**mi-nu ho-tell**	*minu hotell*
market	**turrg**	*turg*
police	**po-lit-say**	*politsei*
post office	**post-kon-torr**	*postkontor*
toilet	**tua-lett**	*tualett*
tourist office	**tu-rris-mi-bü-rroo**	*turismibüroo*

ESTONIAN

ESTONIAN I AM

The power and imagery of 'Estonian I Am' are very difficult to convey in translation, but some of the emotion may be visible. The poet Jüri Leesment wrote the lyrics to Alo Mattiisen's music.

Eestlane olen

Estonian I Am

Tuhat korda kas
või alata,
Tuhat aastat tõusu,
mitte luigelend.

We can have a thousand
beginnings
A thousand years rising,
not just a solitary
swan's flight.

Oma rahvust maha salata
sama ränk on nagu
orjaks müüa end.

To deny your own nation
is like selling yourself
into slavery.

Eestlane olen
ja eestlaseks jään,
kui mind eestlaseks loodi.

Estonian I am and
Estonian I will stay
Since Estonian I was born.

Eestlane olla on
uhke ja hää,
vabalt vaarisa moodi,
nende teiste meeste moodi.

To be an Estonian is a
proud and good thing.
As free as our forefathers,
Yes, like those other men.

Tuhat kõuehäälset küsijat,
vaba meri, põlistanud
püha muld.
Tuhat korda tuhat püsijat
kõige kiuste elus
hoiab püha tuld.

A thousand thundering
questioners, our open sea,
our homeland's inviolate soil.
A thousand times a thousand
who prevail against all odds
to keep the sacred
flame burning.

At the Bank

The Estonian currency is the kroon, which is stable and tied to the German deutschmark. Credit cards are widely accepted. You'll find currency exchange offices everywhere, even in some supermarkets.

Where can I exchange money?
kus mah saahn *vah*-he-tah-dah   *Kus ma saan vahetada*
rrah-hah?   *raha?*
What's the ... rate today?
mis on ... *paeh*-vah-kurrss?   *Mis on ... päevakurss?*
When is the bank open?
mil-lahl on pahnk *ah*-vah-tud?   *Millal on pank avatud?*

cash	*su*-lah-rra-hah	*sularaha*
cashier	kah-*seerr*	*kassiir*
coins	*mün*-did	*mündid*
credit card	krre-*deet*-kaahrrt	*krediitkaart*

At the Post Office

Post offices are open Monday through Saturday. In addition to handling mail, they offer telephone and telegraph services.

Where's the post office?
kus *ah*-sub *post*-kon-torr?   *Kus asub postkontor?*

I'd like to	mah *ta*-hahks	*Ma tahaks*
buy some ...	*os*-tah ...	*osta ...*
envelopes	*ümb*-rrik-ke	*ümbrikke*
postcards	*post*-kaahrr-te	*postkaarte*
stamps	*mahrr*-ke	*marke*

I'd like to send a ...	mah *tah*-hahks	*Ma tahaks*
	saah-tah ...	*saata ...*
fax	*fahk*-si	*faksi*
parcel	*pahk*-ki	*pakki*
telegram	*te*-le-*grrahm*-mi	*telegrammi*

ESTONIAN

I'd like to send this to ...
    mah *tah*-**hahks**   *Ma tahaks*
    saah-**tah** *sel*-**le** ...   *saata selle ...*

How much does it cost?
    kui *pahl*-**yu seh** *mahk*-**sahb?**   *Kui palju see maksab?*

Is there a letter/parcel for me?
    kahs *mul*-**le on**   *Kas mulle on*
    kirr-**yah/** *pahk*-**ki?**   *kirja/pakki?*

airmail	*len*-nu-post	*lennupost*
letter box	*post*-kahst	*postkast*

Telephone & Internet

It's possible to make direct international calls from most private telephones in Estonia. Pay phones need phone cards, sold in kiosks, filling stations and many shops. Mobile phones are very widely used. You can also book telephone calls at post offices through an operator.

I want to make a long-distance
call to ...
    mah *tah*-**han vyt**-**tah**   *Ma tahan võtta*
    kau-ge-ky-ne ...   *kaugekõne ...*

What does it cost per minute?
    kuy *pahl*-**yu**   *Kui palju*
    mahk-**sahb** *mi*-**nut?**   *maksab minut?*

I was cut off.
    ky-**ne** *kaht*-**kes**   *Kõne katkes.*

It's the wrong number.
    seh on *vah*-**le** *num*-**berr**   *See on vale number.*

It's engaged.
    seh on *kin*-**ni**   *See on kinni.*

I'd like to speak to ...
    mah *soo*-**vin** *rraa*-**ki-dah** ...   *Ma soovin rääkida ...*

I want to leave a message.
    mah *tah*-**han** *yat*-**tah** *sy*-**na**   *Ma tahan jätta sõna.*

ESTONIAN

telephone	*te*-le-fon	*telefon*
telephone number	*te*-le-fo-ni-*num*-berr	*telefoninumber*

I need to get on the Internet.
> **mah** *vah*-yahn
> *in*-terr-ne-ti-ü-hen-dust

> *Ma vajan*
> *internetiühendust.*

I need to check my email.
> **mah pean** *vaah*-tah-mah
> *o*-mah e-*lekt*-rron-pos-ti

> *Ma pean vaatama oma*
> *elektronposti.*

Sightseeing

Tallinn and many other towns in Estonia are picturesque and lend
themselves to walking. During summer there are organised walking
and bus tours. Guidebooks, maps and brochures are available in
tourist information offices and bookstores.

ESTONIAN

Do you have a ...?	**kahs tayl on ...?**	*Kas teil on ...?*
town guidebook	*lin*-nah-yuh-ti	*linnajuhti*
town map	*lin*-nah-plaah-ni	*linnaplaani*

What are the main attractions?
> **mis on** *pea*-mi-sed
> *vaah*-tah-mis-vaarr-su-sed?

> *Mis on peamised*
> *vaatamisväärsused?*

What's that?
> **mis seh on?**

> *Mis see on?*

How old is it?
> **kuy** *vah*-nah seh on?

> *Kui vana see on?*

Can I take photographs?
> **kahs mah** *to*-hin
> *pil*-dis-tah-dah?

> *Kas ma tohin*
> *pildistada?*

What time does it open/close?
> **mis kell seh** *ah*-vah-tahk-se/
> su-le-tahk-se?

> *Mis kell see*
> *avatakse/suletakse?*

What street is this?
> **mis** *ta*-nahv seh on?

> *Mis tänav see on?*

I'd like to go to ...
  mah *tah*-haks *min*-nah ...   *Ma tahaks minna ...*
I'd like to go on a guided tour.
  mah *tah*-haks *min*-nah   *Ma tahaks minna*
  eks-kurr-*siaw*-ni-le   *ekskursioonile.*
I'd like to hire a guide.
  mah *tah*-hahks *tel*-li-da *gee*-di *Ma tahaks tellida giidi.*

Useful Words

building	*haw*-ne	*hoone*
castle	loss	*loss*
cemetery	*kahl*-mis-tu	*kalmistu*
church	*ki*-rrik	*kirik*
exhibition	*nai*-tus	*näitus*
fortress	*kind*-lus	*kindlus*
historical	a-*yah*-law-li-ne	*ajalooline*
library	*rraah*-mah-tu-ko-gu	*raamatukogu*
monument	*mo*-nu-ment	*monument*
museum	*moo*-se-um	*muuseum*
national park	*rrah*-vus-pahrk	*rahvuspark*
nature trail	*low*-du-se	*looduse*
	yp-pe-rrah-dah	*õpperada*
park	pahrrk	*park*
ruins	*vah*-rre-med	*varemed*
statues	*ku*-yud	*kujud*
university	*ü*-li-kawl	*ülikool*

ESTONIAN

Going Out

Restaurants abound throughout Estonia, nearly all of them opened since independence. Prices are close to western levels and you'll also find fast food places and pizza parlours. Estonia's long musical heritage is reflected in the wide range of classical music performances, and events like the enormous song festivals. Theatre is vibrant and popular. Discos, cabaret shows, and casinos are booming. They often have a cover charge.

What's there to do here
in the evenings?
    mi-dah vyiks sehn   *Mida võiks siin*
    yh-tu-ti *te*-hah?   *õhtuti teha?*
Are there any discos?
    kahs sehn on *dis*-ko-sid?   *Kas siin on diskosid?*
Are there places where I can hear
Estonian folk music?
    kahs *ku*-sah-gil saahb   *Kas kusagil saab*
    koo-lah-tah *ehs*-ti   *kuulata Eesti*
    rrah-vah-moo-si-kaht?   *rahvamuusikat?*

Please recommend *pah*-lun *saw*-vi-tah-ge *Palun soovitage*
a good ...   *mu*-le head ...   *mulle head ...*
    bar   *baah*-rri   *baari*
    cafe   *koh*-vi-kut   *kohvikut*
    nightclub   *err*-klu-bi   *ööklubi*

What's on tonight at the theatre?
    mis on *ta*-nah *teaht*-rris?   *Mis on täna teatris?*
What time does it begin?
    mis kell seh *al*-gab?   *Mis kell see algab?*
Where can I buy tickets?
    kust saahb *os*-tah *pi*-le-tayd?   *Kust saab osta pileteid?*
One ticket/two tickets, please.
    üks *pi*-let/kahks   *Üks pilet/kaks*
    pi-le-tit *pah*-lun   *piletit, palun.*
Is this seat free?
    kahs seh koht on *vah*-bah?   *Kas see koht on vaba?*

ESTONIAN

ESTONIAN

cabaret	kah-bah-*rray*	*kabaree*
casino	*kah*-seh-no	*kasiino*
cinema	*ki*-no	*kino*
concert	*kont*-serrt	*kontsert*
disco	*dis*-ko	*disko*
theatre	*teah*-terr	*teater*

PAPERWORK

name	*ni*-mi	*nimi*
address	*aahd*-rress	*aadress*
age	*vah*-nus	*vanus*
birth certificate	*sün*-ni-tun-nis-tus	*sünnitunnistus*
border	*rree*-gi-peerr	*riigipiir*
car registration	*syi*-du-ki	*sõiduki*
document	*rre*-gist-*rreh*-rri-mis-tun-nis-tus	*registreerimis-tunnistus*
citizenship	*ko*-dah-kond-sus	*kodakondsus*
customs	toll	*toll*
date of birth	*sün*-ni-aeg	*sünniaeg*
driver's licence	*yu*-hi-lu-bah	*juhiluba*
identification	*i*-si-ku-tun-nis-tus	*isikutunnistus*
immigration	im-mig-*rraht-siawn*	*immigratsioon*
marital status	*pe*-rre-kon-nah-says	*perekonnaseis*
passport	pahss	*pass*
passport number	*pahs*-si *num*-berr	*passi number*
place of birth	*sün*-ni-koht	*sünnikoht*
profession	e-lu-*kut*-se	*elukutse*
reason for travel	*rray*-si *pyh*-yus	*reisi põhjus*
religion	kon-fes-*siawn*	*konfessioon*
sex	*su*-gu	*sugu*
visa	*vee*-sah	*viisa*

IN THE COUNTRY
Weather

Today the weather is ...	*ta*-nah on ... ilm	*Täna on ... ilm.*
nice	*i*-lus	*ilus*
bad	hahlb	*halb*
cold	külm	*külm*
warm	soe	*soe*
windy	*too*-li-ne	*tuuline*
foggy	*u*-du-ne	*udune*

It will ... tomorrow.	*hom*-me *sah*-yahb ...	*Homme sajab ...*
rain	*vih*-mah	*vihma*
snow	lund	*lund*
sleet	*lert*-si	*lörtsi*

Directions

How far is it?		
kuy kau-gel seh on?		*Kui kaugel see on?*
Can we walk there?		
kahs *sin*-na sahb *yahlg*-si?		*Kas sinna saab jalgsi?*

north	*py*-hi	*põhi*
south	*lyu*-nah	*lõuna*
east	*i*-dah	*ida*
west	laas	*lääs*

ESTONIAN

RAINING SPRATS & DOGS

Kui müristab ja välku lööb, siis Vanapagan silku sööb.
'When it thunders and lightning strikes, then Old
Pagan eats sprats.' – Estonian folk saying.

ESTONIAN

Animals

beaver	**kob-rrahs**	*kobras*
bird	**lind**	*lind*
boar	**mets-sigah**	*metssiga*
cat	**kahss**	*kass*
cow	**lehm**	*lehm*
deer	**hirrv**	*hirv*
dog	**koerr**	*koer*
fish	**kah-lah**	*kala*
fox	**rre-bah-ne**	*rebane*
horse	**ho-bu-ne**	*hobune*
lynx	**il-ves**	*ilves*
moose	**py-derr**	*põder*
otter	**saahrr-mahs**	*saarmas*
rabbit	**yah-nes**	*jänes*
sheep	**lahm-mahs**	*lammas*
wolf	**hunt**	*hunt*

Plants

birch	**kahsk**	*kask*
fir	**koosk**	*kuusk*
flower	**lill**	*lill*
oak	**tahmm**	*tamm*
pine	**mand**	*mänd*
tree	**poo**	*puu*

DID YOU KNOW ...   Estonia's national bird is the barn swallow, *suitsupääsuke*, and the national flower is the cornflower, *rukkilill*.

Camping

Where's a camp site?
kus on *kam*-ping?   *Kus on kämping?*
Can we set up a tent here?
kahs seen vyib *tel*-ki-dah?   *Kas siin võib telkida?*

ESTONIAN

air mattress	*yhk*-mahd-rrahts	õhkmadrats
axe	*kirr*-ves	kirves
backpack	*sel*-yah-kott	seljakott
can opener	*ah*-vah-yah	avaja
compass	*kom*-pahss	kompass
firewood	*lyk*-ke-pood	lõkkepuud
gas cylinder	*maht*-kah-gaahs	matkagaas
matches	*ti*-kud	tikud
penknife	*tahs*-ku-nu-gah	taskunuga
rope	kyis	köis
sleeping bag	*mah*-gah-mis-kott	magamiskott
stove	*ah*-hi	ahi
tent	telk	telk
tent pegs	*tel*-gi-vai-ahd	telgivaiad
torch (flashlight)	*tahs*-ku-lahmp	taskulamp

ESTONIAN

Useful Words

beach	rrahnd	*rand*
county/province	*maah*-kond	*maakond*
forest	mets	*mets*
island	saahrr	*saar*
lake	yarrv	*järv*
river	*yo*-gi	*jõgi*
sea	*me*-rri	*meri*
village	*kü*-lah	*küla*
weather forecast	*il*-mah-tea-de	*ilmateade*
windmill	*too*-le-ves-ki	*tuuleveski*

ISLAND HOPPING

Estonia's long coastline includes many islands. The two largest, Saaremaa and Hiiumaa, are among the most unspoiled and idyllic parts of Europe, thanks in large part to the 50-year Soviet occupation, during which they were off limits for all but the locals, and no significant industrialisation took place.

Saaremaa is the larger, about the size of Luxembourg, and it's a place for quiet wandering and looking at ancient churches, windmills, and manor houses. In the sleepy main town of Kuressaare is the only entirely preserved stone castle in the Baltics, dating back to the 14th century. With moat and towers, it fulfills any child's fantasy. Even more intriguing for many is the meteor crater at Kaali. The last giant meteorite to fall in an inhabited place, it may be the source of stories in Pytheas and northern mythology about the sun falling to earth.

Even wilder and more tranquil is the second island, Hiiumaa. Many writers, artists and musicians have summer houses here. In addition to churches and manor houses, worth seeing is the enormous lighthouse at *Kõpu*, first lit in 1531.

FOOD

Estonians prefer entertaining in their own homes, and while the food may not be exotic you'll be served tasty fish and pork, fresh vegetables and fruits. Even city dwellers take off weekends in the spring and autumn to tend allotments and visit family farms, and they bring back home-grown food to use during the rest of the year.

Estonians start any meal by saying *Head isu!* which is the equivalent of 'Bon appetit!'. When enjoying a drink, you'll often hear *Terviseks!*, 'To your health!'. In an informal situation, your host may say *Söö kõht täis*, 'Eat until your stomach is full'.

Restaurants can be found featuring every cuisine and they often provide multilingual menus. Tipping does not follow firmly established rules. In better restaurants, add 10%.

ESTONIAN

At the Restaurant

Please recommend a good ...	*pah*-lun *saw*-vi-tah-ge *mu*-le head ...	*Palun soovitage mulle head ...*
restaurant	*rres*-to-rrah-ni	*restorani*
cafe	*koh*-vi-kut	*kohvikut*

I'd like to make a reservation
for ... people at ... pm.
    mah *saw*-vin *tel*-li-dah   *Ma soovin tellida*
    lau-dah ... *i*-ni-me-se-le   *lauda ... inimesele*
    kel-lah ...   *kella ...*

I have a reserved table.
    mul on *tel*-li-tud laud   *Mul on tellitud laud.*

Do you have a free table?
    kas tayl on *vah*-bah *lau*-dah?   *Kas teil on vaba lauda?*

May I have a menu?
    kas mah *saahk*-sin me-*nüü*?   *Kas ma saaksin menüü?*

I'd like ...
    ma *saw*-vik-sin ...   *Ma sooviksin ...*

ESTONIAN

This isn't my order.
   seh ay *o*-le *mi*-nu
   tel-li-mus

See ei ole minu
tellimus.

I'd like the bill, please.
   pah-lun *ahrr*-ve

Palun arve.

Can I pay by credit card?
   kas tayl saab *mahks*-tah
   krre-*deet*-*kaahrr*-di-ga?

Kas teil saab maksta
krediitkaardiga?

I've had enough.
   sel-lest *pee*-sahb

Sellest piisab.

Useful Words

ashtray	*tu*-hah-taws	*tuhatoos*
bill	*ahrr*-ve	*arve*
cold	külm	*külm*
cup	tahss	*tass*
drink	yawk	*jook*
fork	*kah*-vel	*kahvel*
fresh	*varrs*-ke	*värske*
glass	klaahs	*klaas*
greasy	*rrahs*-vah-ne	*rasvane*
knife	*nu*-gah	*nuga*
plate	*tahld*-rrik	*taldrik*
spoon	*lu*-si-kahs	*lusikas*
stale	*vah*-nah	*vana*
sweet	*mah*-gus	*magus*

MENU DECODER

Special Dishes

These traditional foods are usually served during special holidays and festivals:

hani	**hah**-ni	goose (served at Christmas and Kadripäev)
heeringas	**heh**-rrin-gahs	herring
hernesupp	**herr**-ne-supp	pea soup
kilu	**ki**-lu	sprat
klimbisupp	**klim**-bi-supp	dumpling soup
mulgikapsas	**mul**-gi-kahp-sahs	sauerkraut with pork and barley
räim	rraim	Baltic herring

seajalad ubadega	**sea**-yah-lad **u**-bah-de-gah	pigs' legs with beans (served on Shrove Tuesday)
suitsuangerjas	**suyt**-su-ahn-gerr-yahs	smoked eel
suitsulest	**suyt**-su-lest	smoked flounder
sült	sült	'headcheese' (meat or fish in aspic)
verivorst	**ve**-rri-vorrst	blood sausage (served at Christmas)

ESTONIAN

Vegetarian Meals

It's not impossible to be a vegetarian in Estonia. Tallinn has at least one vegetarian restaurant, and most restaurants offer some vegetarian dishes.

I'm a vegetarian.
mah o-len tai-me-toyt-lah-ne   *Ma olen taimetoitlane.*

I don't eat ...	mah ay serr ...	*Ma ei söö ...*
meat	*li*-hah	*liha*
chicken	*kah*-nah	*kana*
fish	*kah*-lah	*kala*
ham	*sin*-ki	*sinki*
pork	*sea*-li-hah	*sealiha*

Breakfast

Estonians usually start the day with coffee. In the country, milk and buttermilk are also served. Porridge, eggs and open sandwiches with cheese, fish or sausages are also popular.

Rye bread (*leib*) is very much a part of Estonian culture and is eaten at every meal. *Jätku leiba!* – 'May the bread never run out!'.

breakfast	*hom*-mi-ku-serrk	*hommikusöök*

Would you like ...?	kahs te *saw*-vi-te ...?	*Kas te soovite ...?*
coffee	*koh*-vi	*kohvi*
tea	teed	*teed*
milk	*pee*-mah	*piima*
juice	*mah*-lah	*mahla*

ESTONIAN

barley porridge	krroo-bi-pu-derr	*kruubipuder*
bread (white)	sai	*sai*
cheese	yoost	*juust*
cornflakes	mai-si-hel-bed	*maisihelbed*
egg	mu-nah	*muna*
ground wheat porridge	mahn-nah-pu-derr	*mannapuder*
mashed potato	kahrr-tu-li-pu-derr	*kartulipuder*
pancake	pahn-kawk	*pannkook*
rice porridge	rree-si-pu-derr	*riisipuder*
riceflakes/puffed rice	rri-si-hel-bed	*riisihelbed*
rye bread	layb	*leib*
sausage	vorrst	*vorst*

Lunch & Dinner

There's no great distinction between lunch (*lōuna*) and dinner (*õhtusöök*) in Estonia. Either could be the main meal of the day. It typically consists of soup (*supp*), a main course (*praad*) and dessert (*magustoit*).

Meat, Poultry & Game

beef	law-mah-li-hah	*loomaliha*
boar meat	mets-sea-li-hah	*metssealiha*
chicken	kah-nah	*kana*
ham	sink	*sink*
lamb	lahm-bah-li-hah	*lambaliha*
pork	sea-li-hah	*sealiha*
turkey	kahl-kun	*kalkun*
veal	vah-si-kah-li-hah	*vasikaliha*

ESTONIAN

AT THE MARKET

Basics

bread	sai	*sai*
butter	vyi	*või*
cheese	yoost	*juust*
chocolate	*sho*-ko-lahd	*šokolaad*
cornflakes	*mai*-si-hel-bed	*maisihelbed*
egg	*mu*-nah	*muna*
margarine	*mahrr*-ga-rreen	*margariin*
marmalade	*mahrr*-me-lahd	*marmelaad*
milk	peem	*piim*
olive oil	*y*-li	*õli*
pasta	*pahs*-tah	*pasta*
rice	rrees	*riis*
sugar	*suh*-kurr	*suhkur*
water	*ve*-si	*vesi*
yogurt	*yo*-gurrt	*jogurt*

Meat & Poultry

beef	*law*-mah-li-hah	*loomaliha*
boar meat	*mets*-sea-li-hah	*metssealiha*
chicken	*kah*-nah	*kana*
ham	sink	*sink*
lamb	*lahm*-bah-li-hah	*lambaliha*
pork	*sea*-li-hah	*sealiha*
turkey	*kahl*-kun	*kalkun*
veal	*vah*-si-kah-li-hah	*vasikaliha*

Vegetables

beet	peht	*peet*
broad beans	oahd	*oad*
cabbage	*kahp*-sahs	*kapsas*
capsicum	*pap*-rri-kah	*paprika*
carrot	*porr*-gahnd	*porgand*
cauliflower	*lill*-kahp-sahs	*lillkapsas*
celery	*sel*-lerr	*seller*
cucumber	kurrk	*kurk*

AT THE MARKET

green beans	*aed*-oahd	*aedoad*
lettuce	*sah*-laht	*salat*
mushrooms	*seh*-ned	*seened*
onion	*si*-bul	*sibul*
peas	*herr*-ned	*herned*
potato	*kahrr*-tul	*kartul*
pumpkin	*kyrr*-vits	*kõrvits*
spinach	*spi*-naht	*spinat*
tomato	*to*-maht	*tomat*
turnip	*kaah*-li-kahs	*kaalikas*
vegetables	*yoorr*-vil-yahd	*juurviljad*
zucchini	*su*-vi-kyrr-vits	*suvikõrvits*

Seafood

Baltic herring	rraim	*räim*
cod	turrsk	*tursk*
crayfish	vahk	*vähk*
fish	*kah*-lah	*kala*
herring	*heh*-rrin-gahs	*heeringas*
lobster	*me*-rri-vahk	*merivähk*
mussels	*rran*-nah-karr-bid	*rannakarbid*
salmon	*ly*-he	*lõhe*

Fruit

apple	own	*õun*
apricot	*ahp*-rri-koos	*aprikoos*
banana	bah-*naahn*	*banaan*
berries	*mahrr*-yahd	*marjad*
fruit	*poo*-vil-yahd	*puuviljad*
grapes	*vee*-nah-mahrr-yahd	*viinamarjad*
lemon	*sid*-rrun	*sidrun*
orange	*ah*-pel-sin	*apelsin*
peach	*virr*-sik	*virsik*
pear	pirrn	*pirn*
plum	plawm	*ploom*
strawberry	*maah*-si-kahs	*maasikas*

ESTONIAN

ESTONIAN

Seafood

Baltic or small herring	rraim	*räim*
cod	turrsk	*tursk*
crayfish	vahk	*vähk*
fish	*kah*-lah	*kala*
herring	heh-rrin-gahs	*heeringas*
lobster	me-rri-vahk	*merivähk*
mussels	rran-nah-karr-bid	*rannakarbid*
oysters	ahust-rrid	*austrid*
salmon	*ly*-he	*lõhe*
shrimp	krre-ve-tid	*krevetid*
sprats	*ki*-lud	*kilud*

Vegetables & Salads

beet	peht	*peet*
broad beans	oahd	*oad*
cabbage	*kahp*-sahs	*kapsas*
capsicum	*pap*-rri-kah	*paprika*
carrot	*porr*-gahnd	*porgand*
cauliflower	*lill*-kahp-sahs	*lillkapsas*
celery	*sel*-lerr	*seller*
cucumber	kurrk	*kurk*
green beans	*aed*-oahd	*aedoad*
lettuce	*sah*-laht	*salat*
mushrooms	*seh*-ned	*seened*
onion	*si*-bul	*sibul*
peas	*herr*-ned	*herned*
pickle	hah-pu-kurrk	*hapukurk*
potato	kahrr-tul	*kartul*
potato salad	kahrr-tu-li-sah-laht	*kartulisalat*
pumpkin	*kyrr*-vits	*kõrvits*
spinach	*spi*-naht	*spinat*
tomato	*to*-maht	*tomat*
turnip	*kaah*-li-kahs	*kaalikas*
vegetables	*yoorr*-vil-yahd	*juurviljad*
zucchini	*su*-vi-kyrr-vits	*suvikõrvits*

Fruit

apple	own	*ōun*
apricot	*ahp*-rri-koos	*aprikoos*
banana	bah-*naahn*	*banaan*
berries	*mahrr*-yahd	*marjad*
fruit	*poo*-vil-yahd	*puuviljad*
grapes	vee-nah-mahrr-yahd	*viinamarjad*
lemon	*sid*-rrun	*sidrun*
nuts	*pahk*-lid	*pähklid*
orange	*ah*-pel-sin	*apelsin*
peach	*virr*-sik	*virsik*
pear	pirrn	*pirn*
plum	plawm	*ploom*
strawberry	*maah*-si-kahs	*maasikas*
watermelon	ahrr-*boos*	*arbuus*

Desserts

biscuits	*küp*-si-sed	*küpsised*
cake	kawk	*kook*
fruit preserve	kom-*pott*	*kompott*
ice cream	*jaa*-tis	*jäätis*
whipped cream	vah-hu-kawrr	*vahukoor*

Condiments, Herbs & Spices

butter	vyi	*või*
dill	till	*till*
honey	*me*-si	*mesi*
jam	maws	*moos*
mustard	*si*-nep	*sinep*
oil	*y*-li	*õli*
pepper	*pi*-pahrr	*pipar*
salt	sawl	*sool*
sauce	*kahs*-te	*kaste*
sour cream	hah-pu-kawrr	*hapukoor*
sugar	*suh*-kurr	*suhkur*
vinegar	aa-di-kahs	*äädikas*

ESTONIAN

Cooking Methods

baked	*küp*-se-tah-tud	*küpsetatud*
boiled	*keh*-de-tud	*keedetud*
fried	*prrae*-tud	*praetud*
raw	*taw*-rres	*toores*

Non-Alcoholic Drinks

bottled mineral water	*ahl*-li-kah-ve-si	*allikavesi*
buttermilk	*keh*-firr	*keefir*
juice	*mahhl*	*mahl*
milk	*peem*	*piim*
water	*ve*-si	*vesi*

Alcoholic Drinks

champagne	*sham*-pus	*šampus*
cocktail	kok-*tayl*	*kokteil*
cognac	*kon*-yahk	*konjak*
home-brewed beer	*ko*-du-y-lu	*koduõlu*
mulled wine	*hyyg*-vayn	*hõõgvein*
squash	*morrs*	*morss*
vodka	veen	*viin*
wine	vayn	*vein*

SHOPPING

The big malls and grocery stores are usually open seven days a week but most other shops have reduced hours on Saturdays and are closed on Sundays. Estonians do not bargain when they go shopping, although they may haggle a bit at the colourful outdoor markets.

Shoppers usually bring their own bags, but plastic bags are available for a small fee from the cashier or checkout.

Where's a/an/the ...?	**kus on ...?**	*Kus on ...?*
antique shop	**ahn-tik-vah-rri-*aaht***	*antikvariaat*
bakery	***lay*-vah-pawd**	*leivapood*
bookshop	**rraah-mah-tu-pawd**	*raamatupood*
clothes shop	**rryi-vah-pawd**	*rõivapood*
department store	***kau*-bah-mah-yah**	*kaubamaja*
pharmacy/ chemist	***ahp*-tehk**	*apteek*
florist	***lil*-le-pawd**	*lillepood*
food shop	***toy*-du-pawd**	*toidupood*
gift shop	***kin*-gi-tus-te pawd**	*kingituste pood*
hairdresser	***yook*-surr**	*juuksur*
market	**turrg**	*turg*
shoe shop	***kin*-gah-pawd**	*kingapood*
shop	**pawd/*kaup*-lus**	*pood/kauplus*

ESTONIAN

Making a Purchase

In pharmacies and some other stores you must pay for your goods at the cashier's desk and then present your receipt to collect them.

May I have ...?	***pah*-lun ...?**	*Palun ...?*
I'd like to buy ...	**mah *tah*-hahk-sin *os*-tah ...**	*Ma tahaksin osta ...*
Please show it to me.	***pah*-lun *nai*-dah-ke *mul*-le se-dah**	*Palun näidake mulle seda.*
I'll take it.	**mah *vy*-tahn *sel*-le**	*Ma võtan selle.*
I won't take it.	**mah ay *vy*-tah se-dah**	*Ma ei võta seda.*
What size is this?	**mis *soo*-rrus see on?**	*Mis suurus see on?*
I'd like to try this.	**mah *tah*-hahks se-dah *prraw*-vi-dah**	*Ma tahaks seda proovida.*
It fits.	**seh on *pah*-rrahs**	*See on paras.*
It's too ...	**see on *lee*-gah ...**	*See on liiga ...*
big	**soorr**	*suur*
small	***vai*-ke**	*väike*
long	**pikk**	*pikk*
short	***lü*-hi-ke**	*lühike*

ESTONIAN

Have you anything else like this?
  kahs tayl on *mi*-dah-gi muud   *Kas teil on midagi muud*
  tao-list?   *taolist?*
It's too expensive.
  see on *lee*-gah *kahl*-lis   *See on liiga kallis.*
Does it have a guarantee?
  kahs *sel*-lel on *gah*-rrahn-tee?   *Kas sellel on garantii?*
Can I pay by credit card?
  kahs tayl saahb *mahks*-tah   *Kas teil saab maksta*
  krre-*deet*-kaahrr-di-gah?   *krediitkaardiga?*
Please wrap it in paper.
  pah-lun *pahk*-ki-ge seh   *Palun pakkige see*
  pah-be-rris-se   *paberisse.*
Do you have a plastic bag?
  kahs tayl on *ki*-le-kot-ti?   *Kas teil on kilekotti?*

Essential Groceries

batteries	*pah*-tah-rrayd	*patareid*
bread (white)	sai	*sai*
butter	vyi	*või*
candles	*küün*-lahd	*küünlad*
cheese	yoost	*juust*
chocolate	*sho*-ko-laahd	*šokolaad*
egg	*mu*-nah	*muna*
flour	*yah*-hu	*jahu*
gas cylinder	*maht*-kah-gaahs	*matkagaas*
ham	sink	*sink*
honey	*me*-si	*mesi*
jam	*keh*-dis/maws	*keedis/moos*
margarine	*mahrr*-gah-rreen	*margariin*
marmalade (orange)	*mahrr*-me-laahd	*marmelaad* (also means a type of sweet)
matches	*ti*-kud	*tikud*
milk	peem	*piim*

pasta	*pahs*-tah	*pasta* (older people may say *makaronid*)
pepper	*pi*-pahrr	*pipar*
rice	rrees	*riis*
salt	sawl	*sool*
shampoo	shahm-*poon*	*šampoon*
soap	sehp	*seep*
sugar	*suh*-kurr	*suhkur*
toilet paper	tua-*lett*-pah-berr	*tualettpaber*
toothpaste	*hahm*-bah-pahs-tah	*hambapasta*
washing powder	*pe*-su-pul-berr	*pesupulber*
yogurt	*yo*-gurrt	*jogurt*

ESTONIAN

Souvenirs

Where can I buy ...?	kust mah saahn *os*-tah ...?	*Kust ma saan osta ...?*
a traditional brooch	*sy*-le	*sõle*
Estonian handicrafts	*ehs*-ti *ka*-si-terrd	*eesti käsitööd*
folk costumes	*rrah*-vah-*rryi*-vahd	*rahvarõivad*
paintings	*maah*-le	*maale*
rugs and wall hangings	*vai*-pu	*vaipu*
souvenirs	su-ve-*neerr*-e	*suveniire*

ESTONIAN

Clothing

blouse	**ploos**	*pluus*
coat	**mahn**-tel	*mantel*
dress	klayt	*kleit*
gloves	*kin*-dahd	*kindad*
hat	*kü*-bahrr/	*kübar/*
	kaah-bu	*kaabu*
jacket	yahkk	*jakk*
scarf	sahll	*sall*
shirt	sarrk	*särk*
shoes	*kin*-gahd	*kingad*
skirt	*seh*-lik	*seelik*
socks	**so**-kid	*sokid*
suit (woman's)	kos-*tüüm*	*kostüüm*
(man's)	*ü*-li-kond	*ülikond*
trousers/pants	*pük*-sid	*püksid*

Materials

brass	vahsk	*vask*
cotton	*poo*-vill	*puuvill*
gold	kuld	*kuld*
handmade	*ka*-si-terr	*käsitöö*
leather	nahk	*nahk*
silk	seed	*siid*
silver	*hy*-be	*hõbe*
woollen	*vil*-lah-ne	*villane*

Toiletries

comb	kahmm	*kamm*
condoms	kon-*daw*-mid	*kondoomid*
deodorant	deo-do-*rrant*	*deodorant*
disinfectant	*peerr*-i-tus	*piiritus*
nappies	*mahk*-med	*mähkmed*
razor	zhi-*lett*	*žilett*
sanitary napkins	hü-gi-*eh*-ni-si-de-med	*hügieenisidemed*
shampoo	shahm-*poon*	*šampoon*
shaving cream	*hah*-be-me-ah-yah-mis-krrehm	*habemea jamiskreem*
soap	sehp	*seep*
sunblock cream	*paeh*-vi-tus-krrehm	*päevituskreem*
tampons	tahm-*paw*-nid	*tampoonid*
toilet paper	tua-*lett*-pah-berr	*tualettpaber*
toothbrush	*hahm*-bah-hah-rri	*hambahari*
toothpaste	*hahm*-bah-pahs-tah	*hambapasta*

Stationery & Publications

Newspapers and magazines are sold in small roadside kiosks. Larger shops and hotels often also carry some foreign language publications.

Do you have (a/an) ...?	kahs tayl on ...?	*Kas teil on ...?*
books about Estonia	*rraah*-mah-tuyd *ehs*-tist	*raamatuid Eestist*
Estonian text book	*ehs*-ti *keh*-le y-pi-kut	*eesti keele õpikut*
English-Estonian dictionary	*ing*-li-se – *ehs*-ti sy-nah-rraah-mah-tut	*inglise-eesti sõnaraamatut*
Tallinn guidebook	*tahl*-lin-nah *yuh*-ti	*Tallinna juhti*
map of Tallinn	*tahl*-lin-nah *kaahrr*-ti	*Tallinna kaarti*
books in English	*rrah*-mah-tuyd *ing*-li-se *keh*-les	*raamatuid inglise keeles*

ESTONIAN

envelope	*ümb*-rrik	*ümbrik*
magazine	*a*-yah-ki-rri	*ajakiri*
newspaper	*a*-yah-leht	*ajaleht*
notebook	*vi*-hik	*vihik*
paper	*pah*-berr	*paber*
pen	*pahs*-ta-plee-ahts	*pastapliiats*
wrapping paper	*pahk*-ke-pah-berr	*pakkepaber*

Photography

I'd like to buy	ma *saw*-vin *os*-tah	*Ma soovin osta*
some ... film.	... *fil*-mi	*... filmi.*
B&W	*must*-vahl-get	*mustvalget*
colour	*varr*-vi	*värvi*
print	*ne*-gah-teev	*negatiiv*
slide	*slai*-di	*slaidi*

Do you develop film?
    kahs te *il*-mu-tah-te *fil*-me?   *Kas te ilmutate filme?*
When will it be ready?
    mil-al seh *vahl*-mis saahb?   *Millal see valmis saab?*

Smoking

Smoking isn't allowed in shops. It's permitted in cafes and bars, but in restaurants guests usually don't light up until the end of the meal.

A pack of cigarettes and
matches, please.
    pah-lun pahkk si-gah-rret-te   *Palun pakk sigarette*
    yah ti-kud   *ja tikud.*
May I smoke?
    kas mah to-hin   *Kas ma tohin*
    suyt-se-tah-dah?   *suitsetada?*

Colours

beige	behzh	*beež*
black	must	*must*
blue	*si*-ni-ne	*sinine*
brown	prroon	*pruun*
green	*rro*-he-li-ne	*roheline*
grey	hahll	*hall*
purple	*lil*-lah	*lilla*
red	*pu*-nah-ne	*punane*
white	*vahl*-ge	*valge*
yellow	*kol*-lah-ne	*kollane*

ESTONIAN

Sizes & Comparisons

big	soorr	*suur*
small	*vai*-ke	*väike*
heavy	*rrahs*-ke	*raske*
light	*kerr*-ge	*kerge*
more	*rroh*-kem	*rohkem*
less	va-hem	*vähem*
many	*pahl*-yu	*palju*
too much	*leh*-gah *pahl*-yu	*liiga palju*
enough	*ai*-tahb	*aitab*

ESTONIAN

HEALTH

Since regaining independence in 1991, Estonia has been working to raise standards of health and medicine. However, most visitors turn to privately-run medical and dental clinics for their health needs. Pharmacies are able to recommend over-the-counter medicines and toiletries, but visitors should bring prescription medicines with them. There's a 24-hour pharmacy in Tallinn. And when in the countryside, one should guard against ticks.

At the Doctor

I'm ill.
mah *o*-len *hai*-ge   *Ma olen haige.*

My friend is ill.
mu *sy*-berr on *hai*-ge   *Mu sõber on haige.*

I need a doctor who speaks English.
ma *vah*-yan *ahrrs*-ti kes   *Ma vajan arsti, kes*
rraa-gib *ing*-li-se kehlt   *räägib inglise keelt.*

Where's the nearest ...?	kus on *la*-him ...?	*Kus on lähim ...?*
chemist	*ap*-tehk	*apteek*
dentist	*hahm*-bah-ahrrst	*hambaarst*
doctor	*ahrrst*	*arst*
hospital	*haig*-lah	*haigla*

Ailments

I'm ill.	mah *o*-len *hai*-ge	*Ma olen haige.*
I've been vomiting.	mah *o*-len *ok*-sen-dah-nud	*Ma olen oksendanud.*
I feel nauseous.	mul on *ee*-vel-dus	*Mul on iiveldus.*
I can't sleep.	mah ay sah *mah*-gah-dah	*Ma ei saa magada.*

I feel ...	mul on ...	*Mul on ...*
dizzy	*pea*-perr-ri-tus	*peapööritus*
shivery	*kül*-mah-vah-rri-nahd	*külmavärinad*
weak	*nyrr*-kus	*nõrkus*

I have (a/an) ...	mul on ...	*Mul on ...*
allergy	ahl-*lerr*-gi-ah	*allergia*
bronchitis	brron-*heet*	*bronhiit*
burn	*py*-le-tus	*põletus*
cold	*kül*-me-tus	*külmetus*
constipation	*ky*-hu-kin-ni-sus	*kõhukinnisus*
cough	*ker*-hah	*köha*
diarrhoea	*ky*-hu-lah-ti-sus	*kõhulahtisus*
fever	*pah*-lah-vik	*palavik*
glandular fever	*naarr*-me-pah-lah-vik	*näärmepalavik*
hayfever	*hay*-nah-pah-lah-vik	*heinapalavik*
headache	*peah*-vah-lu	*peavalu*
infection	in-fekt-*siawn*	*infektsioon*
migraine	mig-*rrehn*	*migreen*
pain	*vah*-lud	*valud*
stomachache	*ky*-hu-vah-lu	*kõhuvalu*
thrush	*soo*-vahl-ge	*suuvalge*
travel sickness	*syi*-dust *sü*-dah *pah*-hah	*sõidust süda paha*
urinary infection	urr-i-naahrr-in-fekt-siawn	*urinaar infektsioon*
venereal disease	*su*-gu-hai-gus	*suguhaigus*

ESTONIAN

Useful Phrases

It hurts there.
 mul *vah*-lu-tahb seet   *Mul valutab siit.*
I feel better/worse.
 mul on *pah*-rrem/ *hahl*-vem   *Mul on parem/halvem.*
This is my usual medicine.
 seh on mu *tah*-vah-li-ne *rro*-hi   *See on mu tavaline rohi.*

I don't want a blood transfusion.
> mah ay *tah*-hah
> ve-rre-ü-le-kahn-net

Ma ei taha
vereülekannet.

Can I have a receipt for my insurance?
> kahs mah *saahk*-sin
> *kvee*-tun-gi o-mah
> *kind*-lus-tu-se yaoks?

Kas ma saaksin
kviitungi oma
kindlustuse jaoks?

Parts of the Body

My ... hurts.	mu ... *vah*-lu-tahb	*Mu ... valutab.*
I have a pain in my ...	mul on ... *vah*-lu	*Mul on ... valu.*
I can't move my ...	mah ay saah *lee*-gu-tah-dah o-mah ...	*Ma ei saa liigutada oma ...*
ankle	*pahk*-lood	*pahkluud*
arm	*ka*-si-varrt	*käsivart*
back	*sel*-gah	*selga*
bone	loo	*luu*
chest	rrind	*rind*
ears	*kyrr*-vahd	*kõrvad*
eye	silm	*silm*
foot	*jah*-lah-lah-bah	*jalalaba*
head	peah	*pea*
knee	pylv	*põlv*
leg	yahlg	*jalg*
lungs	*kop*-sud	*kopsud*
mouth	soo	*suu*
nose	*ni*-nah	*nina*
shoulders	*y*-lahd	*õlad*
skin	nahk	*nahk*
spine	*selg*-rrawg	*selgroog*
stomach	kyht	*kõht*
teeth	*hahm*-bahd	*hambad*
throat	kurrk	*kurk*

At the Chemist

Is there an all-night chemist nearby?
kahs seen *lah*-he-dahl **on**
err-paeh-vah-rring-set
ahp-teh-ki?

Kas siin lähedal on
ööpäevaringset
apteeki?

I have a prescription.
mul on *rret*-sept

Mul on retsept.

How many times a day?
mi-tu *korr*-dah *paeh*-vahs?

Mitu korda päevas?

with food	kaws *toi*-du-gah	*koos toiduga*
antibiotics	*ahn*-ti-bi-aw-ti-ku-mid	*antibiootikumid*
Band-Aids	*plahst*-rrid	*plaastrid*
contraceptives	*rrah*-ses-tu-mis-vahst- tah-sed *vah*-hen-did	*rasestumisvastased* *vahendid*
cough medicine	*ker*-hah-rro-hi	*köharohi*
laxatives	*lah*-tis-ti	*lahtisti*
painkillers	*vah*-lu-vai-gis-ti	*valuvaigisti*

ESTONIAN

At the Dentist

I have a toothache.
mul on *hahm*-bah-vah-lu

Mul on hambavalu.

My gums hurt.
mu *i*-ge-med *vah*-lu-tah-vahd

Mu igemed valutavad.

I don't want my tooth extracted.
mah ay *tah*-hah *hahm*-mahst
val-yah *tym*-mah-tah

Ma ei taha hammast
välja tõmmata.

Please give me an anaesthetic.
pah-lun *teh*-ke *mul*-le
tuy-mes-tus

Palun tehke mulle
tuimestus.

Ouch!
ai!

Ai!

ESTONIAN

Useful Words & Phrases

I'm ...	mul on ...	*Mul on ...*
diabetic	*suhk*-rru-hai-gus	*suhkruhaigus*
asthmatic	*ahst*-mah	*astma*
anaemic	*ah*-neh-miah	*aneemia*
addiction	*ai*-ne-syl-tu-vus	*ainesõltuvus*
bite	*hahm*-mus-tus	*hammustus*
blood test	*ve*-rre-prrawv	*vereproov*
contraceptive	*rrah*-ses-tu-mis-vahs- tah-ne *vah*-end	*rasestumisvastane* *vahend*
injection	süst	*süst*
injury	*vi*-gahs-tus	*vigastus*
vitamins	*vi*-tah-mee-nid	*vitamiinid*
wound	haahv	*haav*

THEY MAY SAY ...

kus tayl *vah*-lu-tahb?	Where does it hurt?
kuy *kau*-ah seh on nee *ol*-nud?	How long have you been like this?
kahs te *vy*-tah-te *rroh*-tu?	Are you on medication?
kahs tayl on *mil*-le-gi *vahs*-tu ahl-*lerr*-gi-aht?	Are you allergic to anything?
kahs te o-le-te *rrah*-se?	Are you pregnant?

SPECIFIC NEEDS
Disabled Travellers

I'm disabled/handicapped.
> mah *o*-len *poo*-de-gah
> *i*-ni-me-ne

Ma olen puudega inimene.

I need assistance.
> mah *vah*-yan *ah*-bi

Ma vajan abi.

What services do you have for disabled people?
> mis *ah*-bi-va-hen-dayd
> *sah*-vahd *kah*-su-tah-dah
> *poo*-e-te-gah *i*-ni-me-sed?

Mis abivahendeid saavad kasutada puuetega inimesed?

Is there wheelchair access?
> kahs *sin*-nah sahb kah
> *rrah*-tahs-taw-li-gah?

Kas sinna saab ka ratastooliga?

I'm partly deaf.
> mah *koo*-len *hahl*-vahs-ti

Ma kuulen halvasti.

Speak more loudly, please.
> *pah*-lun *rraa*-ki-ge
> *vahl*-ye-mi-ni

Palun rääkige valjemini.

I have a hearing aid.
> mul on *kool*-de-ah-pah-rraaht

Mul on kuuldeaparaat.

I'm blind.
> mah *o*-len *pi*-me

Ma olen pime.

Are guide dogs permitted?
> kahs mah *to*-hin *kaah*-sah
> *vyt*-tah *yuht*-koe-rrah?

Kas ma tohin kaasa võtta juhtkoera?

I'm mute.
> mah *o*-len tumm

Ma olen tumm.

library for the blind	*pi*-me-dah-te *rraah*-mah-tu-ko-gu	*pimedate raamatukogu*
disabled person	*poo*-de-gah *i*-ni-me-ne	*puudega inimene*
guide dog	*yuht*-koerr	*juhtkoer*
wheelchair	*rrah*-tahs-tawl	*ratastool*

ESTONIAN

ESTONIAN

A NATION OF MUSIC

In few other countries in the world is music such an integral part of the culture as in Estonia. From the birth of national identity in the mid-19th century to the regaining of freedom from the Soviet Union, music has played a vital role in the nation's history. Today Estonian musicians continue to exert worldwide influence. Best-known abroad are Neeme Järvi, the Musical Director of the Detroit Symphony, and the modern composer Arvo Pärt.

The oral tradition of folk singing in Estonia goes back probably thousands of years, and consists of long narrative songs based on mythological tales. In the mid-19th century, as part of the 'national awakening', these songs started to be written down. Much later, starting in the 1920's, they were also recorded. By the 1980's there were 41,000 melodies collected, and many more with written text only.

Estonian choir singing began early in the century and led to one of the earliest public manifestations of national identity, a Song Festival in Tartu in 1869. Later moved to Tallinn, the two-day song festival continues to be held every five years, and is perhaps the largest event of its kind in the world. The Song Festival grounds on the outskirts of Tallinn, with an enormous half-dome stage facing a sweeping natural amphitheatre, hosts choruses of up to 28,000 voices singing to an audience which can number 250,000 people, or one-quarter of all the Estonians in the world. Student and children's song festivals are held in the years between the big ones.

Estonia takes its turn with Latvia and Lithuania to host the Baltika festival every three years, in mid-July. Music, art and dance are included in the week-long event. Exhibitions and parades celebrate the nation's folklore heritage.

TIME & DATES

Telling the time in Estonian is very simple. Just state the hour and then the minutes. See pages 93–94 for a list of numbers.

Excuse me, what time is it?
vah-bahn-dah-ge mis kell on?   *Vabandage, mis kell on?*

It's ...	kell on ...	*Kell on ...*
3.25	**kolm *kahks*-küm-**	*kolm kaksküm-*
(three twenty-five)	**mend vees**	*mend viis*
5.15	**vees *vees*-tayst**	*viis viisteist*
11.48	***üks*-tayst *ne*-li-küm-**	*üksteist*
	mend	*nelikümmend*
8.00	***kah*-hek-sah**	*kaheksa*
1.00	**üks**	*üks*

Take note of the following expressions:

12.30	**pawl üks**	*pool üks*
		(lit: half one)
12.15	***veh*-rrahnd üks**	*veerand üks*
		(lit: quarter one)
12.45	***kolm*-veh-rrahnd üks**	*kolmveerand üks*
		(lit: three-quarters one)

To indicate 'am' and 'pm', Estonians use the expressions *enne lõunat* ('before midday') and *pärast lõunat* ('after midday'):

It's 5 am.	**kell on vees *en*-ne *lyu*-nat**	*Kell on viis enne lõunat.*
It's 6 pm.	**kell on kuus *pa*-rrast *lyu*-nat**	*Kell on kuus pärast lõunat.*

ESTONIAN

second	*se*-kund	*sekund*
minute	*mi*-nut	*minut*
hour	tund	*tund*
in the morning	*hom*-mi-kul	*hommikul*
in the evening	*yh*-tul	*õhtul*

Days of the Week

Monday	es-mahs-paehv	*esmaspäev*
Tuesday	*tay*-si-paehv	*teisipäev*
Wednesday	*kol*-mah-paehv	*kolmapäev*
Thursday	*nel*-yah-paehv	*neljapäev*
Friday	*rreh*-de	*reede*
Saturday	*lau*-paehv	*laupäev*
Sunday	*pü*-hah-paehv	*pühapäev*

Months

January	*yaah*-nuahrr	*jaanuar*
February	*vehb*-rruahrr	*veebruar*
March	marrts	*märts*
April	ahp-*rrill*	*aprill*
May	mai	*mai*
June	*joo*-ni	*juuni*
July	*joo*-li	*juuli*
August	*au*-gust	*august*
September	sep-*tem*-berr	*september*
October	ok-*taw*-berr	*oktoober*
November	no-*vem*-berr	*november*
December	det-*sem*-berr	*detsember*

Seasons

spring	*ke*-vahd	*kevad*
summer	*su*-vi	*suvi*
autumn	*sü*-gis	*sügis*
winter	tahlv	*talv*

ESTONIAN

Dates

What's the date today?	mis *koo*-paehv *ta*-nah on?	*Mis kuupäev täna on?*
Today is ...	*ta*-nah on ...	*Täna on ...*
24 February	**kah-he-küm-ne** **nel-yahs veeb-rruahrr**	*kahekümne* *neljas veebruar*
9 March	**ü-hek-sahs marrts**	*üheksas märts*
16 August	**kooe-tayst-küm-nes** **au-gust**	*kuueteist-* *kümnes august*

Present

today	*ta*-nah	*täna*
this ...	sel ...	*sel ...*
year	*aah*-stahl	*aastal*
month	kool	*kuul*
week	*na*-dah-lahl	*nädalal*

Past

yesterday	*ay*-le	*eile*
day before yesterday	*ü*-le-*ay*-le	*üleeile*
last week	**merr-du-nud** **na-dah-lahl**	*möödunud* *nädalal*

Future

tomorrow	*hom*-me	*homme*
day after tomorrow	*ü*-le-*hom*-me	*ülehomme*
next week	*tu*-le-vahl *na*-dah-lahl	*tuleval nädalal*

ESTONIAN

During the Day

It's early.	aeg on *vah*-rrah-ne	*Aeg on varane.*
It's late.	aeg on *hi*-li-ne	*Aeg on hiline.*

afternoon	*pa*-rrahst-lyu-nah	*pärastlõuna*
dawn	koit	*koit*
day	paehv	*päev*
early	*vah*-rrah	*vara*
evening	*yh*-tu	*õhtu*
lunchtime	*lyu*-nah	*lõuna*
midnight	*sü*-dah-err	*südaöö*
morning	*hom*-mik	*hommik*
night	err	*öö*
noon/midday	*lyu*-nah	*lõuna*
sunrise	*paik*-se-tyus	*päiksetõus*
sunset	*law*-yang	*loojang*

Useful Words

a year ago	*aahs*-tah ehst	*aasta eest*
always	*ah*-lah-ti	*alati*
at once	*ko*-he	*kohe*
at the moment/now	*prrae*-gu	*praegu*
early	*vah*-rrah	*vara*
earlier	*vah*-rrem	*varem*
every day	*i*-gah paehv	*iga päev*
late	*hil*-yah	*hilja*
later	*hil*-yem	*hiljem*
never	*mit*-te *ku*-nah-gi	*mitte kunagi*
not yet	vehl *mit*-te	*veel mitte*
sometimes	*my*-ni-korrd	*mõnikord*
soon	*vahrrs*-ti	*varsti*
still	*ik*-kah	*ikka*

ESTONIAN

FESTIVALS & HOLIDAYS
National Holidays

Uusaasta	1 Jan	New Year's Day
Vabariigi aastapäev	24 Feb	Independence Day
Ülestõusmispühad	March/April	Easter
Võidupüha	23 Jun	Victory Day
Jaanipäev	24 Jun	St John's Day (Midsummer)
Jõulud	24-26 Dec	Christmas
Jõululaupäev	24 Dec	Christmas Eve
Jõulu esimene püha	25 Dec	First Christmas Day
Jõulu teine püha	26 Dec	Second Christmas Day

ESTONIAN

Festivals

New Year   *Uusaasta*

As Christmas was prohibited during the Soviet occupation, New Year's Eve served as a substitute and good children received presents from a Santa Claus-like figure called Father Frost. Nowadays, New Year's Eve is a time for champagne and fireworks and a time for friends to visit. As elsewhere, New Year's Day is for recuperation.

Independence Day – February 24   *Vabariigi aastapäev*

On this day in 1918, the Estonian Republic was proclaimed. It's marked by parades, speeches, flag ceremonies, concerts, and the President's reception on TV.

Easter – Spring   *Ülestõusmispühad*

Also called *Lihavõttepühad*, this was another holiday repressed during the Soviet period. Only old people who had little to fear from the government dared to go to church. But in the home eggs were painted and they still are. Some people send Easter cards.

THE SINGING REVOLUTION

During the Soviet era, the Song Festivals (see 'A Nation of Music' on page 86) continued, and were a rallying point for the Estonian national spirit, even though they had to include Russian and other pan-Soviet music. In 1980, the festival ended with an Estonian patriotic song, and the audience kept on singing it over and over and over, sending a clear message to the Soviets. In 1985, the authorities chose for the final song one which would not lead to a repeat of this.

In June of 1988, a festival in Tallinn's historic Old Town stirred up a wave of nationalist fervor. As it ended, a large part of the audience wanted to continue, and headed out to the Song Festival grounds where they stood in the twilight and sang Estonian patriotic songs. The following night an even larger crowd showed up. They broke into the maintenance buildings and turned the lights and sound system on. And the blue, black and white Estonian flag, forbidden for over forty years, appeared and was run up a flagpole. Each night more flags appeared, and the cheering crowds grew to over 200,000, with well-known popular singers leading them in song after patriotic song.

In addition to old anthems and traditional songs they sang new ones written by the young composer Alo Mattiisen. His 'Five Patriotic Songs' incorporated older musical elements and included 'Estonian I am'. It was sung over and over again during those fervent nights at the Song Festival grounds, and in the cafes and on the streets during the following months. The 'Singing Revolution' had replaced violence with music, and the overwhelming impact of the entire nation demonstrating forcefully but peacefully sent a signal to the Soviet authorities that their demand for freedom would not be repressed.

That year the Soviet Estonian legislature was the first in the USSR to declare sovereignty, and in 1990 it declared a transition to independence. In January 1991 the Soviets threatened a crackdown, but by August Estonia was free again.

ESTONIAN

Victory Day – June 23 *Võidupüha*

After the proclamation of the republic in 1918, Estonia had to fight both German and Soviet armies in the country. A decisive battle on this date in 1919 ensured the new nation's independence, so this day honours all who fought for Estonian freedom. Not surprisingly, the holiday was prohibited during the Soviet occupation but, conveniently, the following day was St John's Day. So for Estonians the bonfires of St John's Eve burned also for freedom and independence.

St John's Day – June 24 *Jaanipäev*

For Estonians, this is the biggest holiday after Christmas, and its ancient pagan roots mark the longest day of the year. All over Estonia on St John's Eve bonfires, both public and private, burn late into the short night. Jumping over the fire brings good luck, but that's hardly possible with the great fires towns put up nowadays. Often folk song or dance groups perform in traditional costume. Games like tug-of-war and sack races take place. More interesting for lovers is the custom of going into the forest to search for the fern flower, said to bloom only on this night. The search often takes a long time. Meanwhile around the fire people sing, dance, eat and drink, right up to dawn.

Souls' Visiting Day – November 2 *Hingedepäev*

The souls of forefathers are expected home on this day, and in olden times a set table was left for them. The holiday largely disappeared during the Soviet occupation but lately there's been a revival. Visits are made to the graves of relatives in the afternoon, and a lit candle is placed in the window of the home.

ESTONIAN

ESTONIAN

St Martin's Day – November 10   *Mardipäev*
St Catherine's Day – November 25 *Kadripäev*

These two holidays are for Estonian kids what Halloween is for American kids. They're most popular in rural areas. Although originally pagan festivals related to the start of winter which were taken over by the church, they're now occasions when children go door to door in costume. On St Martin's Eve boys dress in rough clothes and sing the associated songs (if they know them). On St Catherine's Eve it's the girls' turn (some cross-dressing may occur) and they go around in clean and light-coloured clothes. In both cases they're rewarded with sweets. Some families serve beans and roast goose on St Catherine's Day.

Christmas – December 25   *Jõulud*

Christmas really starts on Christmas Eve, when Santa Claus *(jõuluvana)* arrives and presents are given out. Children are expected to perform, reciting a verse or singing a song they have learned for the occasion. There's also a newer tradition of invisible elves *(päkapikk)* leaving sweets in children's slippers, which are left on the window sill for the night. Children often dress up as elves or at least wear a pointed red hat.

On December 24 the President of Estonia, following a 350-year tradition, declares Christmas Peace and attends a Christmas service. December 25 and 26 are called first and second Christmas day, and are a time for visiting friends and relatives.

The Christmas tree is a fir tree and is decorated with candles, ornaments and sweets. An older tradition is to bring a large pile of straw (as in Jesus' manger) into the main room for children to play in. The making of Christmas crowns, another old tradition, has had a revival in recent years. Made from straw, they're hung with ornaments and ribbons.

Food, and lots of it, is part of Christmas, and it symbolises enough food for the coming year. The traditional Christmas dinner features pork with sauerkraut, potatoes, potato salad with red beets and barley sausages, usually made with cows' blood. A bowl of ginger snaps is never absent from the coffee table. The traditional Christmas drink is home-brewed beer or mead, but store-bought beer is more common nowadays.

Happy Holiday!	**haid** *pü*-hi!	*Häid pühi!*
Happy New Year!	**head oot** *aahs*-taht!	*Head uut aastat!*
Happy Easter!	**haid ü-les-yus-mis-pü-hahd!**	*Häid ülestõus-mispühad!*
Merry Christmas!	**haid** *yow*-lu-pü-hi!	*Häid jõulupühi!*

ESTONIAN

NUMBERS & AMOUNTS
Cardinal Numbers

0	null	*null*
1	üks	*üks*
2	kahks	*kaks*
3	kolm	*kolm*
4	*ne*-li	*neli*
5	vees	*viis*
6	koos	*kuus*
7	*sayt*-se	*seitse*
8	*kah*-hek-sah	*kaheksa*
9	*ü*-hek-sah	*üheksa*
10	*küm*-me	*kümme*

ESTONIAN

11	*üks*-tayst	*üksteist*
12	*kahks*-tayst	*kaksteist*
13	*kolm*-tayst	*kolmteist*
14	*ne-li*-tayst	*neliteist*
15	*vees*-tayst	*viisteist*
16	*koos*-tayst	*kuusteist*
17	*sayt-se*-tayst	*seitseteist*
18	*kah-hek-sah*-tayst	*kaheksateist*
19	*ü-hek-sah*-tayst	*üheksateist*
20	*kahks*-küm-mend	*kakskümmend*
21	*kahks*-küm-mend-*üks*	*kakskümmend üks*
30	*kolm*-küm-mend	*kolmkümmend*
40	*ne-li*-küm-mend	*nelikümmend*
50	*vees*-küm-mend	*viiskümmend*
60	*koos*-küm-mend	*kuuskümmend*
70	*sayt-se*-küm-mend	*seitsekümmend*
80	*kah-hek-sah*-küm-mend	*kaheksakümmend*
90	*ü-hek-sah*-küm-mend	*üheksakümmend*
100	*sah-dah*	*sada*
1000	*tu*-haht	*tuhat*

Ordinal Numbers

1st	*e-si-me-ne*	*esimene*
2nd	*tay-ne*	*teine*
3rd	*kol-mas*	*kolmas*
4th	*nel-jas*	*neljas*
5th	*vee-es*	*viies*
6th	*koo-es*	*kuues*
7th	*sayts-mes*	*seitsmes*
8th	*kah-hek-sahs*	*kaheksas*
9th	*ü-hek-sahs*	*üheksas*
10th	*küm-nes*	*kümnes*
20th	*kah-he-küm-nes*	*kahekümnes*
21st	*kah-he-küm-ne e-si-me-ne*	*kahekümne esimene*

Fractions

1/4	**veh-rrahnd**	*veerand*
1/2	**pawl**	*pool*
3/4	**kolm-veh-rrand**	*kolmveerand*
1 1/2	**pawl-tayst**	*poolteist*

Useful Words

a little (amount)	**nah-tu-ke**	*natuke*
double	**to-pelt**	*topelt*
less	**va-hem**	*vähem*
many	**pahl-yu**	*palju*
more	**rroh-kem**	*rohkem*
percent	**prrot-sent**	*protsent*
some	**my-ni**	*mõni*
too much	**lee-gah pahl-yu**	*liiga palju*

ESTONIAN

SETU PEOPLE

The Setu are a Finno-Ugric people native to the area of Setumaa. This politically unrecognised territory straddles part of Estonia and Russia. The Setu never fully assimilated into Russian culture and have retained many of their old traditions. One of the most important of these is the day of the Setu kingdom which usually falls around 20 August every year. On this day, a representative of the Setu king (who according to folklore sleeps all day and night in his sand cave) is found. Competitions are held to find the king's royal singer and strongman, and the Setu kingdom is declared for another year.

The Setu are known for their songs, called *leelo*, which consist of solo spoken verses, followed by a refrain chanted by the whole group. *Leelo* are particularly the domain of women folk singers, who improvise new words every time they chant a verse.

ABBREVIATIONS

AS	*(aktsiaselts)*	Ltd or Inc
E	*(esmaspäev)*	Monday
e. l.	*(enne lõunat)*	am
e-post		email
hr	*(härra)*	Mr
jne	*(ja nii edasi)*	and so on/etc
jt	*(ja teised)*	and others/etc
K	*(kolmapäev)*	Wednesday
kl	*(kell)*	at (about time)
kr, EEK, s	*(kroon, sent)*	(Estonian currency)
L	*(laupäev)*	Saturday

lk	*(lehekülg)*	page
n	*(näiteks)*	eg
N	*(neljapäev)*	Thursday
P	*(pühapäev)*	Sunday
p. l.	*(pärast lõunat)*	pm
pr	*(proua)*	Mrs
prl	*(preili)*	Miss
R	*(reede)*	Friday
T	*(teisipäev)*	Tuesday
Tln		Tallinn
Trt		Tartu

ESTONIAN

EMERGENCIES

Help!
   ahp-pi!   *Appi!*

Watch out!
   ol-ge *et*-te-vaaht-lik!   *Olge ettevaatlik!*

Go away!
   min-ge a-rrah!   *Minge ära!*

Stop it!
   ly-pe-tah-ge!   *Lõpetage!*

Help, thief!
   ahp-pi vah-rrahs!   *Appi, varas!*

There's been an accident.
   seen *yuh*-tus *yn*-ne-tus   *Siin juhtus õnnetus.*

Call a doctor!
   kut-su-ge ahrrst!   *Kutsuge arst!*

Call an ambulance!
   kut-su-ge *keerr*-ah-bi!   *Kutsuge kiirabi!*

I'm ill/lost.
   mah *o*-len *hai*-ge/*ek*-si-nud   *Ma olen haige/eksinud.*

I've been raped.
   mind *va*-gis-tah-ti   *Mind vägistati.*

I've been robbed.
   mind *rrerr*-vi-ti   *Mind rööviti.*

I'm sorry.
   vah-bahn-dah-ge   *Vabandage.*

I didn't realise I was doing
anything wrong.
   mah ay *tead*-nud et mah   *Ma ei teadnud, et ma*
   teen *mi*-dah-gi *vah*-les-ti   *teen midagi valesti.*

I didn't do it.
   mah *po*-le se-dah *tay*-nud   *Ma pole seda teinud.*

I want to call my embassy/
consulate.
   mah *tah*-hahn *he*-lis-tah-dah   *Ma tahan helistada*
   o-mah *rree*-gi *saaht*-kon-dah/   *oma riigi saatkonda/*
   kon-su-laah-ti   *konsulaati.*

ESTONIAN

Could I use the telephone?
> **kas mah vyin *kah*-su-tah-dah te-le-fo-ni?** — *Kas ma võin kasutada telefoni?*

I have medical insurance.
> **mul on *terr*-vi-se-kind-lus-tus** — *Mul on tervisekindlustus.*

I've lost my ...	**mah *kao*-tah-sin ...**	*Ma kaotasin ...*
bag	***ko*-ti**	*koti*
money	***rrah*-hah**	*raha*
passport	***pahs*-si**	*passi*

LATVIAN

QUICK REFERENCE

Hello.	*svay*-kuh/svayks	Sveika/Sveiks. (f/m)
Goodbye.	uz *redz*-eh-shuhn-aws	Uz redzēšanos.
Yes./No.	yah/neh	Jā./Nē.
Excuse me/	*uht*-vai-naw-yeat/	Atvainojiet/
Sorry.	*pea*-dawd-eat	Piedodiet.
Thank you.	puhl-*deas*	Paldies.
You're welcome.	*loo*-dzu	Lūdzu.

I want to buy a ...	es *vaa*-laws *naw*-	Es vēlos nopirkt
ticket.	pirkt ... *bi*-lyet-i	... biļeti.
one-way	*vean*-virz-ean-uh	vienvirziena
return	turp *uht*-puh-kuhly	turp-atpakaļ

I don't understand.
es *ne*-suh-praw-tu — *Es nesaprotu.*

Do you speak English?
vai yoos *run*-ah-yuht — *Vai jūs runājat*
uhn-glis-ki? — *angliski?*

Where is ...?
kur *uht*-raw-duhs ...? — *Kur atrodas ...?*

Go straight ahead.
uz *preak*-shu — *Uz priekšu.*

Turn left/right.
puh *kray*-si/luh-bi — *Pa kreisi/labi.*

Do you have any rooms
available?
vai yums ir *bree*-vuhs — *Vai jums ir brīvas*
is-tuh-buhs? — *istabas?*

Where's the toilet?
kur ir *tu*-uh-le-tes? — *Kur ir tualetes?*

Help!
pah-lee-gah! — *Palīgā!*

1	veans	viens	6	sesh-i	seši
2	di-vi	divi	7	sep-ti-nyi	septiņi
3	trees	trīs	8	uhs-taw-nyi	astoņi
4	chet-ri	četri	9	de-vi-nyi	deviņi
5	peats-i	pieci	10	des-mit	desmit

LATVIAN

LATVIAN

INTRODUCTION

Latvian is the official language of the Republic of Latvia, which regained independence from the Soviet Union on 21 August 1991 after 50 years of occupation. With just under 2.5 million inhabitants, Latvian is the first language for approximately only 55% of the population (even fewer in the capital, Riga). Although Russian is spoken by just about everyone, Latvians are sensitive towards this fact, as the preservation of their nation's language is vital to their sense of identity and independence.

Latvian is one of the two surviving Baltic Indo-European languages – Lithuanian is the other. There are many similar words in both languages, but not sufficient to make them mutually intelligible. In Latvia there are dialect variations from east to west and this book covers what is known as 'High Latvian', which is the standard language originating from central Latvia.

English is a popular foreign language in Latvia so you may find that local people will be more than pleased to practise their language skills with you. If you manage to grasp at least some basic phrases in Latvian you'll be received warmly.

Latvian uses feminine and masculine forms of words. The feminine form appears first throughout this book and is separated from the masculine form by a slash. All phrases in this book are in the polite form unless otherwise indicated.

Help!

Take the time to learn the following everyday Latvian words and phrases, in order to make your stay more enjoyable:

Hello.	**svay-kuh**	*Sveika.* (to a female)
	svayks	*Sveiks.* (to a male)
Good day/afternoon.	**luhb-*dean***	*Labdien.* (also serves as a general 'hello')

Goodbye.	uz *redz*-eh-shuhn-aws	*Uz redzēšanos.*
Yes./No.	yah/neh	*Jā./Nē.*
Please./	loo-*dzu*	*Lūdzu.*
You're welcome.		
Thank you.	puhl-*deas*	*Paldies.*
Pardon?	kuh loo-*dzu*?	*Kā, lūdzu?*
Do you speak	vai yoos *run*-ah-yuht	*Vai jūs runājat*
English?	*uhn*-glis-ki?	*angliski?*
Cheers!	*prea*-kah!	*Priekā!*

See pages 113-119 for all kinds of small talk phrases to help you get to know the Latvians a little better.

LATVIAN

PRONUNCIATION

There's a consistent relationship between spelling and pronunciation in Latvian. Each letter and each vowel combination has its own constant sound.

Vowels

Latvian uses short and long vowels. As a rule, long and short vowels have the same sound; one is just an extended version of the other. A line above a vowel (called a macron) indicates that it has a long sound. It's important to make the distinction between short and long sounds as they can change the meaning of a word. For example, *istaba* ('a/the room') and *istabā* ('in a/the room'). Note that there are two different ways of pronouncing *e*, *ē* and *o*, so follow the pronunciation guide carefully.

Latvian	Transliteration	Sounds
a	**uh**	as the 'u' in 'fund'
ā	**ah**	as the 'a' in 'father'
e	**e**	as the 'e' in 'bet'
	a	as the 'a' in 'fat'
ē	**eh**	as the 'ai' in 'fair'
	aa	as the 'a' in 'sad', but longer
i	**i**	as the 'i' in 'in'
ī	**ee**	as the 'ee' in 'beet'
o	**o**	as the 'o' in 'pot'
	aw	as the 'oa' in 'oar'
u	**u**	as the 'u ' in 'pull'
ū	**oo**	as the 'u' in 'rule'

Diphthongs

Latvian	Transliteration	Sounds
ai	**ai**	as the 'i' in 'dive'
au	**ow**	as the 'ow' in 'now'
ei	**ay**	as the 'ay' in 'may'
ie	**ea**	as the 'ea' in 'fear'
oi	**oy**	as the 'oy' in 'toy'
ui	**uy**	similar to the 'ui' in 'ruin' (a combination of oo + y, but short)

LATVIAN

DID YOU KNOW ...

Latvian and Lithuanian are the only two surviving Baltic languages in the Indo-European language family. Neither of these languages bears much resemblance to Estonian, which is more closely related to Finnish.

Consonants

Consonants are pronounced as in English with the following exceptions:

Latvian	Transliteration	Sounds
c	ts	as the 'ts' in 'lots'
č	ch	as the 'ch' in 'chew'
dz	dz	as the 'ds' in 'beds'
dž	j	as the 'j' in 'job'
ģ	jy	a 'dy' sound, as the 'd' in British English 'duty'
j	y	as the 'y' in 'yellow'
ķ	ky	as the 'c' in 'cute'
ļ	ly	as the 'll' in 'million'
ņ	ny	as the 'n' in 'onion'
r	r	as the 'r' in 'bring' (slightly rolled)
š	sh	as the 'sh' in 'shop'
ž	zh	as the 's' in 'pleasure'

Stress

In Latvian, the stress is almost always on the first syllable. One notable exception is the word for 'thank you' *paldies* (puhl-**dees**).

Pronunciation Practice

Here are some sentences with transliterations for you to practise your Latvian pronunciation:

He went to the forest.
vinysh *aiz*-gah-yuh uz *mezh*-u   *Viņš aizgāja uz mežu.*

We eat lunch at a restaurant.
mehs *aa*-duhm *pus*-dea-nuhs   *Mēs ēdam pusdienas*
res-to-rah-nah   *restorānā.*

The water in the sea is warm today.
shaw-dean *yoo*-rah   *Šodien jūrā*
ir silts *oo*-dens   *ir silts ūdens.*

I'd like to change my ticket.
    es *vaa*-laws *uhp*-main-eet   *Es vēlos apmainīt*
    ***suh*-vu *bi*-lye-ti**   *savu biļeti.*

Here's my passport.
    shayt ir *muh*-nuh *puh*-se   *Šeit ir mana pase.*

GRAMMAR
The purpose of this section is to give you a brief outline of Latvian grammar so that you'll be able to string together your own simple sentences. Note that in Latvian the endings of nouns, pronouns and adjectives change depending on their use within a sentence and whether or not they are masculine or feminine.

Word Order
The usual word order in Latvian is subject-verb-object, ie, the same as in English. Note that verbs almost always come second in a sentence and that there are no articles (a/an/the) in Latvian.

Nouns
In Latvian nouns can have up to seven different case endings depending on their relationship to other words in the sentence, ie, whether they're the subject, direct object, indirect object, etc. All nouns are either feminine (usually end with a vowel) or masculine (usually end with a consonant). To make a noun plural, the general rule is to add the letter 's' to feminine nouns and the letter 'i' to masculine nouns.

Adjectives

Like pronouns, adjectives precede nouns and adopt the same gender and case.

big	*liels*
I have a big house.	*Man ir liela māja.*
	(lit: to-me is big house)
They live in a big house.	*Viņi dzīvo lielā mājā.*
	(lit: they live big house)
You see a big house.	*Jūs redzat lielu māju.*
	(lit: you see big house)
She sees the big house.	*Viņa redz lielo māju.*
	(lit: she sees big house)

Pronouns

Pronouns adopt the gender, number and case of the nouns they precede. Here they're listed in the nominative case (see page 20 for an explanation of case).

PRONOUNS		
PERSONAL		
I	*es*	*es*
you (sg & inf)	*tu*	*tu*
she	*viny-*uh	*viņa*
he	vinysh	*viņš*
we	mehs	*mēs*
you (pl & pol)	yoos	*jūs*
they	*viny-*uhs/*viny-*i	*viņas/viņi* (f/m)
POSSESSIVE		
my	*muh-*nuh/muhns	*mana/mans* (f/m)
your (sg & inf)	*tuh-*vuh/tuhvs	*tava/tavs* (f/m)
her	*viny-*uhs	*viņas*
his	*viny-*uh	*viņa*
our	moos-u	*mūsu*
your (pl & pol)	yoos-u	*jūsu*
their	*viny-*u	*viņu*

Verbs
Present

I run to the station.   *Es skrienu līdz stacijai.*
                          (lit: I run to station)

He reads the newspaper.   *Viņš lasa avīzi.*
                          (lit: he reads newspaper)

We see the cat.   *Mēs redzam kaķi.*
                          (lit: we see cat)

Past

I ran in the woods.   *Es skrēju pa mežu.*
                          (lit: I ran through/in
                          woods)

He reads a book.   *Viņš lasīja grāmatu.*
                          (lit: he read book)

We saw the monument.   *Mēs redzējam pieminekli.*
                          (lit: we saw monument)

Future

I shall run to town.   *Es skriešu līdz pilsētai.*
                          (lit: I shall-run to town)

She will read the letter.   *Viņa lasīs vēstuli.*
                          (lit: she will-read letter)

We shall see a/the film.   *Mēs skatīsimies filmu.*
                          (lit: we shall/will-see film)

LATVIAN

TO BE

I am	es *as*-mu	es esmu
you are (sg & inf)	tu *es*-i	tu esi
she/he is	*viny*-uh/vinysh ir	viņa/viņš ir
we are	mehs *as*-uhm	mēs esam
you are (pl & pol)	yoos *as*-uht	jūs esat
they are	*viny*-uhs/	viņas/
	viny-i ir	viņi ir (f/m)

TO HAVE

There is no verb meaning 'to have' in Latvian. Instead, Latvians use subject pronouns with the third person of the verb 'to be'. Only one form of the verb is used for each of the present, past and future tenses, irrespective of the subject. Note that it's the subject pronoun that changes.

PRESENT – *ir*
I have a ticket.
Man ir biļete.
(lit: to-me is ticket)

PAST – *bija*
He had a ticket.
Viņam bija biļete.
(lit: to-him was ticket)

FUTURE – *būs*
They will have tickets.
Viņām/viņiem būs biļetes. (f/m)
(lit: to-them will-be tickets)

Questions

Who is there?	*Kas tur ir?*
	(lit: who there is?)
Why did you leave?	*Kāpēc jūs aizgājat?*
	(lit: why you left?)
How shall I dress?	*Kā lai es ģērbjos?*
	(lit: how shall I dress?)

Used at the start of a sentence, *vai* creates a question. It roughly translates as 'do' or 'may' in English.

Do you have a dictionary?	*Vai jums ir vārdnīca?*
	(lit: *vai* to-you is dictionary?)
May I ask you?	*Vai es drīkstu jums uzprasīt?*
	(lit: *vai* I may to-you ask?)

QUESTION WORDS

how?	kaah?	kā?
what?	kahs?	kas?
who?	*kur-ah/kursh?*	kura/kuřš? (f/m)
why?	*kaah*-pehts/*kaah*-dehly?	kāpēc/kādēļ?
when?	kahd?	kad?
where?	kur?	kur?

LATVIAN

Negatives

To make a sentence negative in Latvian, place *ne-* in front of the verb.

He didn't arrive.	*Viņš neatbrauca.*
	(lit: he not-arrive)
I'm not coming with you.	*Es neiešu ar jums.*
	(lit: I not-will-come with you)

Prepositions

with	**ahr**	*ar*
without	**bez**	*bez*
at	**pea(h)**	*pie*
on	**uz**	*uz*
under	**zem**	*zem*
next to	***blah**-kus*	*blakus*
above	**virs**	*virs*

Conjunctions

and	**un**	*un*
because	**yaw**	*jo*
but	**bet**	*bet*
or	**vai**	*vai*
therefore	***taah**-pets*	*tāpēc*

LATVIAN

Useful Words

far	***taah**-luh*	tālu
here	**shayt**	šeit
near	***tu**-vu*	tuvu
that (accusative case)	**taw**	to
that (nominative case)	**taah/tahs**	tā/tas (f/m)
there	**tur**	tur
these	**shees/shea**	šīs/šie (f/m)
this (accusative case)	**shaw**	šo
this (nominative case)	**shee/shis**	šī/šis (f/m)
those	**taahs/tea**	tās/tie (f/m)

GREETINGS & CIVILITIES

Latvians are seen as good-natured, friendly people. They give flowers at almost every opportunity; however, on social occasions flowers should always be given in odd numbers, as an even number of flowers is for funerals. When you're invited to someone's home, you should remove your outdoor shoes and your host will hand you a pair of slippers to wear.

Greetings & Goodbyes

Hello. (inf)	svay-kuh/svayks	*Sveika./Sveiks.* (f/m)
Good morning.	luhb-*reet*	*Labrīt.*
Good day/afternoon.	luhb-*dean*	*Labdien.* (also serves as a general 'hello')
Good evening.	luhb-*vuh*-kuhr	*Labvakar.*
Goodbye.	uz-*redz*-eh-shuhn-aws	*Uz redzēšanos.*
All the best.	*vis*-u *luh*-bu	*Visu labu.*
See you tomorrow.	leedz *reet*-uhm	*Līdz rītam.*
Say hello to ...	*puh*-svayts-in-eat ...	*Pasveiciniet ...*
Good night.	uhr *luh*-bu *nuhkt*-i	*Ar labu nakti.*

LATVIAN

DON'T MENTION IT

If someone thanks you, you should respond with *lūdzu* (*loo-dzu*). This word not only means 'please', but also serves as 'don't mention it' or 'my pleasure'. You'll find that people also use it when handing you something and when addressing you in shops.

Civilities

How are you?	kah yums *klah*-yuhs?	*Kā jums klājas?*
Fine, thank you.	*luh*-bi puhl-*deas*	*Labi, paldies.*
And you?	un yums?	*Un jums?*
It was nice to meet you.	*biy*-uh *puh*-teek-uhm-i ea-puhz-eet-eas	*Bija patīkami iepazīties.*

Forms of Address

Miss	*yown*-kundz-e	*jaunkundze*
Madam/Mrs	*kundz*-e	*kundze*
Sir/Mr	kungs	*kungs*

UH-AH!

Remember, in the transliterations **uh** sounds like the 'u' in 'fund', and **ah** sounds like the 'a' in 'father'.

LATVIAN

Useful Words & Phrases

Yes.	yah	*Jā.*
No.	neh	*Nē.*
Please./ You're welcome.	*loo*-dzu	*Lūdzu.*
Thank you (very much).	(leals) puhl-*deas*	*(Liels) paldies.*
Excuse me.	*uht*-vai-naw-yeat	*Atvainojiet.*
May I?	vai es *dreekst*-u?	*Vai es drīkstu?*
Pardon?	*pea*-doad-eat?	*Piedodiet?*
Sorry/I apologise.	*pea*-doad-eat/ es *uht*-vain-aw-yaws	*Piedodiet/ Es atvainojos.*

SMALL TALK

When meeting people for the first time, always use the polite form
of 'you' (*jūs*), except when speaking to children.

Meeting People

What's your name?
kah yoos sowts?   *Kā jūs sauc?*
My name is ...
muhn-i sowts ...   *Mani sauc ...*
I'd like to introduce you to ...
vaa-laws yoos   *Vēlos jūs*
ea-puhz-eest-in-aht uhr ...   *iepazīstināt ar ...*
I'm pleased to meet you.
preaks ea-puhz-eet-eas   *Prieks iepazīties.*

Nationalities

Where are you from?
naw kur-ean-es yoos as-uht?   *No kurienes jūs esat?*

I'm from ...	es as-mu naw ...	Es esmu no ...
Africa	*ah*-fri-kuhs	*Āfrikas*
Australia	*ow*-strah-li-yuhs	*Austrālijas*
Canada	*kuhn*-ah-duhs	*Kanādas*
China	*kyeen*-uhs	*Ķīnas*
Denmark	*dah*-ni-yuhs	*Dānijas*
England	*uhn*-gli-yuhs	*Anglijas*
Finland	*saw*-mi-yuhs	*Somijas*
France	*fruhn*-tsi-yuhs	*Francijas*
Germany	*vah*-tsi-yuhs	*Vācijas*
Holland	*ho*-luhn-des	*Holandes*
Ireland	*ee*-ri-yuhs	*Īrijas*
Israel	*iz*-ruh-eh-luhs	*Izraēlas*
New Zealand	*yown*-zeh-luhn-des	*Jaunzēlandes*
Norway	*nor*-veh-jyi-uhs	*Norvēģijas*
Spain	*spahn*-i-yuhs	*Spānijas*
Sweden	*zvea*-dri-yuhs	*Zviedrijas*
the USA	*uh*-me-ri-kuhs	*Amerikas*

LATVIAN

Age

How old are you?	tsik yums ir *guh*-du?	*Cik jums ir gadu?*
I'm ... years old.	muhn ir ... *guh*-du	*Man ir ... gadu.*
When's your birthday?	kuhd ir *yoos*-u *dzim*-shuhn-uhs *dean*-uh?	*Kad ir jūsu dzimšanas diena?*

Occupations

What do you do?	uhr kaw yoos *naw*-duhrb-aw-yuht-eas?	*Ar ko jūs nodarbojaties?*
I'm (a/an) ...	es *as*-mu ...	*Es esmu ...*
artist	*mahk*-sl-neats-e	*māksliniece* (f)
	mahk-sl-neaks	*mākslnieks* (m)
business person	*biz*-nes-men-is	*biznesmenis*
doctor	*ahrs*-te	*ārste* (f)
	ahrsts	*ārsts* (m)
engineer	*in*-zhen-ear-e	*inženiere* (f)
	in-zhen-ear-is	*inženieris* (m)
factory worker	*roop*-neets-uhs	*rūpnīcas*
	strahd-neats-e	*strādniece* (f)
	roop-neets-uhs	*rūpnīcas*
	strahd-neaks	*strādnieks* (m)
farmer	*lowk*-saim-neats-e	*lauksaimniece* (f)
	lowk-saim-neaks	*lauksaimnieks* (m)
journalist	*zhur*-nah-list-e	*žurnaliste* (f)
	zhur-nah-lists	*žurnalists* (m)
lawyer	*yur*-is-te	*juriste* (f)
	yu-rists	*jurists* (m)
mechanic	*me*-hah-ni-kyis	*mehāniķis*
musician	*mooz*-i-kye	*mūziķe* (f)
	moo-i-kyis	*mūziķis* (m)
nurse	*med*-mah-suh	*medmāsa*
office worker	*bi*-raw-yuh *duhrb*-in-eats-e	*biroja darbiniece* (f)
	bi-raw-yuh *duhrb*-in-eaks	*biroja darbinieks* (m)

LATVIAN

scientist	zin-aht-neats-e	*zinātniece* (f)
	zin-aht-neaks	*zinātnieks* (m)
student	stud-en-te	*studente* (f)
	stud-ents	*students* (m)
teacher	skaw-law-tah-yuh	*skolotāja* (f)
	skaw-law-tahys	*skolotājs* (m)
unemployed	bez-duhrb-neats-e	*bezdarbniece* (f)
	bez-duhrb-neaks	*bezdarb-nieks* (m)
waiter	of-its-i-uhn-te	*oficiante* (f)
	of-its-i-uhnts	*oficiants* (m)
writer	ruhkst-neats-e	*rakstniece* (f)
	ruhkst-neaks	*rakstnieks* (m)

LATVIAN

THE SINGING REVOLUTION

The song and dance festivals which took place in 1990 were particularly significant events during the 'Singing Revolution', which resulted in Latvia regaining its independence from the Soviet Union in August 1991. For the first time since the end of World War II, Latvians from around the globe were reunited as one nation, with exile-Latvian choirs and dance groups singing and dancing alongside their Latvian peers. At the close of the 1990 Dance Festival the compere announced 'That was the first dance festival in Independent Latvia. Until next time, in a free Latvia!' which sums up the political climate and mood of optimism prevalent at the time.

Religion

What's your religion?
kah-duh ir *yoos*-u *tits*-ee-buh?   *Kāda ir jūsu ticība?*

I'm not religious.
es *ne*-as-mu *tits*-eeg-uh/   *Es neesmu ticīga/*
tits-eegs   *ticīgs.* (f/m)

I'm ...	es *as*-mu ...	Es esmu ...
Buddhist	*bud*-is-te	*budiste* (f)
	bud-ists	*budists* (m)
Catholic	*kuht*-aw-lea-te	*katoliete* (f)
	kuht-aw-lis	*katolis* (m)
Christian	*krist*-ea-te	*kristiete* (f)
	krist-ea-tis	*kristietis* (m)
Hindu	*in*-dea-te	*indiete* (f)
	in-deat-is	*indietis* (m)
Jewish	*e*-brey-eat-e	*ebrejiete* (f)
	e-breys	*ebrejs* (m)
Lutheran	*lut*-er-tits-ee-guh	*luterticīga* (f)
	lut-er-tits-eegs	*luterticīgs* (m)
Muslim	*mus*-ul-muhn-eat-e	*musulmaniete* (f)
	mus-ul-muhn-is	*musulmanis* (m)
Russian	*puhr*-ayz-tits-ee-guh	*pareizticīga* (f)
Orthodox	*puhr*-ayz-tits-eegs	*pareizticīgs* (m)

LATVIAN

Family

Are you married?	**vai yoos** *as*-uht **prets**-eh-yus-eas/ **prets**-eh-yeas?	*Vai jūs esat precējusies/ precējies?* (f/m)

I'm ...	**es** *as*-mu ...	*Es esmu ...*
married	**prets**-eh-yus-eas	*precējusies* (f)
	prets-eh-yeas	*precējies* (m)
single	**ne**-prets-aa-tuh	*neprecēta* (f)
	ne-prets-aats	*neprecēts* (m)
divorced	**shkyee**-ru-seas	*šķīrusies* (f)
	shkyee-reas	*šķīries* (m)
widowed	**uht**-rait-ne	*atraitne* (f)
	uht-rait-nis	*atraitnis* (m)
lesbian/gay	**lez**-bea-te/gays	*lezbiete/gejs*

Do you have any children?
vai yums ir *baar*-ni?   *Vai jums ir bērni?*
I don't have any children.
muhn nuhv *baar*-nu   *Man nav bērnu.*
I have a daughter/son.
muhn ir *may*-tuh/daals   *Man ir meita/dēls.*
How many sisters/
brothers do you have?
tsik yums ir *mah*-su/*brah*-lyu?   *Cik jums ir māsu/brāļu?*
Is your wife/
husband here?
vai yoo-su *sea*-vuh/veers   *Vai jūsu sieva /vīrs*
uht-raw-duhs shayt?   *atrodas šeit?*
Do you have a
girlfriend/boyfriend?
vai yums ir *drow*-dzen-e/   *Vai jums ir draudzene/*
drowgs?   *draugs?*

LATVIAN

brother	*brah*-lis	*brālis*
children	*baar*-ni	*bērni*
family	*jyim*-en-e	*ģimene*
father	taavs	*tēvs*
friend	*drow*-dzen-e	*draudzene* (f)
	drowgs	*draugs* (m)
grandfather	*vats*-taavs	*vectēvs*
grandmother	*vats*-mah-miny-uh	*vecmāmiņa*
mother	*mah*-te	*māte*
sister	*mah*-suh	*māsa*

Kids' Talk

When talking to children, use the familiar form of you (*tu*).

How old are you?
tsik tev ir *guh*-du? *Cik tev ir gadu?*

When's your birthday?
kuhd ir *tuh*-vuh
***dzim*-shuhn-uhs *dea*-nuh?** *Kad ir tava dzimšanas diena?*

What do you do after school?
kaw tu *duh*-ri pehts *skaw*-luhs? *Ko tu dari pēc skolas?*

Do you have a pet at home?
Vai tev *mah*-yahs ir dzeev-neaks? *Vai tev mājās ir dzivnieks?*

I have a ...	muhn ir ...	Man ir ...
bird	*put*-ns	*putns*
canary	*kuhn*-ah-riy-put-ns	*kanārijputns*
cat	*kuh*-kyis	*kaķis*
dog	suns	*suns*
duck	*pee*-le	*pīle*
fish	zivs	*zivs*
frog	*vuhr*-de	*varde*
guinea pig	*yoo*-ruhs *tsoo*-tsiny-uh	*jūras cūciņa*
hamster	*kah*-mee-tis	*kāmītis*
horse	zirgs	*zirgs*
parrot	*puh*-puh-gai-lis	*papagailis*
tortoise	*bru*-nyu-ru-pu-tsis	*bruņrupucis*

Expressing Feelings

The verb 'to be' is not always used to express feelings. The Latvian equivalent of 'I have' (*man ir*) is often used instead.

I'm ...	muhn ir ...	*Man ir ...*
cold	**owk**-sti	*auksti*
hot	**kuhr**-sti	*karsti*
right	**tais**-nee-buh	*taisnība*
well	**luh**-bi	*labi*

The verb 'to be' is used with the following expressions, however.

I'm ...	es **as**-mu ...	*Es esmu ...*
angry	**dus**-mee-guh	*dusmīga* (f)
	dus-meegs	*dusmīgs* (m)
grateful	**puh**-tay-tsee-guh	*pateicīga* (f)
	puh-tay-tseegs	*pateicīgs* (m)
happy	**preats**-ee-guh	*priecīga* (f)
	preats-eegs	*priecīgs* (m)
hungry	**iz**-suhl-ku-si	*izsalkusi* (f)
	iz-suhl-tsis	*izsalcis* (m)
in a hurry	**stay**-gah	*steigā*
sad	**beh**-dee-guh	*bēdīga* (f)
	beh-deegs	*bēdīgs* (m)
sleepy	**mea**-gai-nuh	*miegaina* (f)
	mea-gains	*miegains* (m)
tired	**naw**-gu-ru-si	*nogurusi* (f)
	naw-gu-ris	*noguris* (m)
worried	**suh**-trowk-tuh	*satraukta* (f)
	suh-trowkts	*satraukts* (m)

Expressing Opinions

In my opinion ...	**muh**-nu-praht ...	*Manuprāt ...*
I think (believe)	es **daw**-mah-yu	*Es domāju*
that ...	(**tits**-u) kuh ...	*(ticu), ka ...*
Do you like ...?	vai yums **puh**-teek ...?	*Vai jums patīk ...?*
I like ...	muhn **puh**-teek ...	*Man patīk ...*
I agree.	es **pea**-kree-tu	*Es piekrītu.*
I disagree.	es **ne**-pea-kree-tu	*Es nepiekrītu.*

BODY LANGUAGE

In Latvia there are no significant differences from any other European country as far as the interpretation of body language goes. Latvians shake hands when greeting each other and when saying goodbye, although you should be aware that shaking hands over the threshold is considered unlucky. Social kissing is also the norm nowadays. Women should note that chivalry is very much predominant in Latvia, so don't be surprised when a man helps you on with your coat, pours your drinks and lights your cigarettes for you.

BREAKING THE LANGUAGE BARRIER

Do you speak English?
  vai yoos *run*-ah-yuht   *Vai jūs runājat*
  uhn-gli-ski?   *angliski?*
I don't speak ...
  es *ne*-run-ah-yu ...   *Es nerunāju ...*
I understand.
  es *suh*-praw-tu   *Es saprotu.*
I don't understand.
  es *ne*-suh-praw-tu   *Es nesaprotu.*
Could you speak more
slowly please?
  run-ah-yeat *loo-dzu* laan-ahk   *Runājiet lūdzu lēnāk.*
Could you repeat that please?
  loo-dzu uht-kahr-taw-yeat   *Lūdzu atkārtojiet.*
What does that mean?
  kaw tuhs *naw*-zee-meh?   *Ko tas nozīmē?*
Please write that down.
  loo-dzu pea-ruhk-steat taw   *Lūdzu pierakstiet to.*

LATVIAN

I speak ...	es *run*-ah-yu ...	*Es runāju ...*
English	*uhn*-gli-ski	*angliski*
French	*fruhn*-tsis-ki	*franciski*
German	*vah*-tsis-ki	*vāciski*
Polish	*paw*-lis-ki	*poliski*
Russian	*krea*-vis-ki	*krieviski*

Sports & Interests

I want to go ...	es *vaa*-laws ...	*Es vēlos ...*
bird watching	*vaa*-rawt *put*-nus	*vērot putnus*
bobsleighing	browkt uhr	*braukt ar*
	bob-slay-u	*bobsleju*
canoeing	*ai*-reht uhr *kuh*-nu	*airēt ar kanoe*
cycling	browkt uhr	*braukt ar*
	div-rit-e-ni	*divriteni*
gliding	*li*-dawt uhr	*lidot ar*
	pluhn-ea-ri	*planieri*
hiking	eat *pahr*-gah-yean-ah	*iet pārgājienā*
horse riding	yaht uhr *zir*-gu	*jāt ar zirgu*
ice fishing	*naw*-duhr-baw-teas ar	*nodarboties ar*
	zem-lad-us *muhk*-	*zemledus*
	shkye-reh-shuh-nu	*makšķerēšanu*
jogging	skreat	*skriet*
skating	*sli*-dawt	*slidot*
skiing	*sleh*-pawt	*slēpot*
swimming	*pel*-deht	*peldēt*
tobogganing	browkt uhr	*braukt ar*
	kuh-muh-niny-ahm	*kamaniņām*
yachting	*bu*-raht	*burāt*

I play ...	es *speh*-leh-yu ...	*Es spēlēju ...*
basketball	*buh*-ske-tu	*basketu*
cards	*kahr*-tis	*kārtis*
chess	*shuh*-hu	*šahu*
guitar	*jyi*-tah-ri	*gitāri*
soccer	*fut*-bo-lu	*futbolu*
tennis	*ten*-i-su	*tenisu*

LATVIAN

I play winter sports.
es *naw*-duhr-*baw*-jaws uhr   *Es nodarbojos ar ziemas*
zea-muhs *spor*-tuh *vay*-deam   *sporta veidiem.*

Do you like ...?	vai yums *puh*-teek ...?	*Vai jums patīk ...?*
art	*mahk*-sluh	*māksla*
ballet	*buh*-lets	*balets*
the cinema	*ki*-no	*kino*
(classical) music	(*kluhs*-is-kah)	(*klasiskā*)
	mooz-i-kuh	*mūzika*
exhibitions	*iz*-stah-des	*izstādes*
opera	*o*-per-uh	*opera*
reading	*luh*-seet	*lasīt*
the theatre	*te*-ah-tris	*teātris*
travelling	*tse*-lyot	*ceļot*

LATVIAN

Useful Words & Phrases

Of course.	*praw*-tuhms	*Protams.*
Just a minute.	*uhts*-u-mir-kli	*Acumirkli.*
It's important.	ir *svuh*-ree-gi	*Ir svarīgi.*
It's not important.	nuhv *svuh*-ree-gi	*Nav svarīgi.*
It's not possible.	nuhv *ea*-speh-yams	*Nav iespējams.*
Wait!	*puh*-gai-deat!	*Pagaidiet!*

GETTING AROUND
Directions

Where's the ...?	kur uht-raw-duhs ...?	Kur atrodas ...?
airport	lid-aw-stuh	lidosta
bus station	ow-to-aws-tuh	autoosta
ferry terminal	puh-suh-zhea-ru aw-stuh	pasažieru osta
harbour	aw-stuh	osta
ticket office(s)	bi-lye-shu kuh-ses	biļešu kases
train station	dzelz-ce-lyuh stuhts-i-ya	dzelzceļa stacija
tram/ trolleybus stop	truhm-vuh-yuh/ trol-ey-bu-suh pea-tu-ruh	tramvaja/ trolejbusa pietura

STREETS AHEAD

IELA	STREET
LAUKUMS	SQUARE
PROSPEKTS/BULVĀRIS	AVENUE/BOULEVARD
CEĻŠ	ROAD
LIELCEĻŠ/ŠOSEJA	HIGHWAY
TILTS	BRIDGE

How do I get to ...?
kah es tea-ku leedz ...?   *Kā es tieku līdz ...?*

Is it far from here?
vai tuhs uht-raw-duhs tah-lu?   *Vai tas atrodas tālu?*

Can I walk there?
vai leedz tur-ea-ni vuhr aiz-stai-gaht?   *Vai līdz turieni var aizstaigāt?*

Could you show me
(on the map) please?
loo-dzu puhr-ah-deat muhn (uz kuhrt-es)   *Lūdzu parādiet man (uz kartes)*

Go straight ahead.	**uz** *preak*-**shu**	*Uz priekšu.*
Turn left/right at the ...	puh *kray*-si/*luh*-bi **pea** ...	*Pa kreisi/labi pie ...*
corner	*krus*-**taw-yum-uh**	*krustojuma*
traffic lights	*luks*-**o-for-eam**	*luksoforiem*

Buying Tickets

Where can I buy a ticket to ...?
kur es vuh-ru naw-pirkt   *Kur es varu nopirkt biļeti*
bi-**lyet-i leedz** ...?   *līdz ...?*
How much does it cost?
tsik *muhk*-**sah?**   *Cik maksā?*

I want to buy a ... ticket.	es **vaa-laws** *naw*-**pirkt** ... *bi*-**lyet-i**	*Es vēlos nopirkt ... biļeti.*
one-way	**vean-virz-ean-uh**	*vienvirziena*
return	**turp** *uht*-**puh-kuhly**	*turp-atpakaļ*
student/child	**stud-en-tu/ baar-nu**	*studentu/bērnu*
1st class	*pir*-**mah** *kluh*-**se**	*pirmā klase*
2nd class	**aw-trah** *kluh*-**se**	*otrā klase*
ticket office(s)	*bi*-**lye-shu** *kuh*-**ses**	*biļešu kases*
local train	*pea*-**pil-saat-uhs**	*piepilsētas*
ticket office	**kuh-ses**	*kases*
international train	*stuhrp*-**tow-tis-kahs**	*starptautiskās*
ticket office	**kuh-ses**	*kases*

Air

Riga International airport has recently undergone a revamp and is now a modern user-friendly airport, with English-speaking staff, signs in both Latvian and English and plenty of bars, cafes and duty free shops.

Is there a flight to ...?
    vai ir *lid*-aw-yums uz ...?   *Vai ir lidojums uz ...?*
What's the flight number?
    kahds ir *ray*-suh *num*-urs?   *Kāds ir reisa numurs?*

Bus, Tram & Trolleybus

Tickets are required for buses, trams and trolleybuses and are bought from the conductor on board. Monthly season tickets can be bought from newspaper kiosks.

Does this tram go to ...?
    vai shis *truhm*-vuhys browts   *Vai šis tramvajs brauc*
    leedz ...?   *līdz ...?*
Are you getting off?
    vai yoos *iz*-kahp-seat?   *Vai jūs izkāpsiet?*
Could you let me know
when to get off?
    vai yoos *vuhr*-aa-tu muhn   *Vai jūs varētu man*
    puh-taykt kuhd muhn ir   *pateikt, kad man ir*
    jah-iz-kahpy?   *jāizkāpj?*
I want to get off.
    es *vaa*-laws *iz*-kahpt   *Es vēlos izkāpt.*

What time is	*tsik*-aws *uht*-eat ...	*Cikos attiet ...*
the ... bus to ...?	*ow*-taw-bus uz ...?	*autobuss uz ...?*
next	*nah*-kuhm-ais	*nākamais*
first	*pirm*-ais	*pirmais*
last	*peh*-deh-yais	*pēdējais*

LATVIAN

Train

The train leaves from ...

    vilts-eans *uht*-eat naw ...   *Vilciens attiet no ...*

Is this the right train for ...?

    vai shis ir *puh*-rayz-ais   *Vai šis ir pareizais*

    vilts-eans uz ...?   *vilciens uz ...?*

dining car	*res*-to-rah-nuh	*restorāna*
	vuh-gons	*vagons*
express	*eks*-pres-is	*ekspresis*
local	*pea*-pil-saa-tuhs	*piepilsētas*
platform	*pe*-rawns	*perons*
sleeping car	*kup*-eh-yuh	*kupēja*
timetable	*vilts*-ea-nu *suh*-ruhksts	*vilcienu saraksts*
track	*tselysh*	*ceļš*

Boat

Where does the
boat leave from?

    naw *ku*-rea-nes *uht*-eat *ku*-gyis? *No kurienes attiet kuģis?*

What time does
the boat arrive?

    tsi-kaws *pea*-nahk *ku*-gyis? *Cikos pienāk kuģis?*

Which boat goes to ...?

    kursh *ku*-gyis ir leedz ...? *Kurš kuģis ir līdz ...?*

Which harbour is next?

    kuhs ir *nah*-kuhm-ah *aws*-tuh? *Kas ir nākamā osta?*

Is this the ferry for ...?

    vai shis ir *prah*-mis leedz ...? *Vai šis ir prāmis līdz ...?*

boat (ship)	*ku*-gyis	*kuģis*
ferry	*prah*-mis	*prāmis*
harbour	*aws*-tuh	*osta*
Riga Passenger	*ree*-guhs *puh*-suh-	*Rīgas pasažieru*
Terminal	zhee-ru *aws*-tuh	*osta*

LATVIAN

Taxi

Licensed taxis in Latvia are distinguishable by the white sign on the roof and yellow-number-plates with the prefix TH. There are different tariffs for day and night rides. If the driver does not turn on the meter, make sure you agree on a price to avoid being ripped off.

taxi	*tuhks*-ow-met-rs	*taksometrs*

How much does it
cost to go to ...?
    tsik *muhk*-sah *aiz*-vest leedz ...?   *Cik maksā aizvest līdz ...?*
I want to go to the
next corner, please.
    leedz *nah*-kuhm-ah-yuhm   *Līdz nākamājam*
    krus-taw-yum-uhm *loo*-dzu   *krustojumam, lūdzu.*
Here is fine, thank you.
    te boos *luh*-bi puhl-*deas*   *Te būs labi, paldies.*
Please slow down.
    brow-tseat *loo*-dzu *laa*-nahk   *Brauciet lūdzu lēnāk.*
Please stop.
    loo-dzu uhp-*staht*-eas   *Lūdzu apstāties.*
Please wait.
    loo-dzu uz-gai-deat   *Lūdzu uzgaidiet.*

Car

Where can I rent a car/motorcycle?
    kur es *vuh*-ru *naw*-ee-reht   *Kur es varu noīrēt mašīnu/*
    muh-shee-nu/*mo*-to-tsik-lu?   *motociklu?*
How much is it daily/weekly?
    tsik *muhk*-sah *dea*-nah/   *Cik maksā dienā/nedēļā?*
    ned-eh-lyah?
Is insurance included?
    vai *uhp*-draw-shin-ah-shuhn-uh *Vai apdrošināšana ir*
    ir *ea*-skai-tee-tuh?   *ieskaitīta?*

Where's the next
petrol station?

    kur ir tuv-ah-kah *dag*-veal-uhs   *Kur ir tuvākā degvielas*
    uz-pil-des *stats*-i-yuh?   *uzpildes stacija?*

Please fill the tank.

    pil-nu *bah*-ku *loo*-dzu   *Pilnu bāku, lūdzu.*

air	gais	*gaiss*
battery	*uh*-ku-mu-luh-tors	*akumulators*
brakes	*brem*-zes	*bremzes*
clutch	*suh*-yoogs	*sajūgs*
engine	*mo*-tors	*motors*
lights	*gais*-muhs	*gaismas*
oil	*ely*-lyuh	*eļļa*
road map	*tse*-lyuh *kuhr*-te	*ceļa karte*
tyre	*rea*-puh	*riepa*
windscreen	*preak*-sheh-yais *stik*-ls	*priekšējais stikls*

I need a mechanic.

    muhn ir vuhy-uh-dzeegs
    me-hah-ni-kyis
    Man ir vajadzīgs
    mehāniķis.

> ## DON'T STRESS OUT!
>
> Stress is almost always on
> the first syllable in Latvian.

The car is overheated.

    muh-shee-nuh ir *pahr*-kuhr-   *Mašīna ir pārkarsēta.*
    saa-tuh

The radiator is leaking.

    ruhd-i-uh-tors tak   *Radiators tek.*

The battery is flat.

    uh-ku-mu-luh-tors ir *iz*-lah-   *Akumulators ir izlādējies.*
    deh-yeas

I have a puncture.

    rea-puh ir *pahr*-sprah-gu-si   *Riepa ir pārsprāgusi.*

LATVIAN

ACCOMMODATION
Finding Accommodation

I'm looking for a ...	es *mek*-leh-yu ...	*Es meklēju ...*
cheap hotel	*laa*-tu *veas*-neets-u	*lētu viesnīcu*
clean hotel	*tee*-ru *veas*-neets-u	*tīru viesnīcu*
good hotel	*luh*-bu *veas*-neets-u	*labu viesnīcu*
youth hostel	*yow*-nea-shu *meet*-ni	*jauniešu mītni*

At the Hotel

Do you have any rooms available?
vai yums ir *bree*-vuhs *Vai jums ir brīvas istabas?*
is-tuh-buhs?

Sorry, we're full.
es *uht*-vai-naw-yaws mums *Es atvainojos, mums nav*
nuhv *vea*-tu *vietu.*

I have a reservation.
muhn ir *puh*-soo-teets *Man ir pasūtīts.*

I'd like a ...	es *vaa*-laws ...	*Es vēlos ...*
single room	*vean*-vea-tee-gu	*vienvietīgu*
	is-tuh-bu	*istabu*
double room	*div*-vea-tee-gu	*divvietīgu*
	is-tuh-bu	*istabu*
room with a	*is*-tuh-bu uhr	*istabu ar*
shower/bath	*du*-shu/*vuhn*-nu	*dušu/vannu*
room with a	*is*-tuh-bu uhr	*istabu ar*
balcony	*buhl*-ko-nu	*balkonu*

I'm going to stay for ...	es *puh*-lik-shu ...	*Es palikšu ...*
one night	*vea*-nu *nuhk*-ti	*vienu nakti*
two nights	*di*-vuhs *nuhk*-tis	*divas naktis*
a week	*ne*-deh-lyu	*nedēļu*

How much is it per night?
tsik *muhk*-sah *dean*-nuhk-tee? *Cik maksā diennaktī?*

LATVIAN

Is there (a) ...?	vai ir ...?	*Vai ir ...?*
bathroom	**vuhn**-nuhs *is*-tuh-buh	*vannas istaba*
hot water	**kuhrsts** *oo*-dens	*karsts ūdens*
sauna	**pirts**	*pirts*
shower	**du**-shuh	*duša*
telephone	**te**-le-fons	*telefons*
television	**te**-le-vi-zors	*televizors*

Can I see the ...?	vai es **vuh**-ru **uhp**-skuh-teet ...?	*Vai es varu apskatīt ...?*
room	*is*-tuh-bu	*istabu*
bathroom	**vuhn**-nuhs *is*-tuh-bu	*vannas istabu*

Fine, I'll take it.
luh-bi es taw *nyem*-shu
Labi, es to ņemšu.

I'd like a different room.
es **vaa**-laws *tsi*-tu *is*-tuh-bu
Es vēlos citu istabu.

Is there a reduction for students/children?
vai ir *uht*-lai-de *stud*-en-team/ *baar*-neam?
Vai ir atlaide studentiem/ bērniem?

Does it include breakfast?
vai *braw*-kuhs-tis ir *ea*-skai-teet-uhs?
Vai brokastis ir ieskaitītas?

Is there a lift?
vai ir **lifts**?
Vai ir lifts?

Is there hot water all day?
vai ir *kuhrst*-ais *oo*-dens *vi*-su *dea*-nu?
Vai ir karstais ūdens visu dienu?

Do you have a safe?
vai **yums** ir **sayfs**?
Vai jums ir seifs?

May I have the bill please?
loo-dzu *reh*-kyin-u
Lūdzu rēķinu.

LATVIAN

Requests & Complaints

Please wake me up at ...
   loo-dzu puh-maw-din-eat   *Lūdzu pamodiniet*
   muh-ni pulks-tens ...   *mani pulkstens ...*
The ... doesn't work.
   ... ne-strah-dah   *... nestrādā.*
I can't open the window.
   es ne-vuh-ru uht-vehrt law-gu   *Es nevaru atvērt logu.*
I can't flush the toilet.
   es ne-vuh-ru naw-rowt oo-den-i   *Es nevaru noraut ūdeni*
   tu-uh-le-teh   *tualetē.*

It's too ...	ir puhr ...	Ir par ...
cold	*owk-stu*	*aukstu*
hot	*kuhr-stu*	*karstu*
noisy	*skuh-lyu*	*skaļu*

Laundry

Can you please	vai yoos vuh-reh-tu	Vai jūs varētu
... this?	sho ... loo-dzu?	šo ... lūdzu?
clean	*iz-tee-reet*	*iztīrīt*
iron	*iz-glud-in-aht*	*izgludināt*
mend	*suh-lah-peet*	*salāpīt*
wash	*iz-maz-gaht*	*izmazgāt*

I need it ...	muhn ir	Man ir
	vay-uh-dzeegs ...	vajadzīgs ...
today	*shaw-dean*	*šodien*
tomorrow	*ree-tah*	*rītā*
as soon as	*tsik vean aht-ri*	*cik vien ātri*
possible	*ea-speh-yuhms*	*iespējams*

Useful Words

name	**vahrds**	*vārds*
surname	*uz*-**vahrds**	*uzvārds*
room number	*is*-tuh-**buhs** *num*-urs	*istabas numurs*
address	**uh**-dre-se	*adrese*
air-conditioning	*gai*-**suh**	*gaisa*
	kon-dits-i-on-aa-tahys	*kondicionētājs*
balcony	**buhl**-kons	*balkons*
bathroom	**vuhn**-nuhs *is*-tuh-buh	*vannas istaba*
bed	**gul**-tuh	*gulta*
bill	**reh**-kyins	*rēķins*
blanket	**sa**-guh	*sega*
chair	**kraa**-sls	*krēsls*
clean	**teers**	*tīrs*
dark	**tumsh**	*tumšs*
dirty	*ne*-**teers**	*netīrs*
key	**uht**-slaa-guh	*atslēga*
lift (n)	**lifts**	*lifts*
light bulb	**spul**-dze	*spuldze*
lock (n)	**sleh**-dze	*slēdze*
mattress	**muh**-druh-tsis	*madracis*
pillow	**spil**-vans	*spilvens*
quiet	**klus**	*kluss*
sheet	**puh**-luhgs	*palags*
shower	**du**-shuh	*duša*
soap	**zea**-pes	*ziepes*
suitcase	**ko**-fer-is	*koferis*
table	**guhlds**	*galds*
toilet	*tu*-uh-le-te	*tualete*
toilet paper	*tu*-uh-le-tes *puh*-peers	*tualetes papīrs*
towel	**dvea**-lis	*dvielis*
(hot/cold) water	(**kuhr**-stais/ **auk**-stais)	*(karstais/aukstais)*
	oo-dens	*ūdens*

LATVIAN

AROUND TOWN

Where's the ...?	kur *uht*-raw-duhs ...?	*Kur atrodas ...?*
art gallery	**muhk-sluhs**	*mākslas*
	guh-le-ri-yuh	*galerija*
bank	**buhn-kuh**	*banka*
city/town centre	**pil-saa-tuhs tsent-rs**	*pilsētas centrs*
... embassy	... **vehst-nea-tsee-buh**	*... vēstniecība*
hotel	**veas-nee-tsuh**	*viesnīca*
library	**bib-lio-te-kuh**	*bibliotēka*
market	**tir-gus**	*tirgus*
museum	**muz-eys**	*muzejs*
old town	**vats-pil-saa-tuh**	*vecpilsēta*
post office	**puhsts**	*pasts*

Is there a tourist office here?
vai shayt ir	*Vai šeit ir*
too-ris-muh bi-rawys?	*tūrisma birojs?*

At the Bank

Money can be changed into *lats* at currency exchange booths (*valūtas maiņa*), where exchange rates are posted on the window. It's also possible to withdraw money on your credit card, transfer money and exchange foreign currency and travellers cheques in banks. Be aware that notes that are crumpled, torn or have any writing on them will generally not be accepted – or may be accepted on payment of a surcharge. If you don't wish to bother with exchange booths and banks, simply use your credit card to withdraw money from one of the many cash machines.

I'd like to	es **vaa-laws**	*Es vēlos*
change ...	*iz*-mai-neet ...	*izmainīt ...*
this into lats	**shaw luh-taws**	*šo latos*
a travellers	**tsely-aw-yum-uh**	*ceļojuma*
cheque	**che-ku**	*čeku*

LATVIAN

Can I have money transferred
here/abroad?
  vai ir *ea*-speh-**yuhms**   *Vai ir iespējams*
  ***pahr*-soo-teet** now-du uz   *pārsūtīt naudu uz*
  shay-ea-ni/uz *ahr*-zem-ehm?   *šejieni/uz ārzemēm?*
How long will it take?
  tsik *il*-gah *lai*-kah?   *Cik ilgā laikā?*
Has my money arrived yet?
  vai *muh*-nuh *now*-duh ir   *Vai mana nauda ir*
  pea-nah-ku-si?   *pienākusi?*

coins	*mo*-neh-tuhs	*monētas*
currency exchange booth	*vuh*-loo-tuhs *mai*-nyuh	*valūtas maiņa*
exchange rate	*vuh*-loo-tuhs kurs	*valūtas kurss*
money	*now*-duh	*nauda*
notes	puh-*peer*-now-duh	*papīrnauda*

At the Post Office

Signs above each counter in the post office indicate what you can
do at that particular counter, such as send registered letters and
buy stamps. Post offices also sell newspapers, and telephone cards.

I'd like to	es *vaa*-laws	*Es vēlos*
send a ...	*naw*-soo-teet ...	*nosūtīt ...*
I'm expecting a ...	es *gai*-du ...	*Es gaidu ...*
fax	*fuhks*-u	*faksu*
letter	*vaa*-stu-li	*vēstuli*
postcard	*uht*-klaht-ni	*atklātni*
parcel	*puh*-ku	*paku*
telegram	te-le-*gruhm*-mu	*telegrammu*
I'd like to send	es *vaa*-laws	*Es vēlos*
this (by) ...	*naw*-soo-teet shaw ...	*nosūtīt šo ...*
airmail	uhr *gai*-su *puhst*-u	*ar gaisa pastu*
express	uhr *eks*-pre-si	*ar ekspresi*
ordinary post	uhr *puh*-ruh-staw *puhst*-u	*ar parasto pastu*
registered mail	*ea*-ruhk-stee-tu	*ierakstītu*

I'd like a stamp, please.

es vaa-laws puhst-muhr-ku loodz-u   *Es vēlos pastmarku, lūdzu.*

Has any post arrived for me?

vai muhn ir pea-nah-tsis kahds puhst-uh soo-tee-yums?   *Vai man ir pienācis kāds pasta sūtījums?*

Telephone & Internet

The telephone system in Latvia has undergone significant modernisation over the last few years and most telephone lines are now digital, enabling users to make national and international telephone calls easily. In order to use the public telephone booths, you have to buy a telephone card from a newspaper kiosk or post office. Public telephone booths provide instructions in a number of languages (including English) on how to use the phone system. Making calls from your hotel or someone's home is just as simple. The Internet and email are used widely throughout Latvia, and there are many Internet cafes providing Internet access for a small fee.

SIGNS

IESNIEGŠANA and **IZSNIEGŠANA** – here you can hand in and collect parcels and registered letters at larger post-offices.

APDROŠINĀTAS PAKAS	INSURED PARCELS
BANDROLES	PRINTED MATTER
IERAKSTĪTAS PAKAS	REGISTERED PARCELS
IERAKSTĪTAS SĪKPAKAS	REGISTERED PACKETS
IERAKSTĪTAS VĒSTULES	REGISTERED LETTERS
KOMERCPRECES	COMMERCIAL GOODS
PASTMARKAS	STAMPS
PAKU DAĻA	PARCEL SECTION
TELEGRAMMAS	TELEGRAMS
TELEKARTES	TELEPHONE CARDS
VĒSTULES	LETTERS

LATVIAN

A telephone card, please.
te-le-kuhr-ti *loo-dzu*   *Telekarti, lūdzu.*
How much does it cost?
tsik tuhs *muhk-sah?*   *Cik tas maksā?*
I was cut off.
muh-ni uht-vea-naw-yuh   *Mani atvienoja.*
It was the wrong number.
bi-yuh ne-puh-ray-zais
num-urs   *Bija nepareizais numurs.*
The number is engaged.
num-urs ir *aiz-nyemts*   *Numurs ir aizņemts.*

international	*stuhrp-tow-tis-kahs*	*starptautiskās*
phone calls	**suh-ru-nuhs**	*sarunas*
local phone calls	**vea-teh-yahs**	*vietējās sarunas*
	suh-ru-nuhs	
mobile phone	*mo-bee-lais* **te-le-fons**	*mobīlais telefons*
telephone	**te-le-fons**	*telefons*
telephone booth	**te-le-fo-nuh**	*telefona automāts*
	ow-to-mahts	
telephone number	**te-le-fo-nuh** *num-urs*	*telefona numurs*

I need to use the Internet.
es *vaa-laws lea-tawt*   *Es vēlos lietot*
in-ter-ne-tu   *internetu.*
I need to check my email.
es *vaa-laws pahr-bow-deet*   *Es vēlos pārbaudīt*
suh-vu e-puhst-u   *savu e-pastu.*

Sightseeing

Do you have a guidebook?
vai yums ir *cely-ved-is?*   *Vai jums ir ceļvedis?*
What's worth seeing?
kaw ir vaarts *uhp-skuh-teet?*   *Ko ir vērts apskatīt?*
What time does it open?
naw *tsik-eam ir uht-vaarts?*   *No cikiem ir atvērts?*
What time does it close?
tsik-aws slaadz?   *Cikos slēdz?*

LATVIAN

I'm interested in ...	*muh-ni in-te-re-she* ...	*Man interesē* ...
architecture	*uhr-hi-tek-too-ruh*	*arhitektūra*
art	*mahk-sluh*	*māksla*
history	*vaas-tu-re*	*vēsture*

I want to go	es *vaa-laws*	*Es vēlos*
to the ...	*uhp-me-kleht* ...	*apmeklēt* ...
botanical	*bo-tah-nis-kaw*	*botānisko*
gardens	*dahr-zu*	*dārzu*
castle	*pi-li*	*pili*
cathedral	*kuht-e-drah-li*	*katedrāli*
cemetery	*kuh-pus*	*kapus*
church	*buhz-neets-u*	*baznīcu*
concert hall	*konts-er-tu zah-li*	*koncertu zāli*
exhibition	*iz-stah-di*	*izstādi*
Freedom	*bree-vee-buhs*	*Brīvības*
Monument	*pea-mi-ne-kli*	*pieminekli*
... national park	... *nats-i-o-nah-law*	... *nacionālo*
	puhr-ku	*parku*
opera house	*o-per-u*	*operu*
park	*puhr-ku*	*parku*
ruins	*dru-puhs*	*drupas*
stadium	*stuhd-i-aw-nu*	*stadionu*
synagogue	*sin-uh-go-gu*	*sinagogu*
university	*un-i-versi-tah-ti*	*universitāti*
zoo	*zo-o-lo-jyis-kaw*	*zooloģisko*
	dahr-zu	*dārzu*

LATVIAN

Useful Words

boulevard	*bul*-vah-ris	*bulvāris*
bridge	tilts	*tilts*
building	*tselt*-ne	*celtne*
monument	*pea*-mi-nek-lis	*piemineklis*
road	tselysh	*ceļš*
statues	*stuht*-u-yuhs	*statujas*
street	*ea*-luh	*iela*
square	*low*-kums	*laukums*

Going Out

What's there to do in the evenings?

kaw shayt vuhr *Ko šeit var*
duh-reet *vuh*-kuh-raws? *darīt vakaros?*

Is there a ...?	vai ir ...?	*Vai ir ...?*
bar	bahrs	*bārs*
cafe	*kaf*-ey-neets-uh	*kafejnīca*
casino	*kuh*-zi-no	*kazino*
cinema	*ki*-no	*kino*
concert	*konts*-erts	*koncerts*
disco	*dis*-ko-teh-kuh	*diskotēka*
nightclub	*nuhkts*-klubs	*nakstklubs*
theatre	*te*-ah-tris	*teātris*

How much is it to get in?
tsik *muhk*-sah *ea*-ey-uh? *Cik maksā ieeja?*
Two tickets, please.
di-vuhs *bily*-e-tes *loo*-dzu *Divas biļetes, lūdzu.*

SIGNS

In accordance with the Latvian language laws all signs should be in Latvian, although you do come across the occasional sign in Russian and sometimes English.

SIGNS

AIZŅEMTS	ENGAGED
APSTĀTIES	STOP
APVEDCEĻŠ	DIVERSION
ATVĒRTS	OPEN
BIĻEŠU KASES	TICKET OFFICE
BRĪVS	VACANT
CEĻA REMONTS	ROADWORKS
IEBRAUKT AIZLIEGTS	NO ENTRY
IEEJA AIZLIEGTA	ENTRY PROHIBITED
IEEJA	ENTRANCE
IEKĀPŠANA	DEPARTURES
IELIDOŠANA	ARRIVALS
INFORMĀCIJA	INFORMATION
IZEJA	EXIT
IZEJAS NAV	NO ENTRY
MAKSAS TUALETES	PUBLIC TOILETS
MUITA	CUSTOMS
NESMĒĶĒT/	NO SMOKING
SMĒĶĒT AIZLIEGTS	
NESTRĀDĀ	OUT OF ORDER
PASU KONTROLE	PASSPORT CONTROL
POLICIJAS IECIRKNIS	POLICE STATION
REĢISTRĀCIJA (BIĻEŠU)	CHECK-IN
REMONTS	UNDER REPAIR
REZERVĒTS	RESERVED
SIEVIEŠU TUALETES	WOMEN'S TOILETS
SLĒGTS	CLOSED
STĀVĒT AIZLIEGTS	NO STANDING
STĀVVIETA	PARKING
TAKSOMETRS	TAXI
UZMANĪBU	CAUTION
VĪRIEŠU TUALETES	MEN'S TOILETS
VIETU NAV	NO SEATS/FULL

LATVIAN

PAPERWORK

name	**vahrds**	*vārds*
surname	**uz-vahrds**	*uzvārds*
address	**uh-dre-se**	*adrese*
age	**vats-ums**	*vecums*
border	**raw-be-zhuh**	*robeža*
car registration	**muh-sheen-uhs**	*mašīnas*
	do-ku-men-ti	*dokumenti*
date	**duh-tums**	*datums*
date of birth	**dzim-shuhn-uhs**	*dzimšanas*
	duh-tums	*datums*
driver's licence	**browk-shuhn-uhs**	*braukšanas*
	uht-lyow-yuh	*atļauja*
	(**tea-see-buhs**)	*(tiesības)*

LATVIAN

marital status	**jyim-en-es stah-vaw-klis**	*ģimenes stāvoklis*
passport	**puh-se**	*pase*
passport number	**puh-ses num-urs**	*pases numurs*
place of birth	**dzim-shuhn-uhs vea-tuh**	*dzimšanas vieta*
sex/gender	**dzim-ums**	*dzimums*
signature	**puh-ruhksts**	*paraksts*
visa	**vee-zuh**	*vīza*

IN THE COUNTRY
Weather

What's the weather
like today?
kahds _shaw_-dean ir laiks?   _Kāds šodien ir laiks?_

Will it/there be ... tomorrow?	**vai reet boos ...?**	_Vai rīt būs ...?_
cloudy	_mah_-kaw-nyains	_mākoņains_
cold	owksts	_auksts_
foggy	_mig_-lains	_miglains_
frost	_suhl_-nuh	_salna_
hot	kuhrsts	_karsts_
icy	_lad_-ains	_ledains_
rain	_lea_-tus	_lietus_
snow	sneags	_sniegs_
sunny	_sow_-lains	_saulains_
warm	silts	_silts_
windy	_veh_-yains	_vējains_

LATVIAN

Directions

How far is it?
tsik _tah_-lu?   _Cik tālu?_

Can we walk/drive there?
vai ir _ea_-speh-yuhms leedz   _Vai ir iespējams līdz_
tu-_rea_-ni _aiz_-browkt/   _turieni aizbraukt/_
aiz-stai-gaht?   _aizstaigāt?_

north	zea-me-lyi	_ziemeļi_
south	dean-vi-di	_dienvidi_
east	ow-stru-mi	_austrumi_
west	rea-tu-mi	_rietumi_

Animals, Birds & Insects

beaver	*be*-brs	bebrs
bird	*put*-ns	putns
boar	*me*-zhuh tsoo-kuh	meža cūka
cat	*ka*-kyis	kaķis
chicken	*vis*-tuh	vista
cow	gaws	govs
dog	suns	suns
elk	*uhl*-nis	alnis
fish	zivs	zivs
deer	*stir*-nuh	stirna
horse	zirgs	zirgs
lynx	*loo*-sis	lūsis
mouse	*pe*-le	pele
otter	*oo*-drs	ūdrs
pig	tsoo-kuh	cūka
pigeon	*buh*-law-dis	balodis
sheep	*ai*-tuh	aita
spider	*zir*-ne-klis	zirneklis
wild animals	*me*-zhuh dzeev-nea-ki	meža dzīvnieki
wolf	vilks	vilks

Plants

tree	kawks	koks
birch	baarzs	bērzs
fir	*eg*-le	egle
flower	*pu*-kye	puķe
oak	*aw*-zawls	ozols
pine	*prea*-de	priede

Camping

There aren't many camp sites in Latvia. The solution is to ask a farmer if you may pitch a tent on his or her land. However, please bear in mind that amenities may be somewhat dilapidated and running water will probably be unavailable.

LATVIAN

May we ... here?	vai mehs *dreek*-stuhm shayt ...?	*Vai mēs drīkstam šeit ...?*
camp	*uz*-stah-deet	*uzstādīt*
	suh-vu tel-ti	*savu telti*
light a fire	*kur*-in-aht	*kurināt*
	u-guns-ku-ru	*ugunskuui*
camp site	*kemp*-ings	*kempings*
can opener	(*kon*-ser-vu *kahr*-bu)	*(konservu kārbu)*
	uht-var-uhm-ais	*atveramais*
compass	*kom*-pas	*kompass*
drinking water	*dzar*-uhm-ais *oo*-dens	*dzeramais ūdens*
gas cylinder	*gah*-zes *buh*-lawns	*gāzes balons*
insect repellent	pret *aw*-du *leedz*-ek-lis	*pret odu līdzeklis*
matches	*saar*-kaw-tsiny-i	*sērkociņi*
saucepan	*kuh*-stro-lis	*kastrolis*
sleeping bag	*guly*-uhm-mais	*guļammaiss*
torch	(*kuh*-buh-tuhs)	*(kabatas)*
	buh-ter-i-yuh	*baterija*
tent	telts	*telts*

Useful Words

beach	*plud*-muh-le	*pludmale*
country house	*low*-ku *mah*-yuh	*lauku māja*
farm	*low*-ku *saa*-tuh	*lauku sēta*
farmer	*lowk*-saim-neaks	*lauksaimnieks*
field	lowks	*lauks*
forest	mezhs	*mežs*
lake	a-zars	*ezers*
river	u-pe	*upe*
sea	*yoo*-ruh	*jūra*
tree	kawks	*koks*
well	*uh*-kuh	*aka*
windmill	*dzir*-nuh-vuhs	*dzirnavas*

LATVIAN

FOOD

Over the last few years there's been a terrific boom in the number and variety of bars, cafes and restaurants in Latvia serving authentic food from around the world, with multilingual menus. Riga has become a gourmet's paradise and you'll be hard pressed not to be able to find something to suit both your pocket and palate. The dishes described below are ones you'll come across in places serving traditional Latvian food. Tipping is not generally expected in Latvia, although this depends to some extent on the 'class' of restaurant you go to.

Can you recommend a good ...?	vai yoos muhn vuh-ruht ea-taykt luh-bu ...?	*Vai jūs man varat ieteikt labu ...?*
bar	bah-ru	*bāru*
cafe	kuh-fey-neets-u	*kafejnīcu*
restaurant	res-to-rah-nu	*restorānu*

Is it possible to get something to eat?
    vai shayt ir ea-speh-yuhms puh-ehst?   *Vai šeit ir iespējams paēst?*

At the Restaurant

I have a reservation.
    muhn ir puh-soo-teets   *Man ir pasūtīts.*
A table for ... people please.
    loo-dzu guhl-du ... per-so-nahm   *Lūdzu galdu ... personām.*
Do you have a menu?
    vai yums ir eh-dean-kuhrt-e?   *Vai jums ir ēdienkarte?*
What do you recommend?
    kaw yoos ea-suh-kuht?   *Ko jūs iesakat?*
What's this dish?
    kuhs ir shis eh-deans?   *Kas ir šis ēdiens?*
I'd like ...
    es vaa-laws ...   *Es vēlos ...*
We'd like ...
    mehs vaa-luhm-eas ...   *Mēs vēlamies ...*

LATVIAN

Please may I have a/an ...?	vai *vuh*-raa-tu *puh*-loogt ...?	*Vai varētu palūgt ...?*
ashtray	*pal*-nu *trow*-ku	*pelnu trauku*
fork	*duhk*-shu	*dakšu*
glass	*glah*-zi	*glāzi*
glass of water	*glah*-zi *oo*-dens	*glāzi ūdens*
knife	*nuh*-zi	*nazi*
plate	*shkyee*-vi	*šķīvi*
spoon	*kuh*-raw-ti	*karoti*

This dish is too ...	shis *eh*-deans ir puhr ...	*Šis ēdiens ir par ...*
cold	*owk*-stu	*aukstu*
hot	*kuhr*-stu	*karstu*
salty	*sah*-lee-tu	*sālītu*
sweet	*suhl*-du	*saldu*

This isn't what I ordered.
   es shaw *ne*-puh-soo-tee-yu   *Es šo nepasūtīju.*
Nothing else, thank you.
   tuhs boos vis *puhl*-deas   *Tas būs viss, paldies.*
That was delicious.
   tuhs *bi*-yuh *guhr*-sheegs   *Tas bija garšīgs.*
The bill, please.
   loo-dzu reh-kyi-nu   *Lūdzu rēķinu.*

Can I pay ...?	vai es *vuh*-ru *muhk*-saht ...?	*Vai es varu maksāt ...?*
by credit card	uhr *kred*-eet-kuhr-ti	*ar kredītkarti*
with foreign currency	*ahr*-zehm-yu *vuhl*-oo-tah	*ārzemju valūtā*

MENU DECODER

Starters

desa	*da*-suh	sausage (usually smoked)
kūpināts/ sālīts lasis	*koo*-pin-ahts/ *sah*-leets *luh*-sis	smoked/ salted salmon
marinētas sēnes	*muh*-rin-aa-tuhs *seh*-nes	pickled mushrooms
mēle majonēzē	*meh*-le *muhy*-o-neh-zeh	tongue in mayonnaise
siļķe kažokā	*sil*-kye *kuh*-zhaw-kah	pickled herring with sour cream, egg and beetroot
šprotes	*shpro*-tes	smoked sprats in vegetable oil
žāvēts zutis	*zhah*-vaats *zu*-tis	smoked eel

Soup

biešu zupa	*bea*-shu *zu*-puh	beetroot soup (similar to borscht)
buljons ar pīradziņiem	*bul*-yawns uhr *pee*-ruhdz-iny-eam	clear broth with meat-filled buns
frikadeļu zupa	*fri*-kuh-de-lyu *zu*-puh	clear broth with meatballs
kāpostu zupa	*kah*-paw-stu *zu*-puh	cabbage soup
soļanka	*so*-lyan-kuh	tomato soup with sausage and pickles
zivju zupa	*ziv*-yu *zu*-puh	fish soup

Meat

karbonāde ar piedevām	*kuhr*-bo-nah-de uhr *pea*-dev-ahm	fried pork chop with potatoes, pickled and fresh vegetables
kotletes	*kot*-le-tes	meatballs
kurzemes stroganovs	*kur*-zem-es *stro*-guh-novs	'Courland' stroganoff

LATVIAN

MENU DECODER

mednieku desiņas	*med*-nea-ku *de*-siny-uhs	'Hunter's' sausages (pork)
pelēkie zirņi ar speķi	*pa*-laa-kea *zir*-nyi uhr *spe*-kyi	grey peas with pork fat and onions (best washed down with a glass of buttermilk)
sīpolu sitenis	*see*-paw-lu *si*-ten-is	beefsteak with fried onions
šašliks	*shuh*-shliks	shish kebab (usually lamb)

Seafood
cepts lasis ar piedevām	tsapts *luh*-sis uhr *pea*-dev-ahm	fried salmon with potatoes, pickled and fresh vegetables
lasis poļu mērcē	*luh*-sis *paw*-lyu *mehrts*-eh	salmon in cream sauce
lasis sēņu un diļļu mērcē	*luh*-sis *seh*-nyu un *dily*-lyu *mehrts*-eh	salmon in mushroom and dill sauce

Salads
biešu salāti	*bea*-shu *suh*-lah-ti	grated beetroot in sour cream
dārzeņu salāti	*dahr*-ze-nyu *suh*-lah-ti	diced vegetable salad in sour cream and mayonnaise
kokteiļu salāti	*kok*-tay-lyu *suh*-lah-ti	diced mixture of sausages, peas and cucumber in sour cream and mayonnaise
kāpostu salāti	*kah*-paw-stu *suh*-lah-ti	fresh grated cabbage

LATVIAN

MENU DECODER

krevešu salāti	*kre*-ve-shu *suh*-lah-ti	diced mixture of shrimp and vegetables in sour cream and mayonnaise
siera salāti	*sea*-ruh *suh*-lah-ti	diced cheese and carrots in sour cream and mayonnaise
svaigo gurķu salāti	*svai*-gaw *gur*-kyu *suh*-lah-ti	fresh cucumbers with sour cream
svaigo tomātu salāti	*svai*-gaw *to*-mah-tu *suh*-lah-ti	fresh tomatoes with sour cream

Desserts & Cakes

putukrējums (ar riekstiem)	*pu*-tu-kray-yums (uhr *reak*-steam)	whipped cream (with nuts)
buberts ar augļu mērci	*bu*-berts uhr *ow*-glyu *mehr*-tsi	egg mousse with fruit sauce
debesmanna	*de*-bes-muhn-nuh	'manna from heaven' – a semolina and berry-based pudding with fruit sauce
ķīselis	*kyee*-se-lis	stewed fruit jelly

Vegetarian Meals

Despite the fact that meat is considered an important part of the meal in Latvia, dining opportunities for vegetarians have certainly improved over the last few years. If in doubt, ask if the chef would be willing to rustle you up something off-menu.

I'm a vegetarian.

es *as*-mu *ve*-jye-tah-rea-te/	*Es esmu veģetāriete/*
ve-jye-tah-rea-tis	*veģetārietis.* (f/m)

Do you have any vegetarian dishes?

vai yums ir *ve*-jye-tah-rea	*Vai jums ir veģetārie*
eh-dea-ni?	*ēdieni?*

I don't eat ...	es *ne*-aa-du ...	*Es neēdu ...*
chicken	**vis-tu**/*vis*-tuhs	*vistu/vistas*
	guh-lyu	*gaļu*
fish	**zivs**	*zivs*
meat	**guh-lyu**	*gaļu*
pork	**tsook-guh-lyu**	*cūkgaļu*

Breads

You may not automatically be served bread with your restaurant meal, but don't hesitate to ask the waiter for some – especially the dark rye bread.

rye bread	**ru-dzu mai-ze**	*rudzu maize*
sour-sweet bread	**suhld-skahb-mai-ze**	*saldskābmaize*
white bread	**buhlt-mai-ze**	*baltmaize*

Dairy Produce

butter	*sveasts*	*sviests*
buttermilk	*ke-feers*	*kefīrs*
cheese	*sears*	*siers*
cottage cheese	*beaz-peans/*	*biezpiens/*
	mah-yuhs sears	*mājas siers*
cream	*kray-yums*	*krējums*
ice cream	*suhl-day-yums*	*saldējums*
milk	*peans*	*piens*
boiled eggs	*vah-ree-tuhs*	*vārītas*
	aw-luhs	*olas*
fried eggs	*tsep-tuhs*	*ceptas*
	aw-luhs	*olas*

Meat

beef	*leal-law-pu*	*liellopu*
	guh-lyuh	*gaļa*
ham	*shkyiny-kyis*	*šķiņķis*
lamb	*yaar-guh-lyuh*	*jērgaļa*
pork	*tsook-guh-lyuh*	*cūkgaļa*
sausage (sliced)	*da-suh*	*desa*
sausages	*tsee-siny-i*	*cīsiņi*
veal	*te-lyuh guh-lyuh*	*teļa gaļa*

Seafood

carp	*kuhr-puh*	*karpa*
cod	*mants-uh*	*menca*
eel	*zu-tis*	*zutis*
herring	*sil-kye*	*silķe*
mackerel	*skum-bri-yuh*	*skumbrija*
plaice	*bu-te*	*bute*
salmon	*luh-sis*	*lasis*
shrimp	*guhr-ne-le*	*garnele*
trout	*fo-re-le*	*forele*

LATVIAN

Poultry & Game

chicken	*vis*-tuh	*vista*
elk meat	*uhl*-nyu *guh*-lyuh	*aļņu gaļa*
turkey	*tee*-tuhrs	*tītars*
wild boar	*mezh*-tsoo-kuh	*mežcūka*

Vegetables

beans	*pu*-piny-uhs	*pupiņas*
beetroot	*bea*-tes	*bietes*
cabbage	*kah*-paw-sti	*kāposti*
capsicum	*suhl*-dea *pi*-puh-ri	*saldie pipari*
carrots	*bur*-kah-ni	*burkāni*
cauliflower	*puky*-*kah*-paw-sti	*puķkāposti*
cucumber	*gur*-kyis	*gurķis*
eggplant	*buhk*-luh-zhahns	*baklažāns*
lettuce	*suh*-lah-ti	*salāti*
mushrooms	*seh*-nes	*sēnes*
onions	*see*-paw-li	*sīpoli*
peas	*zir*-nyi	*zirņi*
pickled	*muhr*-in-aa-ti	*marinēti*
cucumbers	*gur*-kyi	*gurķi*
potatoes	*kuhr*-tu-pe-lyi	*kartupeļi*
spinach	*spin*-ah-ti	*spināti*
tomatoes	*to*-mah-ti	*tomāti*

Legumes

broad beans	*tsook*-pu-puhs	*cūkpupas*
grey peas	*pal*-aa-kea *zir*-nyi	*pelēkie zirņi*
pearl barley	*groo*-buhs	*grūbas*
semolina	*muhn*-nuh	*manna*

LATVIAN

LATVIAN

AT THE MARKET

Basics

bread	*mai*-ze	maize
butter	sveasts	sviests
cereal	*braw*-kuhs-tu	brokastu
	pahr-sluhs	pārslas
cheese	sears	siers
chocolate	*sho*-ko-lah-de	šokolāde
eggs	*aw*-luhs	olas
flour	*mil*-ti	milti
margarine	*muhr*-guh-reens	margarīns
mineral water	*min-er-uhl-oo-dens*	minerālūdens
jam	*ea*-vah-ree-yums	ievārījums
milk	peans	piens
oil	*ely*-lyuh	eļļa
pasta	*muh*-kuh-raw-ni	makaroni
rice	*ree*-si	rīsi
sugar	*tsuk*-kurs	cukurs
yogurt	*yo*-gurts	jogurts

Meat & Poultry

beef	*leal*-law-pu *guh*-lyuh	liellopu gaļa
chicken	*vis*-tuh	vista
ham	*shkyiny*-kyis	šķiņķis
lamb	*yaar*-guh-lyuh	jērgaļa
sausage (sliced)	*da*-suh	desa
pork	*tsook*-guh-lyuh	cūkgaļa
turkey	*tee*-tuhrs	tītars
veal	*te*-lyuh -guh-lyuh	teļa gaļa

Vegetables

beans	*pu*-piny-uhs	pupiņas
beetroot	*bea*-tes	bietes
cabbage	*kah*-paw-sti	kāposti
carrots	*bur*-kah-ni	burkāni
cauliflower	*puky- kah*-paw-sti	puķkāposti
cucumber	*gur*-kyi	gurķi

AT THE MARKET

eggplant	*buhk*-luh-zhahn	*baklažāns*
lettuce	*suh*-lah-ti	*salāti*
mushrooms	*seh*-nes	*sēnes*
onions	*see*-paw-li	*sīpoli*
peas	*zir*-nyi	*zirņi*
potatoes	*kuhr*-tu-pe-lyi	*kartupeļi*
spinach	*spin*-ah-tai	*spināti*
tomatoes	*to*-mah-ti	*tomāti*

Seafood

carp	*kuhr*-puh	*karpa*
cod	*mants*-uh	*menca*
eel	*zu*-tis	*zutis*
herring	*sil*-kyeh	*silķe*
mackerel	*skum*-bri-yuh	*skumbrija*
plaice	*bu*-te	*bute*
salmon	*luh*-sis	*lasis*
shrimp	*guhr*-ne-le	*garnele*
trout	*fo*-re-le	*forele*

Fruit

apples	*ah*-baw-li	*āboli*
apricot	*uhp*-ri-kawzs	*aprikozs*
bananas	*ban*-ah-ni	*banāni*
berries	aw-guhs	*ogas*
cherries	*kyir*-shi	*ķirši*
fruit	ow-glyi	*augli*
grapes	*veen*-aw-guhs	*vīnuogas*
lemon	*tsit*-rons	*citrons*
oranges	*uhp*-el-see-ni	*apelsīni*
peach	*per*-si-kyis	*persiķis*
pears	*bum*-bea-ri	*bumbieri*
plums	*ploom*-es	*plūmes*
raspberries	*uh*-ve-nes	*avenes*
strawberries	ze-me-nes	*zemenes*
watermelon	*uhr*-boozs	*arbūzs*

LATVIAN

Fruit

apples	*ah*-baw-li	*āboli*
apricot	*uhp*-ri-kawzs	*aprikozs*
bananas	*ban*-ah-ni	*banāni*
berries	*aw*-guhs	*ogas*
blueberries	*mell*-en-es	*mellenes*
cherries	*kyir*-shi	*kirši*
cranberries	*dzehr*-ve-nes	*dzērvenes*
fruit (pl)	*ow*-glyi	*augli*
grapes	*veen*-aw-guhs	*vīnogas*
lemon	*tsit*-rons	*citrons*
oranges	*uhp*-el-see-ni	*apelsīni*
peach	*per*-si-kyis	*persiķis*
pears	*bum*-bea-ri	*bumbieri*
pineapple	*uhn*-uhn-uhs	*ananass*
plums	*ploom*-es	*plūmes*
quinces	*tsid*-o-ni-yuhs	*cidonijas*
raspberries	*uh*-ve-nes	*avenes*
red/white	*suhr*-kuhn-ahs/	*sarkanās/*
currants	*buhl*-tahs	*baltās*
	yahny-aw-guhs	*jāņogas*
strawberries	*ze*-me-nes	*zemenes*
watermelon	*uhr*-boozs	*arbūzs*

Desserts & Cakes

apple cake	*ah*-bawl-koo-kuh	*ābolkūka*
baked cheese cake	*beaz*-pea-nu *koo*-kuh	*biezpienu kūka*
biscuits	*tsap*-u-mi	*cepumi*
chocolate	*sho*-ko-lah-de	*šokolāde*
ice cream	*suhl*-day-yums	*saldējums*
pancakes	*puhn*-koo-kuhs	*pankūkas*
pastry	*smuhlk*-mai-zee-te	*smalkmaizīte*
poppyseed cake	*muh*-gaw-nyu *mai*-zee-te	*magoņu maizīte*

BUN IN THE OVEN

Recipe for *pīrāgi* (Buns filled with meat)
(Eaten at Latvian festivals, on Latvian holidays, at names days, birthdays etc. Every Latvian family has its own version of this recipe.)

Ingredients
approx 500g smoked bacon (diced)
1 onion (finely chopped)
1 cup of milk
100g butter or margarine
2 tablespoons sugar
half teaspoon salt
2 egg yolks
500g flour
1 packet dry yeast (dissolved in warm water)
seasoning (salt, pepper, nutmeg, caraway seeds) to taste
1 egg (beaten)

Melt the butter in the milk, add sugar and salt and leave to cool. Add about half a cup of the flour, egg yolks and yeast. Stir well and add the rest of the flour. Knead the mixture and then cover and leave it to rise in a warm place.

Mix the diced bacon with the onion and season according to taste.

Once the dough has risen, roll it out on a floured surface. Cut out circles of dough, put the bacon/onion filling on one side of each circle of dough, fold over, seal the edges and put on a greased baking tray with the sealed side underneath. Once prepared, leave to rise for around half an hour, brush with beaten egg. Bake for around 10 – 15 minutes at 400°F (205°C) until golden brown.

LATVIAN

Condiments

honey	*mad*-us	*medus*
horseradish	*mah*-rut-ki	*mārrutki*
jam	ea-vah-ree-yums	*ievārījums*
mustard	*sin*-e-pes	*sinepes*
oil	*ely*-lyuh	*eļļa*
pepper	*pi*-puh-ri	*pipari*
salt	sahls	*sāls*
sugar	*tsu*-kurs	*cukurs*
vinegar	e-ti-kyis	*etiķis*

Cooking Methods

baked	*krah*-snee tsapts	*krāsnī cepts*
boiled	*vah*-reets	*vārīts*
fried	tsapts	*cepts*
grilled	*gril*-aats	*grilēts*

Non-Alcoholic Drinks

Coffee and tea are usually served black, so if you want milk, you'll generally have to ask for it.

coffee	*kuh*-fi-yuh	*kafija*
(fruit) juice	(*ow*-glyu) *su*-luh	(*augļu*) *sula*
lemonade	*li*-mo-nah-de	*limonāde*
milk	peans	*piens*
mineral water	*min*-er-ahl-oo-dens	*minerālūdens*
tea (with lemon)	*teh*-yuh	*tēja*
	(uhr *tsit*-raw-nu)	*(ar citronu)*

Alcoholic Drinks

Aldaris beer is known worldwide and in Latvia the Aldaris brewery offers the largest selection of beers (and mineral water) to suit all tastes. Wine has grown in popularity over the last several years, but locally produced vodka, cognac, sparkling wine and other spirits remain firm favourites. Riga Black Balsam is very much an acquired taste, but well worth a try.

beer	*uh-lus*	*alus*
local beer	*vea-teh-yais uh-lus*	*vietējais alus*
cognac	*kon-yuhks*	*konjaks*
liqueur	*li-kyear-is*	*liķieris*
red wine	*suhr-kuhn-veens*	*sarkanvīns*
white wine	*buhlt-veens*	*baltvīns*
sparkling wine	*shuhm-puhn-ea-tis*	*šampanietis*
vodka	*shnyuh-bis/ dag-veens*	*šņabis/degvīns*

BOTTOMS UP!

Rīgas Melnais Bālzams is a thick, jet-black alcoholic drink (very alcoholic – 45% proof!) that's been produced in Latvia since 1755. It was created by Abraham Kunze, a druggist, and was supposedly administered to Catherine the Great, when she was struck down in Riga by a mystery illness. The story goes that after drinking Riga Black Balsam, she made an instant recovery.

LATVIAN

Useful Words

breakfast	*braw-kuhs-tis*	*brokastis*
lunch	*pus-dea-nuhs*	*pusdienas*
dinner	*vuh-kuh-riny-uhs*	*vakariņas*
canned	*kon-ser-vaats*	*konservēts*
food	*pahr-ti-kuh*	*pārtika*
fresh	*svaigs*	*svaigs*
pickled	*muh-ri-naats*	*marinēts*

| Bon appetit! | *luh-bu uh-pe-tee-ti!* | *Labu apetīti!* |
| Cheers! | *prea-kah!* | *Priekā!* |

SHOPPING

In Latvia you'll find everything your heart desires in small specialist shops, large department stores, supermarkets or the open-air markets. Be aware that prices of imported goods can often be higher than in Western countries, but the significant increase in choice allows you to be selective as to where you spend your money. Happily, the days of queuing and rationing are just a distant memory.

SIGNS	
DIENNAKTS VEIKALS	24-HOUR SHOP
KASE	CASH REGISTER/
	CHECK-OUT
SLĒGTS	CLOSED
ATVĒRTS	OPEN
DARBA LAIKS	OPENING HOURS
VILKT	PULL
GRŪST	PUSH
(CENU) ATLAIDE	SALE

Making a Purchase

In smaller shops goods are sometimes located on shelves behind the sales assistants and y ou have to ask them to show you what you are interested in. You may also have to pay a cashier first and then present your receipt to the sales assistant to pick up your goods.

May I help you?	*loo-dzu* yoos *vaa-luh-teas?*	*Lūdzu jūs vēlaties?*
Do you have ...?	**vai** yums **ir** ...?	*Vai jums ir ...?*
I'd like to buy ...	es **vaa-**laws *naw-*pirkt ...	*Es vēlos nopirkt ...*

Please show me	*loo-dzu*	*Lūdzu*
this/that ...	*puh-rah-deat*	*parādiet*
	muhn shaw/taw ...	*man šo/to ...*

Do you have	*vai yums ir*	*Vai jums ir*
a ... one?	*kowt-kuhs ...?*	*kautkas ...?*
better	*luhb-ahks*	*labāks*
bigger	*leal-ahks*	*lielāks*
cheaper	*laat-ahks*	*lētāks*
different	*tsits*	*cits*
smaller	*muhz-ahks*	*mazāks*

Can I try it on?
    vai es *vuh*-ru uz-meh-jyin-aht?   *Vai es varu uzmēģināt?*
I don't like it.
    neh muhn tuhs *ne*-puh-teek   *Nē, man tas nepatīk.*
I don't want it.
    neh es taw *ne*-vaa-laws   *Nē, es to nevēlos.*
I'll take it.
    es taw *nyem*-shu   *Es to ņemšu.*
How much is it?
    tsik tuhs *muhk*-sah?   *Cik tas maksā?*
Can I pay by credit card?
    vai es *vuh*-ru *muhk*-saht uhr *kred*-eet-kuhr-ti?   *Vai es varu maksāt ar kredītkarti?*
Could you wrap it please?
    vai *vuh*-raa-tu *loo*-dzu ea-sai-nyawt?   *Vai varētu lūdzu iesaiņot?*
Do you have a bag?
    vai yums ir *mais*-inysh?   *Vai jums ir maisiņš?*

When asking for a specific amount of something in Latvian, use the word *gabalu* (pieces/items) after the number.

One (piece/item), please.
    vea-nu *guh*-buh-lu *loo*-dzu   *Vienu gabalu, lūdzu.*

LATVIAN

Two (pieces/items), please.
   di-vus *guh*-buh-lus *loo*-dzu   *Divus gabalus, lūdzu.*
Five (pieces/items), please.
   peats-us *guh*-buh-lus *loo*-dzu   *Piecus gabalus, lūdzu.*

Shops

Window-shopping in Latvia can be a time-saver when the name of the shop offers no clues as to what is for sale inside. Window-shopping is also an enjoyable way to spend a few hours, especially around midsummer and Christmas, when window dressers' artistic talents and imaginations run wild.

bakery	*mai*-z-neets-uh	*maiznīca*
bookshop	*gruh*-muh-tu *vay*-kuhls	*grāmatu veikals*
chemist/pharmacy	*uhp*-tea-kuh	*aptieka*
clothing shop	*uhp*-jyaar-bu *vay*-kuhls	*apģērbu veikals*
department store	*un*-i-ver-sahl-vay-kuhls	*universālveikals*
drycleaners	*kyee*-mis-kah *tee*-ree-tuh-vuh	*ķīmiskā tīrītava*
electrical shop	*el*-ek-tro-pre-chu *vay*-kuhls	*elektropreču veikals*
food shop	*pahr*-ti-kuhs *vay*-kuhls	*pārtikas veikals*
greengrocer	*suhk*-nyu *vay*-kuhls	*sakņu veikals*
hairdresser	*friz*-aa-tuh-vuh	*frizētava*
jewellery shop	*yu*-vel-ear-iz-strah-dah-yum-i	*juvelieriz-strādājumi*
laundrette	*vely*-uhs *muhz*-gah-tu-ve	*veļas mazgātuve*
shoe shop	*uh*-puh-vu *vay*-kuhls	*apavu veikals*
souvenir shop	*su*-ven-ea-ru *vay*-kuhls	*suvenīru veikals*
stationers	*ruhk*-stahm-pea-dar-um-u *vay*-kuhls (*ruhk*-stahm-pea-dar-um-i)	*rakstāmpiederumu veikals* (*rakstāmpie-derumi*)

LATVIAN

Essential Groceries

batteries	*buh*-te-ri-yuhs	*baterijas*
bread	*mai*-ze	*maize*
butter	sveasts	*sviests*
candles	*sve*-tses	*sveces*
cereal	*braw*-kuhs-tu	*brokastu*
	pahr-sluhs	*pārslas*
cheese	sears	*siers*
chocolate	*sho*-ko-lah-de	*šokolāde*
eggs	*aw*-luhs	*olas*
flour	*mil*-ti	*milti*
gas cylinder	*gah*-zes	*gāzes*
	buh-lawns	*balons*
ham	*shkyiny*-kyis	*šķiņķis*
honey	*mad*-us	*medus*
insect repellent	pret *aw*-du	*pret odu*
	leedz-ek-lis	*līdzeklis*
jam	ea-vah-ree-yums	*ievārījums*
margarine	*muhr*-guh-reens	*margarīns*
matches	*saar*-kaw-tsiny-i	*sērkociņi*
milk	peans	*piens*
pepper	*pi*-puh-ri	*pipari*
pasta	*muh*-kuh-raw-ni	*makaroni*
rice	*ree*-si	*rīsi*
salt	sahls	*sāls*
shampoo	*shuhm*-poons	*šampūns*
soap	*zea*-pes	*ziepes*
sunblock cream	*sow*-les krehms	*saules krēms*
sugar	*tsu*-kurs	*cukurs*
toilet paper	*tu*-uh-le-tes	*tualetes*
	puh-peers	*papīrs*
toothpaste	*zaw*-bu *puhs*-tuh	*zobu pasta*
washing powder	*vely*-uhs *pul*-ve-ris	*veļas pulveris*
yogurt	*yo*-gurts	*jogurts*

LATVIAN

Souvenirs

amber	*dzin*-tuhrs	*dzintars*
art work	*mahk*-sluhs *duhr*-bi	*mākslas darbi*
folk art (articles)	*tow*-tis-kea *preaksh*-mati	*tautiskie priekšmeti*
handicrafts	*raw*-ku *duhr*-bi	*roku darbi*
jewellery	*yu*-vel-ear-iz-strah-dah-yum-i	*juvelier-izstrādājumi*
leather goods	*ah*-duhs iz-strah-dah-yum-i	*ādas izstrādājumi*
Latvian mittens/ socks	*tow*-tis-kea *tsim*-di/ *tow*-tis-kahs ze-kyes	*tautiskie cimdi/ tautiskās zeķes*
linen	lins	*lins*
pottery	*ke*-ruh-mi-kuh	*keramika*
souvenirs	*su*-ve-nee-ri	*suvenīri*
tapestries	*go*-be-lah-ni	*gobelēni*
wood carvings	*kawk*-grea-zu-mi	*kokgriezumi*
weavings	*ow*-du-mi	*audumi*

Clothing

blouse	*bloo*-ze	*blūze*
clothing	*uhp*-jyaar-bi	*apģērbi*
coat	*meh*-te-lis	*mētelis*
dress	*klay*-tuh	*kleita*
hat	*tsa*-pu-re	*cepure*
jacket	*yuh*-kuh/ *zhuh*-ke-te	*jaka/ žakete*
jumper/ sweater	*jem*-per-is	*džemperis*
scarf	*shuhl*-le	*šalle*
shirt	*kra*-kls	*krekls*
shoes	*uh*-puh-vi	*apavi*
skirt	*svahr*-ki	*svārki*
socks	ze-kyes	*zeķes*
trousers	*bik*-ses	*bikses*

Materials

cotton	*kawk*-vilnuh	*kokvilna*
gold	zalts	*zelts*
handmade	*raw*-ku duhrbs	*roku darbs*
leather	*ah*-duh	*āda*
linen	lins	*lins*
metal	*me*-tahls	*metāls*
silver	*su*-druhbs	*sudrabs*
wood	kawks	*koks*
wool	*vil*-nuh	*vilna*

Toiletries

comb	*kyem*-me	*ķemme*
condoms	*prez*-er-vuh-tee-vi	*prezervatīvi*
deodorant	*dez*-o-do-ruhnts	*dezodorants*
razor	*zhi*-le-te	*žilete*
sanitary napkins	*bin*-des	*bindes*
shampoo	*shuhm*-poons	*šampūns*
shaving cream	*skuy*-uhm-ahs	*skujamās*
	pu-tuhs	*putas*
soap	*zea*-pes	*ziepes*
sunblock cream	*sow*-les krehms	*saules krēms*
tampons	*tuhm*-po-ni	*tamponi*
toilet paper	*tu*-uh-le-tes *puh*-peers	*tualetes papīrs*
toothbrush	*zaw*-bu *su*-kuh	*zobu suka*
toothpaste	*zaw*-bu *puhs*-tuh	*zobu pasta*

LATVIAN

IT'S NEWS TO ME

A large selection of Western newspapers and magazines are widely available in the well-stocked newspaper kiosks. Most kiosks also sell stamps, telephone cards, monthly transport tickets, cigarettes, confectionary and other items, too numerous to mention. For Baltic news and events get hold of a copy of 'The Baltic Times', published weekly in Riga. Failing that, you can always read the Internet version.

Stationery & Publications

Do you have ...?	vai yums ir ...?	*Vai jums ir ...?*
books/	*grah-muh-tuhs/*	*grāmatas/*
newspapers/	*uh-vee-zes/*	*avīzes/*
magazines in	*zhur-nah-li*	*žurnāli*
English	*uhn-glyu*	*angļu*
	vuh-law-dah	*valodā*
an English-	*uhn-glyu*	*angļu-*
Latvian	*luht-vea-shu*	*latviešu*
dictionary	*vahrd-neets-uh*	*vārdnīca*
a textbook	*luht-vea-shu*	*latviešu*
to learn	*vuh-law-duhs*	*valodas*
Latvian	*mahts-ee-bu*	*mācību*
	grah-muh-tuh	*grāmata*
books	*gruh-muh-tuhs*	*grāmatas*
guidebook	*tsely-ve-dis*	*ceļvedis*
map	*kuhr-te*	*karte*
newspaper	*laik-ruhksts/uh-vee-ze*	*laikraksts/avīze*
pen	*pild-spuhl-vuh*	*pildspalva*
postcard	*uht-klaht-ne*	*atklātne*
writing paper	*ruhk-stahm-puh-peers*	*rakstāmpapīrs*

Photography

How much is it to process this film?		
tsik muhk-sah uh-tees-teet		*Cik maksā attīstīt šo*
shaw fil-mu?		*filmu?*
When will it be ready?		
kuhd boos guh-tuhvs?		*Kad būs gatavs?*
I'd like a ... film	es vaa-laws ... fil-mu	*Es vēlos ... filmu*
for this camera.	shim fo-to-uh-puh-	*šim fotoaparātam.*
	rah-tuhm	
B&W	*maln-buhl-tu*	*melnbaltu*
colour	*krah-sai-nu*	*krāsainu*
slide	*di-uh-poz-i-tee-vu*	*diapozitīvu*

LATVIAN

Smoking

A packet of cigarettes, please.
    pats-iny-u *tsig*-uh-re-tes *loo*-dzu   *Paciņu cigaretes, lūdzu.*
May I smoke?
    vai es *dreek*-stu smeh-kyeht?   *Vai es drīkstu smēķēt?*
Do you have a light?
    vai yums ir *u*-guns?   *Vai jums ir uguns?*

cigarettes	*tsig*-uh-re-tes	*cigaretes*
matches	*saar*-kaw-tsiny-i	*sērkociņi*
tobacco	*tuh*-buh-kuh	*tabaka*

Colours

black	malns	*melns*
blue	zils	*zils*
brown	broons	*brūns*
green	zuhlysh	*zaļš*
orange	*o*-ruhnzh	*oranžs*
pink	*ro*-zah	*rozā*
red	*suhr*-kuhns	*sarkans*
white	buhlts	*balts*
yellow	*dzal*-tans	*dzeltens*

Sizes & Comparisons

big	leals	*liels*
enough	*pea*-tea-kuhm-i	*pietiekami*
heavy	smuhgs	*smags*
less	*muh*-zahk	*mazāk*
light	veagls	*viegls*
a little	*muhz*-leat	*mazliet*
long	guhrsh	*garš*
many	dowdz	*daudz*
more	*vai*-rahk	*vairāk*
short	ees	*īss*
size	*lea*-lums	*lielums*
small	muhzs	*mazs*
too much	puhr dowdz	*par daudz*

HEALTH

Hotels and embassies in Riga will be able to provide you with lists of English speaking doctors in Latvia. Many Western brands of medicine are readily available, but make sure you bring any prescription medicines with you. Ticks can be a problem in rural areas and forests during the summer months, so if you plan to go hiking or camping you should make sure you're vaccinated prior to travelling to Latvia.

At the Doctor

Please call a doctor.	*loo-dzu iz-sow-tseat ahrs-tu*	*Lūdzu izsauciet ārstu.*
Where can I find a/an ...?	kur es *vuh*-ru uht-ruhst ...?	*Kur es varu atrast ...?*
chemist	*uhp*-tea-ku	*aptieku*
dentist	*zawb*-ahr-stu	*zobārstu*
doctor	*ahr*-stu	*ārstu*
English-speaking doctor	*ahr*-stu kuhs *ru*-nah *uhn*-gli-ski	*ārstu, kas runā angliski*
hospital	*slim*-neets-u	*slimnīcu*
I'd like to see a female doctor.	es *vaa*-laws *redz*-eht *ahr*-stu-*sea*-vea-ti	*Es vēlos redzēt ārstu-sievieti.*
I feel nauseous.	muhn ir *slik*-tuh *doo*-shuh	*Man ir slikta dūša.*
I've been vomiting.	muhn *bi*-yuh *yah*-vemy	*Man bija jāvemj.*
I feel dizzy.	muhn ir *ray*-baw-nis	*Man ir reibonis.*

Ailments

I'm sick.
 es *as*-mu slim-uh/slims *Es esmu slima/slims.* (f/m)

My friend is sick.
 muhn-uh drow-dze-ne ir slim-uh *Mana draudzene ir slima.* (f)
 muhns drowgs ir slims *Mans draugs ir slims.* (m)

LATVIAN

Where does it hurt?
  ku-rah *vea*-tah sahp?   *Kurā vietā sāp?*
It hurts here.
  muhn sahp shayt   *Man sāp šeit.*

I have a/an ...	man sahp ...	*Man sāp ...*
earache	ows	*auss*
headache	*guhl*-vuh	*galva*
sore throat	*kuh*-kls	*kakls*
stomachache	vaa-dars	*vēders*

I have (a/an) ...	muhn ir ...	*Man ir ...*
She/He has (a/an) ...	*viny*-ai/*viny*-uhm ir ...	*Viņai/Viņam ir ...*
asthma	*uhst*-muh	*astma*
backache	mu-gur-sah-pes	*mugursāpes*
burn	*uhp*-dag-ums	*apdegums*
cold	eas-nuhs	*iesnas*
constipation	aiz-tsea-teh-yums	*aizcietējums*
cough	*klap*-us	*klepus*
cramps	kruh*mp*-yi	*krampji*
diabetes	*di*-uh-behts	*diabēts*
diarrhoea	tsowr-e-yuh	*caureja*
epilepsy	ep-i-lep-si-yuh	*epilepsija*
fever	dru-dzis	*drudzis*
food poisoning	suh-in-deh-shuhn-ahs	*saindēšanās*
	uhr eh-dea-nu	*ar ēdienu*
headache	*guhl*-vuhs sah-pes	*galvas sāpes*
hepatitis	he-puh-teets	*hepatīts*
high/low blood	owgsts/zams	*augsts/zems*
pressure	uhs-ins-spea-deans	*asinsspiediens*
indigestion	gram-aw-shuhn-uhs	*gremošanas*
	trau-tseh-yum-i	*traucējumi*
infection	ea-kai-sums	*iekaisums*
influenza	gri-puh	*gripa*
rash	*iz*-sit-um-i	*izsitumi*
sprain	*iz*-mezh-jyee-yums	*izmežģījums*
temperature	tem-pe-ruh-too-ruh	*temperatūra*
venereal disease	ven-e-ris-kah	*veneriskā*
	slim-ee-buh	*slimība*

LATVIAN

Allergies

I have an allergy.

| muhn ir *uh*-ler-jyi-yuh | *Man ir alerģija.* |

I'm allergic to penicillin.

es *as*-mu *uh*-ler-jyis-kuh/	*Es esmu alerģiska/*
uh-ler-jyisks pret	*alerģisks pret*
pen-its-i-lee-nu	*penicilīnu.* (f/m)

Parts of the Body

ankle	*paw*-tee-te	*potīte*
arm	*raw*-kuh	*roka*
back	*mu*-gu-ruh	*mugura*
chest	*kroo*-tis	*krūtis*
ear	ows	*auss*
eye	uhts	*acs*
finger	pirksts	*pirksts*
foot	*paa*-duh	*pēda*
gums	*smuh*-guh-nuhs	*smaganas*
hand	*raw*-kuh	*roka*
head	*guhl*-vuh	*galva*
heart	sirds	*sirds*
knee	*tse*-lis	*celis*
leg	*kah*-yuh	*kāja*
mouth	*mu*-te	*mute*
nose	*da*-guns	*deguns*
shoulder	plats	*plecs*
throat/neck	*kuh*-kls	*kakls*
tongue	*meh*-le	*mēle*

At the Chemist

Do you have
something for ...?

| vai yums ir *kowt*-kuhs pret ...? | *Vai jums ir kaut kas pret ...?* |

I have a prescription.

| muhn ir *rets*-ep-te | *Man ir recepte.* |

At the Dentist

I have a toothache.
muhn sahp zawbs *Man sāp zobs.*

I've lost a filling.
muhn ir *iz*-kri-tu-si *plom*-buh *Man ir izkritusi plomba.*

I've broken a tooth.
muhn ir *naw*-loo-zis zawbs *Man ir nolūzis zobs.*

My gums hurt.
muhn sahp *smuh*-guh-nuhs *Man sāp smaganas.*

I don't want it extracted.
***loo*-dzu ne-iz-row-yeat** *Lūdzu neizraujiet.*

Useful Words & Phrases

I've been vaccinated.
es *as*-mu *paw*-taa-tuh/ *paw*-taats *Es esmu potēta/ potēts.* (f/m)

I haven't had my
period for ... months.
muhn nuhv *bi*-yu-shuhs *ray*-zes jow ... *meh*-ne-shus *Man nav bijušas reizes jau ... mēnešus.*

I have my own syringe.
muhn *puh*-shai/ *puh*-sham ir *suh*-vuh *shlir*-tse *Man pašai/pašam ir sava šlirce.* (f/m)

I'm pregnant.
es *as*-mu *stah*-vaw-klee *Es esmu stāvoklī.*

I feel better/worse.
muhn ir *luh*-bahk/ *slik*-tahk *Man ir labāk/sliktāk.*

LATVIAN

accident	*ne*-lai-me/	*nelaime/*
	uh-vah-ri-yuh	*avārija*
animal bite	kaw-deans	*kodiens*
antibiotic	uhn-ti-bi-o-ti-kuh	*antibiotika*
aspirin	uhs-pi-reens	*aspirīns*
bleeding	uhs-i-nyaw-shuh-nuh	*asiņošana*
blood pressure	uhs-ins-spea-deans	*asinsspiediens*
blood test	uhs-ins-uhn-uh-lee-ze	*asinsanalīze*
cough medicine	kla-pus zah-les	*klepus zāles*
injury	ea-vai-naw-yums	*ievainojums*
insect bite	dzeh-leans	*dzēliens*
medicine	zah-les	*zāles*
menstruation	men-stru-ah-tsi-yuh	*menstruācija*
oxygen	skah-be-klis	*skābeklis*
vitamins	vit-uh-mee-ni	*vitamīni*

SPECIFIC NEEDS
Disabled Travellers

I'm disabled/handicapped.
  es *as*-mu in-vuh-lee-de/   *Es esmu invalīde/*
  in-vuh-leeds   *invalīds.* (f/m)
I need assistance.
  muhn ir *vuhy*-uh-dzee-guh   *Man ir vajadzīga*
  puh-lee-dzee-buh   *palīdzība.*
What services are there
for disabled people?
  kah-di *puh*-kuhl-paw-yu-mi ir *Kādi pakalpojumi ir*
  in-vuh-lee-deam?   *invalīdiem?*
Is there wheelchair access?
  vai tur vuhr *pea*-klyoot uhr *Vai tur var piekļūt ar*
  brauts-uhm-kraas-lu?   *braucamkrēslu?*
I'm deaf. Speak more loudly, please.
  es *as*-mu *kur*-luh/kurls   *Es esmu kurla/kurls*
  (ne-dzir-dee-guh/ne-dzir-deegs). *(nedzirdīga/nedzirdīgs).*
  loo-dzu *run*-ah-yeat *skuh*-lyahk *Ludzu runājiet skaļāk.* (f/m)

I have a hearing aid.
    muhn ir dzir-des uh-puh-rahts   *Man ir dzirdes aparāts.*

I'm blind.
    es as-mu *uh*-kluh/*uh*-kls   *Es esmu akla/akls.* (f/m)

I'm blind.
    es as-mu *ne*-re-dzee-guh/   *Es esmu neredzīga/*
    ***ne*-re-dzeegs**   *neredzīgs.* (f/m)

Are guide dogs permitted?
    vai shayt dreekst vest *su*-nyus   *Vai šeit drīkst vest suņus*
    ***puh*-vuh-daw-nyus?**   *pavadoņus?*

I'm mute.
    es as-mu maa-muh/maams   *Es esmu mēma/mēms.*(f/m)
                                   (NB Colloquially this
                                   means 'I'm lost for words'.)

Braille library	**ne-re-dzee-gaw ruhk-stu**	*Neredzīgo rakstu*
	bib-li-o-te-kuh	*bibliotēka.*
disabled person	***in*-vuh-lee-de/**	*invalīde/*
	***in*-vuh-leeds**	*invalīds* (f/m)
guide dog	**suns *puh*-vuh-daw-nis**	*suns pavadonis*
wheelchair	***brauts*-uhm-kraa-sls**	*braucamkrēsls*

LATVIAN

TIME & DATES
The 24-hour clock is used in Latvia. You may find that Latvians also use it when speaking. The easiest way to tell the time in Latvian is to say the hour and then the minutes, eg, 'three-twenty'. However, there are a few simple rules to learn to be able to tell the time correctly.

hour	***stun*-duh**	*stunda*
minute	***min*-oo-te**	*minūte*
o'clock	***pulk*-sten-is**	*pulkstenis*

What time (is it)?
  tsik (ir) *pulk*-sten-is?   *Cik (ir) pulkstenis?*
It's one o'clock.
  ir *pulk*-sten-is veans   *Ir pulkstenis viens.*

You'll find that the word *pulkstenis* is often omitted:

It's ...	ir ...	*Ir ...*
two o'clock	***di*-vi**	*divi*
		(lit: it's two)
five o'clock	***peats*-i**	*pieci*
ten o'clock	***des*-mit**	*desmit*

To tell the time between the half-hour and the hour, use the word *bez* at the beginning of the phrase, which literally means 'without':

It's ...	ir ...	*Ir ...*
20 (minutes)	bez *div*-des-mit	*bez divdesmit*
to two	(*min*-oo-tehm) ***di*-vi**	*(minūtēm)*
		divi
10 (minutes)	bez *des*-mit	*bez desmit*
to seven	(*min*-oo-tehm)	*(minūtēm)*
	***sep*-ti-nyi**	*septiņi*

LATVIAN

To tell the time between the hour and the half-hour, use the word *pāri* between the two numbers, which literally means 'over':

It's ...	ir...	*Ir ...*
25 past three	**div-des-mit**	*divdesmit*
	peats-i pah-ri	*pieci pāri*
	tri-yeam	*trijiem*
five past eight	**peats-uhs**	*piecas*
	(**min-oo-tes**)	(*minūtes*)
	pah-ri uhs-taw-nyeam	*pāri astoņiem*

To say 'half past ...', use the word *pus* ('half') with the next hour of the clock:

It's half past three.	**ir pus chet-ri**	*Ir pus četri.* (lit: half before four)

Days of the Week
Monday	**pirm-dea-nuh**	*pirmdiena*
Tuesday	**aw-tr-dea-nuh**	*otrdiena*
Wednesday	**tresh-dea-nuh**	*trešdiena*
Thursday	**tsat-urt-dea-nuh**	*ceturtdiena*
Friday	**peakt-dea-nuh**	*piektdiena*
Saturday	**sast-dea-nuh**	*sestdiena*
Sunday	**sveht-dea-nuh**	*svētdiena*

Months
January	**yuhn-vah-ris**	*janvāris*
February	**feb-ru-ah-ris**	*februāris*
March	**muhrts**	*marts*
April	**uhp-ree-lis**	*aprīlis*
May	**maiys**	*maijs*
June	**yoo-niys**	*jūnijs*
July	**yoo-liys**	*jūlijs*
August	**ow-gusts**	*augusts*
September	**sep-tem-bris**	*septembris*
October	**ok-to-bris**	*oktobris*
November	**no-vem-bris**	*novembris*
December	**dets-em-bris**	*decembris*

LATVIAN

Seasons

summer	*vuh*-suh-ruh	*vasara*
autumn	*ru*-dens	*rudens*
winter	*zea*-muh	*ziema*
spring	*puh*-vuh-suh-ris	*pavasaris*

Dates

What's the date today?
kahds *shaw*-dean ir duh-tums?	*Kāds šodien ir datums?*

It's 5 June.
ir *peak*-tais yoo-niys	*Ir piektais jūnijs.*

It's 18 October.
ir *uhs*-tawny-puhds-mi-tais	*Ir astoņpadsmitais oktobris.*
***ok*-to-bris**	

Present

today	*shaw*-dean	*šodien*
this morning	*shaw*-reet	*šorīt*
this week	shaw *ne*-deh-lyu	*šo nedēļu*
this year	*shaw*-guhd	*šogad*
tonight	*shaw*-vuh-kuhr	*šovakar*
now	*tuh*-guhd	*tagad*

Past

yesterday	*vuh*-kuhr	*vakar*
day before yesterday	*aiz*-vuh-kuhr	*aizvakar*
yesterday morning	*vuh*-kuhr-reet	*vakarrīt*
last night	*vuh*-kuhr *vuh*-kuh-rah	*vakarvakarā*
last week	*puhg*-ah-yu-shah ne-deh-lyah	*pagājušā nedēļā*
last year	*puhg*-ah-yu-shah *guh*-dah	*pagājušā gadā*

IT'S A DATE

Latvians write the year first, then the day and then the month. However, where the situation is not particularly formal, the date will be the same as in British English, ie, day, month, year.

Future

tomorrow	reet	*rīt*
day after tomorrow	*puh*-reet	*parīt*
tomorrow morning	reet naw *ree*-tuh	*rīt no rīta*
tomorrow afternoon/ evening	*reet*-dean/ *reet*-vuh-kuhr	*rītdien/ rītvakar*
next week	*nuh*-kuhm *ned*-eh-lyu	*nākam nedēļu*
next year	*nah*-kuhm-guhd	*nākamgad*

During the Day

afternoon	*pehts*-pus-dea-nuh	*pēcpusdiena*
day	*dea*-nuh	*diena*
early	*uh*-gri	*agri*
midnight	*pus*-nuhkts	*pusnakts*
morning	reets	*rīts*
night	nuhkts	*nakts*
noon	*div*-puhds-mit *dea*-nah	*divpadsmit dienā*
sunset	*sowl*-reats	*saulriets*
sunrise	*sowl*-laakts	*saullēkts*

LATVIAN

Useful Words

a year ago	pirms *guh*-duh	*pirms gada*
always	*vean*-maar	*vienmēr*
at the moment	*puhsh*-laik	*pašlaik*
century	*guhd*-simts	*gadsimts*
early	*uh*-gri	*agri*
every day	*kuh*-tru *dea*-nu	*katru dienu*
forever	*vean*-maar	*vienmēr*
just then	*ti*-kaw	*tikko*
late	*vaa*-lu	*vēlu*
later on	*vaa*-lahk	*vēlāk*
never	ne-*kuhd*	*nekad*
not yet	vehl neh	*vēl ne*
now	*tuh*-guhd	*tagad*
since	kawpsh	*kopš*
sometimes	*dazh*-rayz	*dažreiz*
soon	dreez	*drīz*
still	*vehl*-yaw-praw-yahm	*vēljoprojām*
straight away	too-*leet*	*tūlīt*

LATVIAN

FESTIVALS & HOLIDAYS

An entire book could be devoted to the subject of festivals and holidays in Latvia. Suffice it to say that you're guaranteed to have a memorable time if you're lucky enough to spend midsummer, Easter or Christmas in the company of Latvians, as they love any excuse to sing, dance and celebrate.

The traditional Latvian calendar was divided into eight seasons to coincide with the farming year and there are many days, which are marked in the Latvian calendar – although not necessarily celebrated – to signify these points in the year.

You'll never forget a Latvian song festival if you're fortunate enough to be in Riga when one takes place. Latvia also has a number of historically significant public holidays, when all buildings throughout the country must display the Latvian flag.

National Holidays

New Year's Day (1 January)
   yown-guh-duh *dea*-nuh   *Jaungada diena*
Easter Sunday
   leal-dea-nuhs   *Lieldienas*
   (*leal*-dea-nu *sveht*-dea-nuh)   (*lieldienu svētdiena*)
Midsummer (23 June)
   lee-gaw *svaat*-ki   *Līgo svētki*
St John's Day (24 June)
   yah-nyi   *Jāņi*
Independence Day (18 November)
   ne-uht-kuhr-ee-buhs   *Neatkarības*
   prok-lo-meh-shuhn-uhs   *Proklomēšanas Diena*
   dea-nuh
Christmas (24, 25 & 26 December)
   zeam-uhs-svaat-ki   *Ziemassvētki*
                                  (lit: winter festival)

birthday	*dzim*-shuh-nuhs *dea*-nuh	*dzimšanas diena*
name day	*vahr*-duh *dea*-nuh	*vārda diena*
song festival	*dzeas*-mu *svaat*-ki	*dziesmu svētki*
dance festival	*de*-yu *svaat*-ki	*deju svētki*

Felicitations

Happy New Year!
   lai-mee-gu *yown*-aw *guh*-du!   *Laimīgu Jauno Gadu!*
Happy Easter!
   preats-ee-guhs *leal*-dea-nuhs!   *Priecīgas Lieldienas!*
Happy 'Līgo'!
   preats-ee-gus *lee*-gaw *svaat*-kus!   *Priecīgus Līgo svētkus!*
Happy Midsummer!
   preats-ee-gus *yah*-nyus!   *Priecīgus Jāņus!*
Merry Christmas!
   preats-ee-gus   *Priecīgus*
   zeam-uhs-svaat-kus!   *Ziemassvētkus!*
Happy name day/birthday!
   dowdz *lai*-mes   *Daudz laimes*
   vuhr-da *dea*-nah/   *vārda diena/*
   dzim-shuh-nuhs *dea*-nah!   *dzimšanas diena!*

LATVIAN

HAPPY MIDSUMMER!

The greetings *Priecīgus Līgo svētkus!* 'Happy 'Līgo'!' and *Priecīgus Jāņus!* 'Happy Midsummer!' are pretty much interchangeable.

Festivals

Song & Dance Festivals   *Dziesmu Svētki/Deju Svētki*

The first song festival took place in 1873 as part of a European cultural phenomeon and they have continued to this day. Festivals now take place approximately once every four years (the 22nd Song Festival was in July 1998) and are a culmination of the Latvians' love for their culture and history. Choirs and Latvian folk-dance groups from every corner of Latvia and from overseas (totalling up to 30,000 singers and around 5,000 dancers) join forces to perform in several concerts over the course of approximately one week. This is a cultural event not to be missed!

Midsummer/St John's Night   *Līgo Svētki/Jāņi*

This is celebrated on the shortest night of the year – 23 June, the summer solstice. Latvians head out to the countryside and stay up all night singing songs and dancing around a bonfire.

Traditionally, buildings and livestock are decorated with garlands and women weave wreaths from grasses and flowers gathered in the fields. It is important to decorate the doors of the house in order to keep evil spirits away. Beer is brewed and a special St John's Night cheese with caraway seeds is eaten, along with other Latvian foods such as *pīragi* (see recipe, page 155). Young girls wear flower wreaths and men called Jānis (John) are honoured with a wreath made of oak leaves. Young couples head off to the forest to look for fern, which is said to blossom only on this night – those who find it (or at least try to!) are guaranteed happiness and love.

LATVIAN

Baltica International Folk Festival
The first Baltica folk festival took place in 1987 and is held in each of the Baltic states in rotation. The 1987 festival was again a significant event in the Baltic states' move towards renewed independence, as the flag of the Republic of Latvia was carried openly in the festival parade for the first time in over 40 years.

This international festival continues to this day and aims to popularise traditional folk culture and its spiritual values.

18 November   *Neatkarības*
                                             Proklomēšanas Diena
18 November is the day on which Latvia proclaimed independence in 1918. This first period of independence lasted until 17 June 1940 when Latvia was invaded by Soviet troops. Today 18 November is a significant public holiday in Latvia.

Easter   *Lieldienas*
Many of the traditional Easter rituals which Latvians follow to this day relate to the Spring Equinox, *Lielā diena* (lit: big day), although these traditions are now mixed with the Christian festival of Easter.

Traditionally everyone gets up at sunrise and washes their face in running water. In the countryside men build swings and couples take it in turn to swing, so that they are not bitten by mosquitos during the summer. Eggs – which symbolise the sun – are coloured using onion skins, roots and grasses and are given as gifts. Eggs are also a significant part of the Easter breakfast and are the source of many rituals and superstitions. For example, when cracking hard-boiled eggs against other people around the breakfast table, the person whose egg remains intact is guaranteed fortune and happiness. And the person who eats a hard boiled egg without salt is a liar.

LATVIAN

Christmas   *Ziemassvētki*

Nowadays Christmas, like Easter, is a mixture of old and new.
Preparations for the four days of Christmas involve decorating
the house and lighting candles. Ancient traditions dictate that a
fire is lit in the hearth, which should be kept burning. Logs are
dragged around the house to ward off evil spirits. People wearing
fancy dress go from house to house singing Christmas folk songs.
By feeding these people evil spirits are driven away.

The most important day of Christmas is Christmas Eve, when
Latvian families go to church and then return home to open
presents and eat a traditional meal of pork, sauerkraut, potatoes
and grey peas. The remaining days of Christmas are spent visiting
relatives and friends.

NUMBERS & AMOUNTS
Cardinal Numbers

0	*nul*-le	*nulle*
1	veans	*viens*
2	*di*-vi	*divi*
3	trees	*trīs*
4	*chet*-ri	*četri*
5	*peats*-i	*pieci*
6	*sesh*-i	*seši*
7	*sep*-ti-nyi	*septiņi*
8	*uhs*-taw-nyi	*astoņi*
9	*de*-vi-nyi	*deviņi*
10	*des*-mit	*desmit*
11	*vean*-puhds-mit	*vienpadsmit*
12	*div*-puhds-mit	*divpadsmit*
13	*trees*-puhds-mit	*trīspadsmit*
14	*chet*-r-puhds-mit	*četrpadsmit*
15	*peats*-puhds-mit	*piecpadsmit*
16	*sesh*-puhds-mit	*sešpadsmit*
17	*sep*-tiny-puhds-mit	*septiņpadsmit*
18	*uhs*-tawny-puhds-mit	*astoņpadsmit*

LATVIAN

19	*de*-viny-puhds-mit	*deviņpadsmit*
20	*div*-des-mit	*divdesmit*
21	*div*-des-mit-veans	*divdesmitviens*
30	*trees*-des-mit	*trīsdesmit*
40	*chet*-r-des-mit	*četrdesmit*
50	*peats*-des-mit	*piecdesmit*
60	*sesh*-des-mit	*sešdesmit*
70	*sep*-tiny-des-mit	*septiņdesmit*
80	*uhs*-tawny-des-mit	*astoņdesmit*
90	*de*-viny-des-mit	*deviņdesmit*
100	simts	*simts*
200	*di*-vi *sim*-ti	*divi simti*
500	*peats*-i *sim*-ti	*pieci simti*
1000	*tooks*-tawts	*tūkstots*
100,000	simts *tooks*-tawts	*simts tūkstots*
1 million	*mil*-yawns	*miljons*
2 million	*di*-vi *mil*-yaw-ni	*divi miljoni*

Ordinal Numbers

Ordinal numbers have different forms, depending on the gender of the noun they precede. The feminine ending is *-ā* and the masculine ending is *-ais*:

1st	*pir*-mah/*pir*-mais	*pirmā/pirmais* (f/m)
2nd	*awt*-rah/*awt*-rais	*otrā/otrais* (f/m)
3rd	*tre*-shah/*tre*-shais	*trešā/trešais* (f/m)
4th	*tsat*-ur-tah/*tsat*-ur-tais	*ceturtā/ceturtais* (f/m)
5th	*peak*-tah/*peak*-tais	*piektā/piektais* (f/m)
6th	*sas*-tah/*sas*-tais	*sestā/sestais* (f/m)
7th	*sep*-tee-tah/*sep*-tee-tais	*septītā/septītais* (f/m)
8th	*uhs*-taw-tah/*uhs*-taw-tais	*astotā/astotais* (f/m)
9th	*dev*-ee-tah/*dev*-ee-tais	*devītā/devītais* (f/m)
10th	*des*-mit-ah/*des*-mit-ais	*desmitā/desmitais* ((f/m)
20th	*div*-des-mit-ah/ *div*-des-mit-ais	*divdesmitā/ divdesmitais* (f/m)
21st	*div*-des-mit *pir*-mah/ *div*-des-mit *pir*-mais	*divdesmit pirmā/ divdesmit pirmais* (f/m)

Fractions

1/4	*tsat*-urt-duh-lyuh	*ceturtdaļa*
1/3	*tresh*-duh-lyuh	*trešdaļa*
1/2	*pu*-se	*puse*
3/4	trees *tsat*-urt-duh-lyuhs	*trīs ceturtdaļas*
1 1/2	*pus*-aw-truh *da*-lyuh	*pusotra daļa*

Useful Words

once	*vean*-rayz	*vienreiz*
twice	*div*-rayz	*divreiz*
a little	*drus*-ku	*drusku*
some	*muhz*-*leat*	*mazliet*
double	*du*-bul-ti	*dubulti*
few	*pah*-ris	*pāris*
less	*muh*-zahk	*mazāk*
much	dowdz	*daudz*
more	*vai*-rahk	*vairāk*

JŪS YOU TU

Always use *jūs*, the polite form of 'you' when talking to people you don't know. With children, you should use *tu*.

LATVIAN

ABBREVIATIONS

plkst	*pulkstens*	at (about time)
ls	*lats*	lats (Latvian currency)
PVN	*Pievienotās Vērtības Nodoklis*	sales tax
utt	*un tā tālāk*	and so on/etc
P/O/T/C/P/S/S	*pirmdiena/otrdiena/ trešdiena/ceturtdiena/ piektdiena/sestdiena/ svētdiena*	Monday/Tuesday/ Wednesday/ Thursday/Friday/ Saturday/Sunday

EMERGENCIES

Help!
puh-lee-gah!   *Palīgā!*

There's been an accident!
ir naw-ti-ku-si ne-lai-me/   *Ir notikusi nelaime/*
uh-vah-ri-yuh!   *avārija!*

Call a/an/the ...!   **iz-sowts-eat ...!**   *Izsauciet ...!*
  ambulance   **ah-traw**   *ātro palīdzību*
         puh-lee-dzee-bu
  doctor   **ahr-stu**   *ārstu*
  police   **pol-its-i-yu**   *policiju*

Where's the police station?
kur ir pol-its-i-yuhs   *Kur ir policijas*
ea-tsirk-nis?   *iecirknis?*

I've been raped/robbed.
muh-ni iz-vuh-raw-yuh/   *Mani izvaroja/*
uhp-zuh-guh   *apzaga.*

Go away!
ay-eat praw-yam!   *Ejiet projam!*

I'll call the police!
es iz-sowk-shu pol-its-i-yu!   *Es izsaukšu policiju!*

Thief!
zuh-glis!   *Zaglis!*

I'm lost.
es as-mu uhp-muhl-dee-yu-seas/ *Es esmu apmaldījusies/*
uhp-muhl-dee-yeas   *apmaldījies.* (f/m)

Could I please use the telephone?
vai es vuh-raa-tu loo-dzu   *Vai es varētu, lūdzu,*
iz-muhn-tawt te-le-fo-nu?   *izmantot telefonu?*

Where are the toilets?
kur ir tu-uh-le-tes?   *Kur ir tualetes?*

I'm sorry/I apologise.
pea-daw-deat/   *Piedodiet/*
es uht-vai-naw-yaws   *Es atvainojos.*

I didn't realise I was doing
anything wrong.
> **es ne-zin-ah-yu kuh tah**
> **ne-dreek-stu duh-reet**

*Es nezināju, ka tā
nedrīkstu darīt.*

I didn't do it.
> **es taw ne-iz-duh-ree-yu**

Es to neizdarīju.

I want to contact my
embassy/consulate.
> **es vaa-laws suh-zin-ah-teas
> uhr suh-vu vehst-neats-ee-bu/
> kon-su-lah-tu**

*Es vēlos sazināties
ar savu vēstniecību/
konsulātu.*

I've lost my …	**es as-mu puh-zow-deh-yu-si/puh-zow-deh-yis suh-vu …**	*Es esmu pazau-dējusi/pazaudējis savu … (f/m)*
bag	**saw-mu**	*somu*
money	**now-du**	*naudu*
passport	**puh-si**	*pasi*

LATVIAN

LITHUANIAN

LITHUANIAN

QUICK REFERENCE

Hello.	*svay*-ki-*lah*-bahs	Sveiki/Labas. (pol/inf)
Goodbye.	su-*deah*	Sudie.
Yes./No.	tayp/na	Taip./Ne.
Excuse me/	aht-si-prah-*show*/	Atsiprašau/
Sorry.	aht-*lays*-ki-ta	Atleiskite.
Thank you.	deh-*kaw*-yu/	Dėkoju/
	ah-choo	Ačiū. (pol/inf)
You're welcome.	*prah*-show	Prašau.

I'd like a ...	ahsh naw-*reh*-chow ...	Aš norėčiau ...
one-way	*bil*-eah-tah i	bilietą į
ticket	*veah*-nah	vieną
	gah-lah	galą
return	*bil*-eah-tah i ah-*bu*	bilietą į abu
ticket	gah-*lus*	galus

I don't understand you.
ahsh *yoo*-soo
na-su-prahn-*tu*

*Aš jūsų
nesuprantu.*

Do you speak English?
ahr yoos *kahl*-bah-ta
ahn-glish-kai?

*Ar jūs kalbate
angliškai?*

Where is ...?
kur ee-*rah* ...?

Kur yra ...?

| straight ahead | *teah*-say | tiesiai |
| to the left/right | i *kai*-ra/*dash*-na | į kairę/dešinę |

Do you have any rooms available?
ahr *tu*-ri-ta lais-*voo*
kahm-bahr-yew?

*Ar turite laisvų
kambarių?*

Where's the toilet?
kur tu-ah-*lat*-ai?

Kur tualetai?

Help!
gal-beh-ki-te!

Gelbėkite!

1	*veah*-nahs	vienas	6	shash-*i*	šeši
2	du	du	7	sap-tee-*ni*	septyni
3	trees	trys	8	ahsh-tu-aw-*ni*	aštuoni
4	kat-u-*ri*	keturi	9	dav-ee-*ni*	devyni
5	pan-*ki*	penki	10	*dash*-imt	dešimt

LITHUANIAN

LITHUANIAN

INTRODUCTION

Lithuania is the largest of the three Baltic countries and, in 1990, was the first to regain its independence after more than 50 years of forced annexation to the Soviet Union.

Standard Lithuanian is based on the High West dialect of the country and was declared the official language of Lithuania in 1918. Regional dialects in some provincial areas of Lithuania make communication more difficult, though not impossible. While other Indo-European languages have undergone various metamorphoses over time, Lithuanian, due to its isolation in the past, has preserved its homogeneity and has retained a more archaic character than most other contemporary Indo-European tongues. This makes it particularly interesting to linguists.

However, modernity, advances in technology, commerce and global communication in English are leaving their marks on the Lithuanian lexicon. Words with English roots are found in Lithuanian journalism and increasingly in everyday speech.

Traditionally, Lithuanians strive to accommodate and assist visitors. It's hoped that this phrasebook will provide users with a useful guide while visiting the country. Please note that Lithuanian has feminine and masculine forms of words, separated by a slash and indicated by (f) and (m), the feminine form first.

Help!

While you settle back on your plane, train, ferry or bus ride to Lithuania, take some time to learn a few necessary words to ensure that communication with the locals runs a little more smoothly. One of the phrases you may find yourself inclined to utter is, *Ar kas nors kalba angliškai?* (**ahr kahs nors kahl-bah** *ahn*-**glish-kai?**), which means 'Does anyone speak English?'.

PRONUNCIATION

Pronunciation in Lithuanian is unambiguous. Each letter denotes
a particular sound. The sound may be short or long, depending
on the surrounding letters. Vowel combinations, or diphthongs,
also have short and long sounds.

Vowels

Lithuanian	Transliteration	Sounds
a, ą	**ah**	as the 'u' in 'cut' or longer, as the 'a' in 'arm'
e, ę	**a**	as the 'a' in 'cat' or longer, as the 'a' in 'amber'
ė	**eh**	as the 'e' in 'bed' but longer
i	**i**	as the 'i' in 'it'
y, į	**ee**	as the 'ee' in 'eel'
o	**aw**	as the 'aw' in 'law'
	o	as the 'o' in 'hot'
u	**u**	as the 'u' in 'put'
ū, ų	**oo**	long, as the 'oo' in 'poor'

Diphthongs

Lithuanian	Transliteration	Sounds
ai	**ai**	as the 'i' in 'bite' or longer as the 'ai' in 'aisle'
au	**ow**	as the 'ou' in 'ouch' or longer as the 'ow' in 'owl'
ei	**ay**	as the 'ay' in 'say'
ie	**eah**	as the 'ea' in 'ear'
ių	**ew**	as the 'ew' in 'new'
ui	**wi**	as the 'oui' in 'Louis'
uo	**u-aw**	as the 'wa' in 'wander'

Consonants

Lithuanian	Transliteration	Sounds
c	ts	as the 'ts' in 'ants'
č	ch	as the 'ch' in 'chicken'
ch	h	as the 'h' in 'hot'
dz	dz	as the 'ds' in 'roads'
dž	j	as the 'j' in 'jump'
g	g	as the 'g' in 'gas'
j	y	as the 'y' in 'you'
r	r	trilled like the Italian 'r'
s	s	soft, as the 's' in 'kiss'
š	sh	as the 'sh' in 'shop'
ž	zh	as the 's' in 'treasure'

The following sentences will help you to practise your pronunciation in Lithuanian:

How is this word pronounced?
kaip shis zhaw-dis   *Kaip šis žodis*
tahr-yah-mahs   *tariamas?*

The sun is shining.
shveah-cha sow-leh   *Šviečia saulė.*

Would you please help me?
mah-law-neh-ki-ta mahn   *Malonėkite man*
pah-deh-ti   *padėti.*

I'll be ready in about five minutes.
uzh pan-kew mi-nu-chew ahsh   *Už penkių minučių aš*
boos-yu pah-si-ru-aw-sh(u-si/-as)   *būsiu pasiruoš(usi/ęs).* (f/m)

Stress

Stress and tone variations are very subtle and complex in Lithuanian. You'll be understood without having to worry about this too much. The best way to learn is by listening. Stressed syllables are indicated by italic in the transliterations.

LITHUANIAN

GRAMMAR
Sentence Structure

In everyday speech, sentence structure is subject-verb-object, just as it is in English.

Articles

There are no articles (a/an/the) in Lithuanian. So, *gydytojas* can mean 'doctor', 'the doctor' or 'a doctor'.

Nouns

Nouns in Lithuanian have a more complex structure than in English due to their different forms. Here are two tables showing the different forms of the masculine noun *bičiulis* ('friend/mate') and the feminine noun *draugė* ('friend/girlfriend') for the nominative, genitive, dative and accusative cases:

MASCULINE NOUN	SINGULAR	PLURAL
Nominative	*bičiulis*	*bičiuliai*
Genitive	*bičiulio*	*bičiulių*
Dative	*bičiuliui*	*bičiuliams*
Accusative	*bičiulį*	*bičiulius*

FEMININE NOUN	SINGULAR	PLURAL
Nominative	*draugė*	*draugės*
Genitive	*draugės*	*draugių*
Dative	*draugei*	*draugėms*
Accusative	*draugę*	*drauges*

Gender

Nouns are either masculine or feminine. The range of noun endings in Lithuanian is large and varies for each noun depending on the declension used. Therefore, in general, there's no simple way by looking at the form of a noun in a sentence, to determine whether it's masculine or feminine. This will come gradually as you become more familiar with the language.

Adjectives

Adjectives in Lithuanian agree in number, gender and case with the nouns they describe but the suffixes of adjectives and nouns don't necessarily match letter for letter. Here's the adjective *didelis* ('large') in each of the four cases listed before in both masculine and feminine forms:

SINGULAR	MASCULINE	FEMININE
Nominative	*didelis*	*didelė*
Genitive	*didelio*	*didelės*
Dative	*dideliam*	*didelei*
Accusative	*didelį*	*didelę*

PLURAL	MASCULINE	FEMININE
Nominative	*dideli*	*didelės*
Genitive	*didelių*	*didelių*
Dative	*dideliems*	*didelioms*
Accusative	*didelius*	*didelias*

Comparatives

To form a comparative adjective drop the case ending of the nominative singular form of the adjective and add *-esnė* (f) or *-esnis* (m):

It's a nice day.	*Graži diena.* (lit: nice day)
Today is a nicer day.	*Šiandiena gražesnė diena.* (lit: today it-is-nicer day)
You have a handsome/pretty face.	*Jus turite gražų veidą.* (lit: you have handsome/ pretty face)
Your face is more handsome/prettier.	*Jūsų veidas gražesnis.* (lit: your face is-more-handsome/prettier)

LITHUANIAN

Superlatives

To form a superlative adjective use the endings *-iausia* (f) or *-iausias* (m). If, after dropping the case endings, the word stem ends in *d* or *t*, replace these letters with *dž* and *č* respectively:

Today is the loveliest day. *Šiandiena gražiausia diena.*
(lit: today it-is-loveliest day)

Yours is the most handsome/ *Jūsų yra gražiausias veidas.*
prettiest face. (lit: yours is most-
handsome/prettiest face)

This is the largest house. *Šis yra didžiausias namas*
(lit: this is largest house)

PRONOUNS		
PERSONAL		
I	ahsh	*aš*
you (sg & inf)	tu	*tu*
she	yi	*ji*
he	yis	*jis*
we	mas	*mes*
you (pl & sg pol)	yoos	*jūs*
they	yaws/yeah	*jos/jie* (f/m)
POSSESSIVE		
my	*mah*-naw	*mano*
your (sg & inf)	*tah*-vaw	*tavo*
her	yaws	*jos*
his	yaw	*jo*
our	*moo*-soo	*mūsų*
your (pl & sg pol)	*yoo*-soo	*jūsų*
their	yoo	*jų*

LITHUANIAN

Verbs

The infinitive (dictionary form) of every verb in Lithuanian ends in *-ti*. Verbs belong to three different groups. Each of these groups has its own set of endings for each tense. Which endings to use for the present, past and future tenses, for example, is determined by the last letter of the verb in the third person, present tense. This ending will be either *-a*, *-o* or *-i*. To be able to use the correct tense endings (conjugations), you have to know whether the verb ends in *-a*, *-i* or *-o* in the third person, present tense.

He is going.	*Jis eina.*
	(lit: he goes/is-going)
She loves her daughter.	*Ji myli dukterį.*
	(lit: she loves her-daughter)
He is reading.	*Jis skaito.*
	(lit: he reads/is-reading)

The endings of verbs for each conjugation are consistent so, if you're given a verb stem, ie, the dictionary form of the verb minus the *-ti* ending, and the endings for a particular tense, the correct conjugation of a verb in Lithuanian is possible. It is, however, beyond the scope of this book to list all the possible conjugations.

Imperatives

There are three different forms of the imperative (command) in Lithuanian.

- When *tu* is the subject, drop *-ti* from the infinitive (dictionary form) and add k:

    skaityti 'to read' becomes *Skaityk!* 'Read!'

- When *jūs* is the subject, drop *-ti* from the infinitive and add *-kite*:

    dirbti 'to work' becomes *Dirbkite!* 'Work!'

- When *mes* is the subject, drop *-ti* and add *-kime*:

    daryti 'to do' becomes *Darykime!* 'Let's do it!'

TO BE

I am	*aš esu*
you (sg & inf) are	*tu esi*
she/he is	*ji/jis yra*
we are	*mes esame*
you (pl & sg pol) are	*jūs esate*
they are	*jos/jie yra* (f/m)

TO HAVE

I have	*aš turiu*
you (sg & inf) have	*tu turi*
she/he has	*ji/jis turi*
we have	*mes turime*
you (pl & sg pol) have	*jūs turite*
they have	*jos/jie turi* (f/m)

Questions

To turn a sentence into a question, you can place the word *ar* at the beginning of the sentence or just use rising intonation of your voice as you would in English.

You speak English.	*Jūs kalbate angliškai.*
	(lit: you speak English)
You speak English?	*Jūs kalbate angliškai?*
	(rising intonation)
	(lit: you speak English?)
Do you speak English?	*Ar jūs kalbate angliškai?*
	(lit: is-it-that you speak English?)

(Note: *Ar* at the beginning of a statement changes it into a question.)

She has change.	*Ji turi grąžos.*
	(lit: she has some-change)
Does she have change?	*Ar ji turi grąžos?*
	(lit: is-it-that she has some-change?)

LITHUANIAN

How do I get there?	*Kaip ten nuvažiuoti?*
	(lit: how there to-go?)
What's that?	*Kas tai yra?*
	(lit: what that is?)
Why have we stopped?	*Kodėl mes sustojome?*
	(lit: why we have-stopped?)

QUESTION WORDS		
how?	kaip?	*kaip?*
what?	kahs?	*kas?*
who?	kahs?	*kas?*
why?	kaw-*dehl*?	*kodėl?*
when?	kah-*dah*?	*kada?*
where?	kur?	*kur?*

Negatives

The word *ne-* is placed in front of nouns or joined to the word which it negates, ie, before a verb, adjective or adverb. When used with *ne-*, the verb *yra* ('is/are') is contracted to *nėra*.

She is a relative.	*Ji giminė.*
	(lit: she is relative)
She is not a relative.	*Ji ne giminė.*
	(lit: she is-not relative)

The ticket is legible.	*Bilietas aiškus.*
	(lit: ticket is-legible)
The ticket is not legible.	*Bilietas neaiškus.*
	(lit: ticket is-not-legible)

This has been done correctly.	*Čia gerai padaryta.*
	(lit: this well has-been-done)
This has not been done correctly.	*Čia negerai padaryta.*
	(lit: this not-well has-been-done)

Want & Need

To express desire for someone or something in Lithuanian, use
the verb *norėti* ('to want'). In the present tense its forms are:

I want you.	*Aš tavęs noriu.*
	(lit: I of-you want)
Do you want a drink?	*Ar tu nori atsigerti?*
	(lit: is-it-that you want to-have-drink?)
We want to go home.	*Mes norime važiuoti namo.*
	(lit: we want to-go to-home)

To express need in Lithuanian the keywords in a sentence are *reikia*
for the present tense, *reikėjo* for the past tense and *reikės* for the
future tense:

I need some change.	*Man reikia grąžos.*
	(lit: for-me there-is-need of-some-change)
We needed help.	*Mums reikėjo pagalbos.*
	(lit: for-us there-was-need of-some-help)
He will need a doctor.	*Jam reikės daktaro.*
	(lit: for-him there-will-be-need of-doctor)

TO WANT

I want	*aš noriu*
you (sg & inf) want	*tu nori*
she/he wants	*ji/jis nori*
we want	*mes norime*
you (pl & pol) want	*jūs norite*
they want	*jos/jie nori* (f/m)

Prepositions

above	virsh	*virš*
on	ahnt	*ant*
next to	preah	*prie*
under	paw	*po*
with	su	*su*
without	ba	*be*

Conjunctions

and	ir	*ir*
because	nas	*nes*
but	bat	*bet*
or	*ahr*-bah	*arba*
therefore	taw-*dehl*	*todėl*

Useful Words

after (time)	paw *taw*/kai	*po to*/kai
after (place)	paw	*po*
before (time)	ahnks-*chow*	*anksčiau*
before (place)	preah-sh	*prieš*
here	cha	*čia*
far	taw-*li*	*toli*
from	nu-aw	*nuo*
near	ahr-*ti*	*arti*
that/this	shi-*tah*/shi-*tahs*	*šita/šitas* (f/m)
those/these	shi-*teah*	*šitie*
there	tan	*ten*
this much	teahk	*tiek*

LITHUANIAN

GREETINGS & CIVILITIES
Greetings & Goodbyes

Hello.	*svay*-ki	*Sveiki.*
Hi.	*lah*-bahs	*Labas.*
Good morning.	*lah*-bahs *ree*-tahs	*Labas rytas.*
Good day.	*lah*-bah *deah*-nah	*Laba diena.*
Good evening.	*lah*-bahs *vah*-kah-rahs	*Labas vakaras.*
Welcome.	svay-*ki* aht-*vee*-ka	*Sveiki atvykę.*
Goodbye.	su-*deah*	*Sudie.*
All the best.	*vi*-saw *ga*-raw	*Viso gero.*
So long.	kawl *kahs*	*Kol kas.*
See you later.	i-ki pah-si-*mah*-tee-maw	*Iki pasimatymo.*
Good night.	lah-*baws* nahk-teahs	*Labos nakties.* (pol)
	lah-*bah*-nahk-tis	*Labanaktis.* (inf)
See you soon.	i-ki *gray*-taw pah-si-*mah*-tee-maw	*Iki greito pasimatymo.*

Until ...	i-ki ...	*Iki ...*
this afternoon	paw peah-*too*	*po pietų*
tomorrow	ree-*taw*-yows	*rytojaus*
next week	*sak*-ahn-chaws *sah*-*vai*-tehs	*sekančios savaitės*

Civilities

How are you?	kaip gee-*vu-aw*-yah-ta?	*Kaip gyvuojate?* (pol)
	kaip gee-*vu-aw*-yi?	*Kaip gyvuoji?* (inf)
How are things?	kaip *sak*-ah-si?	*Kaip sekasi?*
How are you going?	kaip yums *ay*-nah-si?	*Kaip jums einasi?* (ir
Well, thanks.	ah-*choo* ga-*rai*	*Ačiū gerai.*
Glad to see you.	mah-*law*-nu yus mah-*tee*-ti	*Malonu jus matyti.*
Have a pleasant trip.	lai-*min*-gaw *kal*-yaw	*Laimingo kelio.*
You're welcome.	prah-*show*	*Prašau.*

Special Occasions

When people meet during a special holiday season such as Christmas or Easter, they greet each other with a handshake or a kiss, saying *Su šventėm!*

Season's greetings!	su *shvan*-tehm!	*Su šventėm!*

I/We wish you ...!	lin-*kyu*/ lin-ki-ma ...!	*Linkiu/Linkime ...!*
happy birthday	il-*gyow*-syew *mat*-oo	*ilgiausių metų*
good health	svay-*kah*-taws	*sveikatos*
happiness	*lai*-mehs	*laimės*
success	sak-*mehs*	*sekmės*

Congratulations!	svay-ki-nu!	*Sveikinu!*
Merry Christmas!	*links*-moo kah-*leh*-doo!	*Linksmų Kalėdų!*
Happy New Year!	lai-*min*-goo now-yoo *mat*-oo!	*Laimingų Naujų Metų!*

Forms of Address

It's important to use the polite singular pronoun *jūs* when you're speaking to someone you don't know well, such as an official, a teacher, elders or the like. Children, family and friends address each other using *tu*.

Miss	pah-*nal*-eh	*Panelė*
Madam/Mrs	pawn-*ya*	*Ponia*
Sir/Mr	pawn-ahs	*Ponas*
Ladies and Gentlemen	pawn-yaws ir pawn-ai	*Ponios ir ponai*

Dear ...	brahn-*goos* ...	*Brangūs ...*
colleagues	ko-*lag*-ehs	*kolegės* (f)
	ko-*lag*-os	*kolegos* (m)
friends	drow-*gai*	*draugai*
guests	svach-*ay*	*svečiai*

Useful Words & Phrases

Yes.	tayp	*Taip.*
No.	na	*Ne.*
No way!	yawk-yu boo-du!	*Jokiu būdu!*
Please.	prah-show	*Prašau.*
Thank you.	deh-kaw-yu	*Dėkoju.* (pol)
	ah-choo	*Ačiū.* (inf)
Excuse me.	aht-si-prah-show	*Atsiprašau.*
Sorry.	aht-lays-ki-ta	*Atleiskite.*
I see. (I understand.)	su-prahn-tu	*Suprantu.*

SMALL TALK

Lithuanians are generally considered very gregarious and self-confident. Meeting and talking with Lithuanians will undoubtedly be a warm and welcoming experience for you.

Meeting People

My name is ...
 mah-naw vahr-dahs ee-rah ... *Mano vardas yra ...*
What's your name?
 kaip yoo-soo vahr-dahs? *Kaip jūsų vardas?*
I'd like to introduce you to ...
 lays-ki-ta mahn yums *Leiskite man jums*
 pri-stah-tee-ti ... *pristatyti ...*
Pleased to meet you.
 mah-law-nu *Malonu.*

Nationalities

Where are you from?	ish kur yoos a-sah-ta?	*Iš kur jūs esate?*

I'm from ...	ahsh a-*su* ish ...	*Aš esu iš ...*
Africa	*ahf*-ri-kaws	*Akrikos*
Australia	ows-*trah*-li-yaws	*Australijos*
Canada	kah-*nah*-daws	*Kanados*
China	*ki*-ni-yaws	*Kinijos*
Denmark	*dah*-ni-yaws	*Danijos*
England	*ahn*-gli-yaws	*Anglijos*
Finland	su-*aw*-mi-yaws	*Suomijos*
France	prahn-tsoo-*zi*-yaws	*Prancūzijos*
Germany	vaw-keah-*ti*-yaws	*Vokietijos*
Holland	aw-*lahn*-di-yaws	*Olandijos*
Ireland	*ai*-ri-yaws	*Airijos*
Israel	iz-rah-*ehl*-yaw	*Izraėlio*
New Zealand	now-*yaws*	*Naujos*
	ze-*lahn*-di-yaws	*Zelandijos*
Norway	nor-*vag*-i-yaws	*Norvegijos*
Scotland	*shko*-ti-yaws	*Škotijos*
Spain	is-*pah*-ni-yaws	*Ispanijos*
Sweden	*shvad*-i-yaws	*Švedijos*
the USA	yung-*ti*-new	*Jungtinių*
	ah-*ma*-ri-kaws	*Amerikos*
	vahl-*sti*-yoo	*Valstijų*

Age

How old are you?	keahk yums mat-oo?	*Kiek jums metų?*
I'm ... years old.	mahn ... mat-oo	*Man ... metų.*

For numbers, see pages 274–275.

Occupations

What (work) do you do?	kawk-*yah* yoo-soo praw-*fas*-i-yah?	*Kokia jūsų profesija?*
I'm (a/an) ...	ahsh a-*su* ...	*Aš esu* ...
artist	*man*-in-in-keh	*menininkė* (f)
	man-in-in-kahs	*menininkas* (m)
business person	ko-mer-*sahn*-teh	*komersantė* (f)
	ko-mer-*sahn*-tahs	*komersantas* (m)
doctor	gee-dee-taw-yah	*gydytoja* (f)
	gee-dee-taw-yahs	*gydytojas* (m)
engineer	in-*zhi*-near-yus	*inžinierius*
farmer	*oo*-ki-nin-keh	*ūkininkė* (f)
	oo-ki-nin-kahs	*ūkininkas* (m)
journalist	zhur-nah-*lis*-teh	*žurnalistė* (f)
	zhur-nah-*lis*-tahs	*žurnalistas* (m)
lawyer	yoo-*ris*-the	*juristė* (f)/
	yoo-*ris*-tahs/	*juristas* (m)/
	ahd-*vaw*-kah-teh	*advokatė* (f)
	ahd-*vaw*-kah-tahs	*advokatas* (m)
mechanic	ma-*hah*-ni-kahs	*mechanikas*
musician	mu-zi-*kahn*-tahs	*muzikantas*
nurse	*slow*-geh	*slaugė*
office worker	tahr-*now*-taw-yah	*tarnautoja* (f)
	tahr-*now*-taw-yahs	*tarnautojas* (m)
scientist	gahm-*taws* *mawks*-li-nin-keh	*gamtos mokslininkė* (f)
	gahm-*taws* *mawks*-li-nin-kahs	*gamtos mokslininkas* (m)
student	stu-*dan*-teh	*studentė* (f)
	stu-*dan*-tahs	*studentas* (m)
teacher	*maw*-kee-taw-yah	*mokytoja* (f)
	maw-kee-taw-yahs	*mokytojas* (m)
unemployed	bad-*ahr*-beh	*bedarbė* (f)
	bad-*ahr*-bis	*bedarbis* (m)
waiter	pah-dah-*veh*-yah	*padavėja* (f)
	pah-dah-*veh*-yahs	*padavėjas* (m)
writer	rah-*shee*-taw-yah	*rašytoja* (f)
	rah-*shee*-taw-yahs	*rašytojas* (m)

Religion

What's your religion?
> **ku-*ray* yoos ra-*li*-gi-yay** *Kuriai jūs religijai*
> **pri-*klow*-saw-ta?** *priklausote?*

I'm not religious.
> **ahsh na-*su* ra-li-*gin*-g(ah/ahs)** *Aš nesu religing(a/as).* (f/m)

I'm ...	ahsh a-*su* ...	*Aš esu ...*
Buddhist	bu-*dis*-teh	*budistė* (f)
	bu-*dis*-tahs	*budistas* (m)
Catholic	kah-tah-*li*-keh	*katalikė* (f)
	kah-tah-*li*-kahs	*katalikas* (m)
Christian	kriksh-*chaw*-neh	*krikščionė* (f)
	kriksh-*chaw*-nis	*krikščionis* (m)
Hindu	*in*-deh	*indė* (f)
	in-dahs	*indas* (m)
Jewish	zhee-*deh*	*žydė* (f)
	zhee-*dahs*	*žydas* (m)
Lutheran	lyew-ta-*raw*-neh	*liuteronė* (f)
	lyew-ta-*raw*-nahs	*liuteronas* (m)
Muslim	mu-sul-*maw*-neh	*musulmonė* (f)
	mu-sul-*maw*-nahs	*musulmonas* (m)
Russian	stah-*chah*-ti-keh	*stačiatikė* (f)
Orthodox	stah-*chah*-ti-kis	*stačiatikis* (m)

LITHUANIAN

Family

Are you married?	ahr yoos ish-tak-*eh*-yu-si?	*Ar jūs ištekėjusi?* (to a female)
	ahr yoos *vad*-as?	*Ar jūs vedęs?* (to a male)
I'm ...	ahsh a-*su* ...	*Aš esu ...*
divorced	ish-si-*skee*-ru-si	*išsiskyrusi* (f)
	ish-si-*skee*-ras	*išsiskyręs* (m)
gay	laz-*beah*-teh	*lezbietė* (f)
	ho-mo-sak-swah-*lis*-tahs	*homosek-sualistas* (m)
married	ish-tak-*eh*-yu-si	*ištekėjus* (f)
	vad-as	*vedęs* (m)
single	na-ish-tak-*eh*-yu-si	*neištekėjusi* (f)
	na-*vad*-as	*nevedęs* (m)
widowed	nahsh-*leh*	*našlė* (f)
	nahsh-*lees*	*našlys* (m)

How many children do you have?
    keahk yoos tu-ri-ta vai-*koo*?   *Kiek jūs turite vaikų?*
I don't have any children.
    ahsh na-tur-*yu* vai-*koo*   *Aš neturiu vaikų.*
I have a daughter/son.
    ahsh tur-*yu* duk-ta-ri/*soo*-nu   *Aš turiu dukterį/sūnų.*
How many sisters/
brothers do you have?
    keahk yoos *tu*-ri-ta sa-sa-*roo*/*brawl*-yoo?   *Kiek jūs turite seserų/brolių?*
Is your wife/husband here?
    ahr *yoo*-soo zhmaw-*nah*/*vee*-rahs cha?   *Ar jūsų žmona/vyras čia?*
Do you have a girlfriend/boyfriend?
    ahr yoos *tu*-ri-ta *drow*-ga/*drow*-gah?   *Ar jūs turite draugę/draugą?*

baby	*koo*-di-kis	*kūdikis*
brother	*braw*-lis	*brolis*
child/children	*vai*-kahs/vai-*kai*	*vaikas/vaikai*
daughter	duk-*teh*	*duktė*
family	shay-*mah*	*šeima*
father	*teh*-vahs	*tėvas*
grandfather	san-*al*-is	*senelis*
grandmother	san-*al*-eh	*senelė*
mother	*maw*-ti-nah	*motina*
sister	sas-*u*-*aw*	*sesuo*
son	soo-*nus*	*sūnus*

Kids' Talk

How old are you?
keahk tow *ma*-too? — *Kiek tau metų?*

When's your birthday?
kah-*dah* tah-vaw
gim-*tah*-deah-nis? — *Kada tavo gimtadienis?*

What do you do after school?
kah tu vay-*ki* paw
pah-maw-koo? — *Ką tu veiki po pamokų?*

Do you have a pet at home?
ahr tu-*ri* nah-*mi*-ni
gee-vu-*lyu*-kah? — *Ar turi naminį gyvuliuką?*

I have a ...	ahsh tu-*ryu* ...	*Aš turiu ...*
bird	powksh-*ta*-li	*paukštelį*
budgerigar	ows-*trah*-lish-kah	*australišką*
	pah-poo-*geh*-la	*papūgėlę*
canary	kah-nah-*reh*-la	*kanarėlę*
cat	kah-*tee*-ta	*katytę*
duck	*ahn*-ti	*antį*
dog	*shu*-ni	*šunį*
fish	zhu-*vee*-ta	*žuvytę*
frog	vahr-*lee*-ta	*varlytę*
guinea pig	*yoo*-raws kyow-*lee*-ta	*jūros kiaulytę*
hamster	zhur-*keh*-nah	*žiurkėną*
horse	*ahrk*-li	*arklį*
tortoise	vehzh-*lyu*-kah	*vėžliuką*

LITHUANIAN

Expressing Feelings

I'm ...	ahsh ...	Aš ...
in a hurry	sku-*bu*	*skubu*
right	tay-*si*/tay-*sus*	*teis/teisus* (f/m)
wrong	klees-*tu*	*klystu*
I'm sorry. (condolence)	uzh-*u*-*aw*-yow-tah	*Užuojauta.*

I'm ...	mahn ...	Man ...
afraid	bai-*su*	*baisu*
angry	*pik*-tah	*pikta*
cold	*shahl*-tah	*šalta*
happy	*links*-mah	*linksma*
hot	*kahr-sh*-tah	*karšta*
sad	*lyood*-nah	*liūdna*
sleepy	im-ah *meah*-gahs	*ima miegas*
well	ga-*rai*	*gerai*

I'm ...	ahsh a-*su* ...	Aš esu ...
full of energy	*pil*-nahs an-*ar*-gi-yaws	*pilnas energijos*
hungry	ish-*ahl*-kusi	*išalkusi* (f)
	ish-*ahl*-kas	*išalkęs* (m)
thirsty	ish-*trawsh*-kusi	*ištroškusi* (f)
	ish-*trawsh*-kas	*ištroškęs* (m)
tired	pah-*vahr*-gusi	*pavargusi* (f)
	pah-*vahr*-gas	*pavargęs* (m)
worried	su-si-*roo*-pi-nusi	*susirūpinusi* (f)
	su-si-*roo*-pi-nas	*susirūpinęs* (m)

Expressing Opinions

I like ...	mahn pah-*tin*-kah ...	*Man patinka ...*
I don't like ...	mahn na-pah-*tin*-kah ...	*Man nepa tinka ...*
What a pity!	kaip *gai*-lah	*Kaip gaila!*
I agree.	ahsh su-*tin*-*ku*	*Aš sutinku.*
I disagree.	ahsh na-su-*tin*-*ku*	*Aš nesutinku.*
We're very upset.	mas lah-*bai* su-*yow*-din-ti	*Mes labai sujaudinti.*
Good!	ga-*rai*!	*Gerai!*

BODY LANGUAGE

When you go visiting it's proper to take gifts such as flowers for her and perhaps a bottle of drink for him. Don't shake hands across the threshold – it brings bad luck!

If you're due to accept some traditional Lithuanian home hospitality, be prepared to loosen your belt several notches and skip breakfast that morning. There'll be a prolonged period of feasting, punctuated by many *Išgeriam!* (Let's drink!) and *Iki dugno!* (Bottoms up!). Be wary and discreetly ration your intake of food and drink from the start to avoid offending your hosts later, when you find you're too full to accept any more. Starter dishes can be deceptively generous, leading unsuspecting guests to think they're the main meal. To decline further helpings may offend and be taken to mean that you don't like the food or the hospitality.

LITHUANIAN

BREAKING THE LANGUAGE BARRIER

Do you speak English?
ahr *kahl*-bah-ta *ahn*-glish-kai?   *Ar kalbate angliškai?*

Do you understand me?
ahr mah-*na* su-*prahn*-tah-ta?   *Ar mane suprantate?*

I understand you.
ahsh *yus* su-prahn-*tu*   *Aš jus suprantu.*

I don't understand you.
ahsh *yoo*-soo na-su-prahn-*tu*   *Aš jūsų nesuprantu.*

What does this word mean?
kah *raysh*-kyah shis *zhaw*-dis?   *Ką reiškia šis žodis?*

Please translate.
***prah*-shom ish-*vars*-ti**   *Prašom išversti.*

We need an interpreter.
mums *ray*-kyah var-*teh*-yaw   *Mums reikia vertėjo.*

What do you mean?
kah yoos tu-ri-ta aw-ma-*nee*-ja?   *Ką jūs turite omenyje?*

What's Lithuanian for ...?
kaip leah-*tu*-vish-kai ...?   *Kaip lietuviškai ...?*

CLAMBERING FOR AMBER

Amber, found throughout the Baltic region, is one of Lithuania's most distinctive souvenirs. Formed 30-50 million years ago (well after the dinosaurs died out, despite what the makers of *Jurassic Park* would have you believe), amber is fossilised resin of coniferous trees. It ranges in colour from opaque to transparent, from ivory through to black. Yellows and reddish browns are the most common colours, although amber can also be green, blue or cherry.

It has been used as a gemstone for hundreds of thousands of years. Many people believe amber has healing properties. It is said to cure sore throats, asthma and bronchitis.

LITHUANIAN

I speak ...	ahsh kahl-*bu* ...	*Aš kalbu* ...
English	*ahn*-glish-kai	*angliškai*
French	**prahn**-*tsoo*-zish-kai	*prancūziškai*
German	*vaw*-kish-kai	*vokiškai*
Polish	*lan*-kish-kai	*lenkiškai*
Russian	*rus*-ish-kai	*rusiškai*

Sports & Interests

Do you like ...?	ahr yoos *mehgs*-tah-ta ...?	*Ar jūs mėgs tate* ...?
art	*man*-ah	*meną*
ballet	bah-*lat*-ah	*baletą*
bird watching	*powksh*-chus	*paukščius*
	stab-*eh*-ti	*stebėti*
the cinema	*ki*-nah	*kiną*
classical music	*klah*-sish-kah	*klasišką*
	mu-zi-kah	*muziką*
exhibitions	*pah*-raw-dahs	*parodas*
fishing	mash-ka-*ryaw*-ti	*meškerioti*
folk dancing	*tow*-ti-nyus	*tautinius*
	shaw-kyus	*šokius*
folk music	*lyow*-deahs	*liaudies*
	mu-zi-kah	*muziką*
gliding	*sklahn*-dee-ti	*sklandyti*
horse riding	yaw-di-*neh*-ti	*jodinėti*
ice fishing	*la*-daw zhuk-la	*ledo žuklę*
opera	*o*-pa-rah	*operą*
reading	skai-*tee*-ti	*skaityti*
rollerblading	rah-*tu*-ki-nehm	*ratukinėm*
	pah-*choo*-zhawm	*pačiūžom*
	vah-zhi-*neh*-tis	*važinėtis*
sailboarding	*bur*-lan-ta	*burlente*
	plowk-ti	*plaukti*
the theatre	teh-*aht*-rah	*teatrą*
travelling	kal-*yow*-ti	*keliauti*

I want to go ...	ahsh *naw*-ryu ...	*Aš noriu ...*
bobsleighing	pah-si-vah-zhi-*neh*-ti	*pasivažinėti*
	bob-*sleh*-yu-mi	*bobslėjumi*
canoeing	pah-*plowk*-yaw-ti	*paplaukioti*
	bai-*dah*-ra	*baidare*
cycling	pah-si-vah-zhi-*neh*-ti	*pasivažinėti*
	dvi-rah-chu	*dviračiu*
hiking	ish-kee-*low*-ti	*iškylauti*
jogging	pah-behg-*yaw*-ti	*pabėgioti*
skating	pah-chu-aw-zhi-*neh*-ti	*pačiuožinėti*
skiing	pah-sli-di-*neh*-ti	*paslidinėti*
swimming	pah-si-*mow*-dee-ti	*pasimaudyti*
tobogganing	pah-si-vah-zhi-*neh*-ti	*pasivažinėti*
	raw-*gu*-teh-mis	*rogutėmis*
yachting	pah-bur-*yaw*- ti	*paburiuoti*

I play ...	ahsh ...	*Aš ...*
basketball	zhai-*ju*	*žaidžiu*
	krap-*shi*-ni	*krepšinį*
cards	lawsh-*yu* kor-	*lošiu kor*
	taw-mis	*tomis*
chess	lawsh-*yu*	*lošiu*
	shah-*mah*-tais	*šachmatais*
guitar	*skahm*-bi-nu	*skambinu*
	gi-*tah*-rah	*gitara*
soccer	zhai-*ju* sok-a-ri	*žaidžiu sokerį*
tennis	lawsh-*yu* tan-i-sah	*lošiu tenisą*
winter sports	zhai-*ju* zheah-*maws*	*žaidžiu žiemos*
	spor-tus	*sportus*

LITHUANIAN

USEFUL PHRASES

Sure.	tik-*rai*	*Tikrai.*
Just a minute.	pah-*low*-ki-ta mi-*nu*-ta	*Palaukite minute.*
It's (not) important.	tai (na)-svahr-*bu*	*Tai (ne)svarbu.*
I can't do it.	ahsh *shi*-taw na-gah-*lyu* pah-dah-*ree*-ti	*Aš šito negaliu padaryti.*
Wait!	pah-*low*-ki-ta!	*Palaukite!*
Good luck!	lai-*min*-gai!	*Laimingai!*
That's great!	pwi-*ku*!	*Puiku!*
How awful!	*syow*-bahs	*Siaubas!*

GETTING AROUND

Where's the ...?	kur ee-*rah* ...?	*Kur yra ...?*
airport	aw-raw u-*aws*-tahs	*oro uostas*
booking office	kah-*sah*	*kasa*
bus stop	ow-*taw*-bu-saw staw-*ta*-leh	*autobuso stotelė*
train station	gal-azh-*in*-kal-yaw staw-*tis*	*geležinkelio stotis*
ferry terminal	*kal*-taw staw-*tis*	*kelto stotis*

Is it far from here?
ahr tai taw-*li*?   *Ar tai toli?*

Can we walk there?
ahr *gah*-li-mah nu-ay-ti pehs-*chom*?   *Ar galima nueiti pėsčiom?*

Can you show me (on the map)?
gah-*leh*-tu-met mahn pah-*raw*-dee-ti (zham-*eh*-lah-pee-ya)?   *Galėtumėt man parodyti (žemėlapyje)?*

Please write down the address.

prah-shom pah-rah-*shee*-ti *ahd*-ras-ah	*Prašom parašyti adresą.*

Are there other means
of getting there?

ahr *gah*-li-mah ki-*taip* tan nu-*veek*-ti?	*Ar galima kitaip ten nuvykti?*

Directions

Turn left at the ...	*su*-ki-ta i *kai*-ra preah ...	*Sukite į kairę prie ...*
Turn right at the ...	*su*-ki-ta i *dash*-na preah ...	*Sukite į dešinę prie ...*
traffic lights	shveah-so-*fo*-ro	*šviesoforo*
next	*sak*-ahn-chaw	*sekančio*
corner	*kahm*-paw	*kampo*

back	aht-*gahl*	*atgal*
behind	uzh	*už*
far	taw-*li*	*toli*
in front of	*preah*-shais	*priešais*
straight ahead	teah-say	*tiesiai*
to the left	i *kai*-ra	*į kairę*
to the right	i *dash*-na	*į dešinę*

STREET CRED

GATVĖ	STREET
AIKŠTĖ	SQUARE
PROSPEKTAS/ BULVARAS	AVENUE/ BOULEVARD
KELIAS	ROAD
PLENTAS	HIGHWAY
TILTAS	BRIDGE

Buying Tickets

Where can I buy tickets?
kur gah-*lyu* nu-si-*pirk*-ti   *Kur galiu nusipirkti*
bil-eah-tus?   *bilietus?*

I want to travel to ...
ahsh *naw*-ryu   *Aš noriu*
nu-vah-*zhu-aw*-ti i ...   *nuvažiuoti į ...*

Do I need to book?
ahr mahn *ray*-kya   *Ar man reikia*
uzh-si-sah-*kee*-ti?   *užsisakyti?*

Is it sold out?
ahr ee-*rah* ish-pahr-*du-aw*-tah?   *Ar yra išparduota?*

I'd like to book a seat to ...
ahsh *naw*-ryu uzh-sah-*kee*-ti   *Aš noriu užsakyti vietą*
veah-tah kal-*yaw*-nay i ...   *kelionei į ...*

I'd like (a) ...	ahsh naw-*reh*-chow ...	*Aš norėčiau ...*
one-way ticket	*bil*-eah-tah i *veah*-nah gah-lah	*bilietą į vieną galą*
return ticket	*bil*-eah-tah i ah-*bu* gah-*lus*	*bilietą į abu galus*
two tickets	*du bil*-eah-tus	*du bilietus*
tickets for all of us	*bil*-eah-tus mums vis-*eahms*	*bilietus mums visiems*
child/pensioner fare	*bil*-eah-tah *vai*-kwi/ *pen*-si-nin-kwi	*bilietą vaikui/ pensininkui*
1st class ticket	pir-*maws klah*-sehs *bil*-eah-tah	*pirmos klasės bilietą*
2nd class ticket	ahn-*traws klah*-sehs *bil*-eah-tah	*antros klasės bilietą*

LITHUANIAN

Air

Is there a flight to ...?
 ahr ee-*rah* ray-sahs i ...? *Ar yra reisas į ...?*
When's the next flight to ...?
 kah-*dah* sak-*ahn*-tis *ray*-sahs i ...? *Kada sekantis reisas į ...?*
What's the flight number?
 kawks ee-*rah* ray-saw *Koks yra reiso*
 ***nu*-ma-ris?** *numeris?*
When will the plane arrive at ...?
 kah-*dah* lehk-*tu*-vahs *Kada lėktuvas*
 aht-*skris* i ...? *atskris į ...?*

airport	**aw-raw *u-aws*-tahs**	*oro uostas*
airport tax	**aw-raw *u-aws*-taw**	*aoro uosto*
	***maw*-kas-tis**	*mokestis*
boarding pass	**tah-*lon*-ahs**	*talonas*
customs	***mwi*-ti-neh**	*muitinė*
customs	***mwi*-ti-nehs**	*muitinės*
declaration	**dak-lah-*rah*-tsi-yah**	*deklaracija*

Bus

Where's the ... stop?	**kur ee-*rah* ...**	*Kur yra ...*
	staw-*ta*-leh?	*stotelė?*
bus	**ow-*to*-bu-saw**	*autobuso*
trolleybus	**tro-*lay*-bu-saw**	*troleibuso*

Which bus goes to ...?
 kaw-*kyu* ow-*to*-bu-su *gah*-li-mah *Kokiu autobusu galima*
 nu-vah-*zhu-aw*-ti i-ki ...? *nuvažiuoti iki ...?*
Does this trolleybus go to ...?
 ahr *shi*-tahs tro-*lay*-bu-sahs *Ar šitas troleibusas*
 vah-*zhu-aw*-yah i ...? *važiuoja į ...?*
Could you let me know
when we get to ...?
 ahr gah-*leh*-tu-met *par*-speh-ti *Ar galėtumėt perspėti,*
 kai pri-vah-*zhu-aw*-sim ...? *kai privažiuosiм ...?*

I want to get off.
    ahsh *naw*-ryu ish-*lip*-ti   *Aš noriu išlipti.*

This is your stop.
    dah-*bahr* yums   *Dabar jums*
    rayk-yah ish-*lip*-ti   *reikia išlipti.*

Train

Is this the right platform for ...?
    ahr ish *shi*-taws plaht-*for*-maws   *Ar iš šitos platformos*
    ish-*veeks*-tah trow-ki-*nees* i ...?   *išvyksta traukinys į ...?*

The train leaves from platform ...
    trow-ki-*nees* ish-vah-*zhu-aw*-yah   *Traukinys išvažiuoja*
    ish ... plaht-*for*-maws   *iš ... platformos.*

Passengers must ...	ka-*lay*-vay tu-ri ...	*Keleiviai turi ...*
change trains	*par*-sehs-ti	*persėsti*
go to platform	*ay*-ti į ... pa-*ro*-nah/	*eiti į ... peroną/*
number ...	plaht-*for*-mah	*platformą*

Boat

To cross from the mainland at Klaipėda to the strip of sand dunes called Neringa (the Curonian Spit) you need to take a short ferry ride. In the summer months you can take a ferry along the Nemunas River between Kaunas and Nida, or a boat tour of the Curonian Bay as well as a boat trip from Nida to the mouth of the Nemunas. Overseas ferry services operate between Klaipėda and Germany, Sweden and Denmark.

When does the ...	kah-*dah*	*Kada išplaukia ...*
sail for ...?	ish-plowk-yah ... į ...?	*į ...?*
When does the ...	kah-*dah*	*Kada atplaukia ...?*
arrive?	aht-plowk-yah ...?	
boat	*lai*-vahs	*laivas*
ferry	*kal*-tahs	*keltas*
hydrofoil	rah-*kat*-ah	*raketa*

boat/ferry landing place	*preah*-plow-kah	*prieplauka*
ferry terminal	*kal*-taw *preah*-plow-kah	*kelto prieplauka*
harbour	*u-aws*-tahs	*uostas*

Where does the boat leave from?
    ish kur *lai*-vahs *ish*-plow-kyah?   *Iš kur laivas išplaukia?*
What time does the boat arrive?
    kah-*dah lai*-vahs *aht*-plow-kyah?   *Kada laivas atplaukia?*
Which boat goes to ...?
    ku-*ris lai*-vahs *plow*-kyah i ...?   *Kuris laivas plaukia į ...?*
Which landing is next?
    kahs bus *sak*-ahn-ti   *Kas bus sekanti*
    preah-plow-kah?   *prieplauka?*
Is this the ferry for ...?
    ahr *shis kal*-tahs *plow*-kyah i ...?   *Ar šis keltas plaukia į ...?*

Taxi

Can you take me to ...?
    ahr gah-*leh*-tu-met mah-na   *Ar galėtumėt mane*
    nu-*vash*-ti i ...?   *nuvežti į ...?*
How much does it cost to go to ...?
    keahk kai-*nu-aw*-yah nu-vah-   *Kiek kainuoja nuvažiuoti*
    zhu-*aw*-ti i ...?   *į ...?*
Here is fine, thank you.
    deh-kwi ish-*lays*-ki-ta cha   *Dėkui, išleiskite čia.*
The next corner, please.
    prah-*show* ish-*lays*-ki-ta preah   *Prašau išleiskite prie*
    sak-ahn-chaw *kahm*-paw   *sekančio kampo.*
Please slow down.
    prah-*show* su-*leh*-tin-ki-ta   *Prašau sulėtinkite*
    gray-ti   *greitį.*
Please wait here.
    prah-*show* cha pah-*lowk*-ti   *Prašau čia palaukti.*

LITHUANIAN

Car

Where can I hire a car
(for a day/week)?

> **kur ahsh gah-*leh*-chow
> pah-si-sahm-*dee*-ti
> ow-to-*mob*-i-li
> (*deah*-nai/sah-*vai*-tay)?**

*Kur aš galėčiau
pasisamdyti
automobilį
(dienai/savaitei)?*

Where's the next petrol station?

> **kur ee-*rah* sak-ahn-ti
> dag-ah-*li*-neh?**

*Kur yra sekanti
degalinė?*

Please fill the tank.

> **prah-*show* pri-*pil*-dee-ki-ta
> ban-*zi*-naw *bah*-kah**

*Prašau pripildykite
benzino baką.*

Please check the oil and water.

> **prah-*show* pah-*tik*-rin-ki-ta
> *tap*-ah-lah ir *vahn*-dan-i**

*Prašau patikrinkite tepalą
ir vandenį.*

Does this road lead to ...?

> **ahr shis *kal*-yahs *vad*-ah i ...?**

Ar šis kelias veda į ...?

I need a mechanic.

> **mahn *rayk*-yah ma-*hah*-ni-kaw**

Man reikia mechaniko.

We've had an accident.

> **mums ish-*tik*-aw ah-*vah*-ri-yah**

Mums ištiko avarija.

I have a flat tyre.

> **mahn prah-*doo*-reh
> *pah*-dahn-gah**

*Man pradūrė
padangą.*

Could you please tow my car?

> **ahr na-gah-*leh*-tu-met
> pah-*vilk*-ti mah-naw
> *mah*-shi-nah?**

*Ar negalėtumėt
pavilkti mano
mašiną?*

The battery is flat.

> **ah-ku-mu-*lah*-taw-rus ee-*rah*
> ish-si-*ayk*-*vaw*-yas**

*Akumuliatorius yra
išsieikvojęs.*

The radiator is leaking.

> **rah-di-*yah*-taw-rus
> prah-*kew*-ras**

*Radiatorius
prakiuręs.*

It's overheating.
    vah-*rik*-lis *par*-kais-tah   *Variklis perkaista.*

It's not working.
    na-vayk-yah   *Neveikia.*

Useful Words

air (for tyres)	aw-raw *pah*-dahn-goms	*oro padangoms*
battery	ah-ku-mu-*lah*-taw-rus	*akumuliatorius*
brakes	*stahb*-jay	*stabdžiai*
clutch	*sahn*-kah-bah	*sankaba*
driving licence	vai-*ru-aw*-taw-yaw	*vairuotojo*
	pah-zhee-*meh*-yi-mahs	*pažymėjimas*
engine	vah-*rik*-lis	*variklis*
lights	shveah-saws	*šviesos*
oil	*tap*-ah-lahs	*tepalas*
puncture	*nu*-lays-tah	*nuleista*
	pah-dahn-gah	*padanga*
radiator	rah-di-*yah*-taw-rus	*radiatorius*
repair shop	*ram*-on-taw *dirb*-tu-vehs	*remonto dirbtuvės*
road map	ow-taw-kal-*yoo*	*autokelių*
	aht-lah-sahs	*atlasas*
spare parts	aht-sahr-*gin*-ehs	*atsarginės*
	dah-lees	*dalys*
spark plug	zhvah-keh	*žvakė*
speed limit	gray-chaw	*greičio*
	ahp-rib-*aw*-yi-mahs	*apribojimas*
tyre	*pah*-dahn-gah	*padanga*
windscreen	preah-ki-nis *stik*-lahs	*priekinis stiklas*

Useful Phrases

The train is delayed/cancelled.
trow-ki-*nees* veh-*lu*-aw-yah/
na-ba-vah-*zhu*-aws
*Traukinys vėluoja/
nebevažiuos.*

How long will it be delayed?
keahk il-*gai* veh-*lu*-aw-yah?
Kiek ilgai vėluoja?

There's a delay of ... hours.
veh-*lu*-aw-yah ... *vah*-lan-doo
Vėluoja ... valandų.

How long does the trip take?
keahk il-*gai* *trun*-kah
kal-*yaw*-neh?
*Kiek ilgai trunka
kelionė?*

Is it a direct route?
ahr kal-*yaw*-neh ba
par-seh-di-moo?
*Ar kelionė be
persėdimų?*

I want to hire a bicycle.
ahsh *naw*-ryu
pah-si-sahm-*dee*-ti *dvi*-rah-ti
*Aš noriu
pasisamdyti dviratį.*

SIGNS

ATIDARA	OPEN
DĖMESIO!	CAREFUL!
DRAUDŽIAMA STOTI	NO STANDING/ PARKING
DRAUDŽIAMA	ENTRY PROHIBITED
DRAUDŽIAMA	NO ENTRY
IĖJIMAS	ENTRANCE
INFORMACIJA	INFORMATION
IŠĖJIMAS	EXIT
NERŪKOMA	NO SMOKING
PATOGUMAI	PUBLIC TOILET
PERĖJA	PEDESTRIAN CROSSING
REZERVUOTAS	RESERVED
STOK!	STOP!
TAISOMAS KELIAS	ROADWORKS
UŽDARA	CLOSED
VAKANSIJA	VACANT

LITHUANIAN

ACCOMMODATION

Over the last few years a number of new quality hotels have sprung up in the major cities of Lithuania, particularly the capital, Vilnius, offering a welcome alternative to the old Soviet-style accommodation.

Tourist, holiday and health resorts have some exceptional facilities, but you'll have to book well in advance as they're very popular with the locals.

Finding Accommodation

I'm looking for (a) ...	ahsh *yeash*-kow ...	Aš ieškau ...
hotel	*veash*-bu-chaw	viešbučio
camp site	staw-veek-*lah*-veah-tehs	stovyklavietės
somewhere to stay	kur nors ahp-si-*staw*-ti	kur nors apsistoti

Could you write down
the address please?
**ahr gah-*leh*-tu-met mahn
uzh-rah-*shee*-ti ah-dras-ah?** *Ar galėtumėt man
užrašyti adresą?*

At the Hotel

Do you have any rooms available?
**ahr *tu*-ri-ta lais-*voo*
kahm-bahr-yew?** *Ar turite laisvų
kambarių?*

I'd like a ...	ahsh *nawr*-yu ...	*Aš noriu ...*
single room	veahn-*veah*-chaw	*vienviečio*
	kahm-bahr-yaw	*kambario*
double room	dvi-*veah*-chaw	*dviviečio*
	kahm-bahr-yaw	*kambario*
room with a	*kahm*-bahr-yaw su	*kambario su*
bathroom	prow-*seek*-lah	*prausykla*
room with a	*kahm*-bahr-yaw su	*kambario su*
television	te-le-*viz*-aw-ryum	*televizorium*
room with a	*kahm*-bahr-yaw su	*kambario su*
window	*lahn*-gu	*langu*

Is there (a) ...?	ahr ee-*rah* ...?	*Ar yra ...?*
hot water	*kahrsh*-tahs	*karštas vanduo*
	vahn-*du*-aw	
bathroom	vawn-*yah*	*vonia*
sauna	pir-*tis*	*pirtis*
shower	*du*-shahs	*dušas*
telephone	te-le-*fo*-nahs	*telefonas*
television	te-le-*viz*-aw-ryus	*televizorius*

How much is it per
day (24 hrs)?
   keahk kai-*nu-ah*-yah
   pah-*rai*?
   Kiek kainuoja parai?

HIP HIP PARAI!

In Lithuania, prices at
hotels are often marked
parai, for a 24-hour day.

How much is it per night,
per person?
   keahk kai-*nu-aw*-yah
   ahp-si-*staw*-ti *nahk*-chay
   ahs-man-wi?

   Kiek kainuoja
   apsistoti nakčiai
   asmeniui?

Does it include breakfast?
   ahr kai-*nah* i-*skai*-taw
   pus-ree-chus?

   Ar karina įskaito
   pusryčius?

Can I see the room?
   ahr gah-*leh*-chow *kahm*-bah-ri
   pah-mah-*tee*-ti?

   Ar galėčiau kambarį
   pamatyti?

LITHUANIAN

Are there any cheaper rooms?
ahr ee-*rah* pi-gas-*new*
kahm-bahr-yew?
Ar yra pigesnių
kambarių?

THEY MAY SAY ...
aht-si-prah-*show*
vi-*si* moo-soo
kahm-bah-*ray*
uzh-im-*ti*
Sorry, we're full.

Is there hot water all day?
ahr ee-*rah* kahrsh-taw
vahn-*dans* vi-sah *deah*-nah?
Ar yra karšto vandens visą dieną?

It's fine, I'll take it.
bus *tin*-kah-mah pah-*ims*-yu   *Bus tinkama, paimsiu.*
I'm not sure how long I'm staying.
ahsh na-su *tik*-rahs   *Aš nesu tikras*
keahk il-*gai* ahsh boos-yu   *kiek ilgai aš būsiu*
ahp-si-*staw*-(yu-si/-yas)   *apsistoj (usilęs).* (f/m)

I'm going   ahsh ahp-si-*staws*-yu ...   *Aš apsistosiu ...*
to stay for ...
  one day   veah-nah *deah*-nah   *vieną dieną*
  two days   dvi deah-*nahs*   *dvi dienas*
  one week   veah-nah sah-*vai*-ta   *vieną savaitę*

I'm leaving ...   ahsh ish-veeks-*tu* ...   *Aš išvykstu ...*
  this afternoon   shan-*deahn* paw   *šiandien po*
                    peah-too   *pietų*
  tonight   shah-nahkt   *šiąnakt*
  tomorrow   ree-*toy* ree-tah   *rytoj rytą*
    morning

We're leaving now.
mas dah-*bahr*   *Mes dabar*
ish-si-*krows*-taw-ma   *išsikraustome.*
I'd like to pay the bill.
ahsh *nawr*-yu su-si-maw-*keh*-ti   *Aš noriu susimokėti*
sah-skai-tah   *sąskaitą.*

Requests & Complaints

Please wake me up at ...
  prah-shom mah-na pah-*zhah*-din-ti ...
  Prašom mane pažadinti ...

The room needs to be cleaned.
  ray-*keh*-tu *kahm*-bah-ri ish-vah-*lee*-ti
  Reikėtų kambarį išvalyti.

Please change the sheets.
  prah-shom pah-*kays*-ti pah-*klaw*-das
  Prašom pakeisti paklodes.

I can't open the window.
  ahsh na-gahl-*yu* ah-ti-dah-*ree*-ti *lahn*-gaw
  Aš negaliu atidaryti lango.

I've locked myself out of my room.
  ahsh a-su ne-*tee*-chah uzh-si-*tran*-kas du-*ris*
  Aš esu netyčia užsitrenkęs duris.

The toilet won't flush.
  ish-veah-tehs vahn-*du*-aw na-nu-si-*lay*-jah
  Išvietės vanduo nenusileidžia.

I don't like this room.
  mahn shi-tahs *kahm*-bah-rees na-pah-*tin*-kah
  Man šitas kambarys nepatinka.

It's too ... here.   cha par-na-*leeg* ...   *Čia pernelyg ...*
  cold   *shahl*-tah   *šalta*
  dark   tahm-*su*   *tamsu*
  expensive   brahn-*gu*   *brangu*
  hot   *kahrsh*-tah   *karšta*
  noisy   truksh-*min*-gah   *triukšminga*

Laundry

Where can I have my things ...?	kur *gah*-li-mah ah-ti-*du*-aw-ti *daik*-tus ...?	*Kur galima atiduoti daiktus ...?*
dry-cleaned	ish-vah-*lee*-ti	*išvalyti*
pressed	ish-*lee*-gin-ti	*išlyginti*
washed	ish-*skahlp*-ti	*išskalbti*

I need my things ...	mah-naw daik-*tai* mahn bus ray-kah-*lin*-gi ...	*Mano daiktai man bus reikalingi ...*
today	shan-*deahn*	*šiandien*
tomorrow	ree-*toy*	*rytoj*
the day after tomorrow	paw-*reet*	*poryt*

Please remove this stain.	*prah*-shom ish-*im*-ti shah deh-ma	*Prašom išimti šią dėmę.*
This isn't mine.	tai ne *mah*-naw daik-tahs	*Tai ne mano daiktas.*

Useful Words

air-conditioning	kon-dits-yo-*neahr*-yus	*kondicionierius*
balcony	bahl-*kon*-ahs	*balkonas*
bathroom	prow-*seek*-lah	*prausykla*
bed	*law*-vah	*lova*
bill	*sah*-skai-tah	*sąskaita*
blanket	vil-*naw*-neh ahnt-klaw-deh	*vilnonė antklodė*
chair	keh-*deh*	*kėdė*
dark	tahm-*su*	*tamsu*
dirty	na-shvah-*ru*	*nešvaru*
electricity	al-ak-trah	*elektra*
fan	veh-sin-*tu*-vahs	*vėsintuvas*
heater	*shil*-dee-mahs	*šildymas*

key	*rahk*-tahs	*raktas*
lift (elevator)	*lif*-tahs	*liftas*
light bulb	*lam*-pah	*lempa*
lock (n)	*uzh*-rahk-tahs	*užraktas*
mattress	maht-*raht*-sahs	*matracas*
pillow	*pah*-gahl-veh	*pagalvė*
plug (basin)	*kahmsh*-tis	*kamštis*
	prows-*tu*-vwi	*praustuvui*
plug (bath)	*kahmsh*-tis *vawn*-yay	*kamštis voniai*
quiet	tee-*lah*	*tyla*
room	*kahm*-bah-rees	*kambarys*
shower	*du*-shahs	*dušas*
soap	*mwi*-lahs	*muilas*
suitcase	lah-gah-*mi*-nahs	*lagaminas*
toilet	tu-ah-*lat*-ahs	*tualetas*
toilet paper	tu-ah-*lat*-aw	*tualeto popierius*
	paw-peahr-yus	
towel	*rahnk*-shlu-aws-tis	*rankšluostis*
water	vahn-*du*-aw	*vanduo*
hot/cold water	*kahrsh*-tahs/*shahl*-tahs	*karštas/šaltas*
	vahn-*du*-aw	*vanduo*
window	*lahn*-gahs	*langas*

AROUND TOWN

How do I get	*prah*-shom	*Prašom*
to the ...?	pah-sah-*kee*-ti	*pasakyti,*
	kaip pah-*tak*-ti i ...?	*kaip patekti į ...?*
art gallery	*man*-aw gah-*la*-ri-yah	*meno galeriją*
cinema	*ki*-nah	*kiną*
exhibition	*pah*-raw-dah	*parodą*
museum	mu-*zeah*-yu	*muziejų*
stadium	stah-di-*yo*-nah	*stadijoną*
university	u-ni-var-si-*tat*-ah	*universitetą*
zoo	zaw-*log*-i-yaws *saw*-dah	*zoologijos sodą*

LITHUANIAN

I'm looking for the ...   ahsh *yeahsh*-kow ...   *Aš ieškau ...*

art gallery	*man*-aw gah-*la*-ri-yaws	*meno galerijos*
barber/	kir-*peek*-laws	*kirpyklos*
hairdresser		
church	bahzh-*nee*-chaws	*bažnyčios*
city centre	*meahs*-taw *tsan*-traw	*miesto centro*
currency	vah-*lyu*-taws	*valiutos*
exchange		
outlet	kay-*teek*-laws	*keityklos*
embassy	ahm-bah-*sah*-daws	*ambasados*
hotel	*veahsh*-buch-aw	*viešbučio*
market	*tur*-gows	*turgaus*
museum	mu-*zeah*-yows	*muziejaus*
old city	san-*ah*-meahs-chaw	*senamiesčio*
police	paw-*lit*-si-yaws	*policijos*
post office	*pahsh*-taw	*pašto*
public toilet	tu-ah-*lat*-aw	*tualeto*
telephone	te-le-*fo*-naw-	*telefono-*
centre	ow-to-*mah*-taw	*automato*
tourist	tu-*ris*-too	*turistų*
information	in-for-*mah*-tsi-yaws	*informacijos*
office	*byoo*-raw	*biuro*

At the Bank

The litas is now the only legal tender in the country. Money can be exchanged at banks and at street kiosks dealing exclusively in money exchange. Cash advances on major credit cards are available from some banks in the major towns.

I want to exchange some money/
travellers cheques.
   ahsh *nawr*-yu ish-*kays*-ti   *Aš noriu iškeisti pinigų/*
   pi-ni-*goo*/kal-ay-*vi*-new chak-ew   *keleivinių čekių.*
What's the exchange rate?
   kawks ee-*rah* kur-sahs?   *Koks yra kursas?*

How many litas per ...?	keahk *li*-too uzh ...?	*Kiek litų už ...?*
Australian dollar	ows-*trah*-li-yaws *do*-la-ri	*Australijos dolerį*
Canadian dollar	kah-*nah*-daws *do*-la-ri	*Kanados dolerį*
English pound	*ahn*-gloo *svah*-rah	*Anglų svarą*
German mark	vaw-keah-*chew mahr*-ka	*Vokiečių markę*
US dollar	ah-*ma*-ri-kaws *do*-la-ri	*Amerikos dolerį*

bank notes	bahnk-*naw*-tai	*banknotai*
cashier	*kah*-si-nin-kahs	*kasininkas*
coins	maw-*nat*-aws	*monetos*
credit card	kra-*di*-taw kor-*ta*-leh	*kredito kortelė*
exchange	ish-kay-*ti*-mahs	*iškeitimas*

At the Post Office

I'd like to send a ...	ahsh naw-*reh*-chow pah-*syoos*-ti ...	*Aš norėčiau pasiųsti ...*
fax	*fahk*-sah	*faksą*
(registered) letter	(rag-is-*tru*-aw-tah) *laish*-kah	*(registruotą) laišką*
postcard	aht-vi-*ru*-kah	*atviruką*
parcel	*syun*-ti-ni pah-*kat*-ah	*siuntinį* (large) *paketą* (small)
telegram	te-le-*grah*-mah	*telegramą*

Where's the poste restante counter?
kur ish-du-aw-dah-*mi* laish-*kai* *Kur išduodami laiškai*
i-ki pah-ray-kah-*lah*-vi-maw? *iki pareikalavimo?*
Are there any letters for me?
ahr mahn ee-*rah* laish-*koo*? *Ar man yra laiškų?*
Here's my passport.
shtai mah-naw *pah*-sahs *Štai mano pasas.*

LITHUANIAN

I'd like some stamps.

    naw-*reh*-chow nu-*pirk*-ti   *Norėčiau nupirkti*
    pahsh*-taw zhank-*loo   *pašto ženklų.*

How much is the postage?

    keahk kai-*nu-aw*-yah   *Kiek kainuoja*
    ***pahsh*-taw zhank-*lai*?**   *pašto ženklai?*

aerogram	**ah-eh-raw-grah-*mah***	*aerograma*
airmail	**aw-raw pahsh-*tu***	*oro paštu*
envelope	**va*w*-kahs**	*vokas*
express mail	**aks-*pras* pahsh-tahs**	*ekspres paštas*
mail box	***pahsh*-taw deh-zheh**	*pašto dėžė*
registered mail	**rag-is-*tru-aw*-tahs**	*registruotas paštas*
	pahsh-tahs	
surface mail	**pah-prahs-*tu* pahsh-*tu***	*paprastu paštu*

Telephone & Internet

Would you please put a
call through to ...?

    ***prah*-shom pri-im-ti uzh-*sah*-**   *Prašom priimti užsakymą*
    kee-mah *paw*-kahl-byui su ...   *pokalbiui su ...*

How much do you charge for a
three-minute call?

    keahk kai-*nu-aw*-yah tri-*yoo*   *Kiek kainuoja trijų*
    mi-*nu*-chew *paw*-kahl-bis?   *minučių pokalbis?*

How much does each
extra minute cost?

    keahk kai-*nu-aw*-yah uzh   *Kiek kainuoja už*
    keahk-*veah*-nah pri-*deh*-ti-na   *kiekvieną pridėtinę*
    mi-*nu*-ta?   *minutę?*

It's engaged.

    ***uzh*-im-tah**   *Užimta.*

I've been cut off.

    kahzh-*kahs* mus *ish*-yun-geh   *Kažkas mus išjungė.*

telephone	te-le-*fo*-nahs	*telefonas*
telephone number	te-le-*fo*-naw *nu*-ma-ris	*telefono numeris*
telephone booth	te-le-*fo*-naw boo-*da*-leh	*telefono būdelė*

I need to get access to the Internet.
mahn *rayk*-yah preah in-ter-*nat*-aw pri-*ay*-ti — *Man reikia prie interneto prieiti.*

I need to check my email.
mahn *rayk*-yah pah-si-*tik*-rin-ti al-ak-*tron*-i-ni *pahsh*-tah — *Man reikia pasitikrinti elektronini paštą.*

Making a Phone Call

Hello.	ahl-*yo*	*Alio.*
I'd like to speak to ...	naw-*reh*-chow pah-kahl-*beh*-ti su ...	*Norėčiau pakalbėti su ...*
Please wait a minute.	*prah*-shom pah-*lowk*-ti mi-nu-*teh*-la	*Prašom palaukti minutėlę*
Speaking!	klow-*sow!*	*Klausau!* (lit: I'm-listening)
This is Tom.	cha *to*-mahs	*Čia Tomas.*

Sightseeing

Do you have a guidebook/local map?
ahr yoos *tu*-ri-ta tu-*ris*-too vah-*daw*-vah/ *veah*-ti-ni zham-*eh*-lah-pi? — *Ar jūs turite turisų vadovą/vietinį žemėlapį?*

What are the main attractions?
kawk-yaws ee-rah pah-grin-*din*-ehs ah-*trahk*-tsi-yaws? — *Kokios yra pagrindinės atrakcijos?*

What's that?
kahs tahs? — *Kas tas?*

How old is it?
    kal-*in*-tah-ma *shimt*-mat-ee-ya   *Kelintame šimtmetyje*
    yis bu-vaw pah-stah-*tee*-tahs?   *jis buvo pastatytas?*
        (lit: what century
          it was built?)

Can I take photographs?
    ahr *lay*-jah-mah fo-to-grah-   *Ar leidžiama fotografuoti?*
    fu-aw-ti?
What time does it open/close?
    kal-*in*-tah *vah*-lahn-dah   *Kelintą valandą*
    aht-si-*dah*-raw/uzh-si-*dah*-raw?   *atsidaro/užsidaro?*

Useful Words

ancient	san-*aw*-vin-is	*senovinis*
archaeological	ar-he-o-*lo*-gin-is	*archeologinis*
building	*pah*-stah-tahs	*pastatas*
castle	pil-*is*	*pilis*
cathedral	*kah*-tad-rah	*katedra*
cemetery	*kah*-pi-nehs	*kapinės*
church	bahzh-*nee*-chah	*bažnyčia*
concert hall	*kon*-tsar-too *sah*-leh	*koncertų salė*
library	bib-*lyo*-tak-ah	*biblioteka*
main square	pah-grin-*di*-neh	*pagrindinė*
	meahs-taw *aiksh*-teh	*miesto aikštė*
monastery	veah-nu-*aw-lee*-nahs	*vienuolynas*
monument	pah-*mink*-lahs	*paminklas*
national park	nah-tsyo-*nah*-li-nis	*nacionalinis*
	pahr-kahs	*parkas*
opera house	o-*per*-aws *roo*-mai	*operos rūmai*
park	*pahr*-kahs	*parkas*
parliament	*say*-maw *roo*-mai	*seimo rūmai*
ruins	groo-*veh*-say	*griuvėsiai*
stadium	stah-di-*yon*-ahs	*stadijonas*
statues	stah-*tu*-laws	*statulos*
synagogue	si-nah-*gog*-ah	*sinagoga*
university	u-ni-var-si-*tat*-ahs	*universitetas*

FOLK SONGS

Lithuanians have many thousands of folk songs in their folkloric treasure chest, most stemming from pre-Christian times. Here is but one of them, heard to be sung by the crowd during a pro-independence demonstration. The song is very old, while the refrain is a popular modern addition:

Augo sode klevelis,	A maple in the garden grew,
Augo sode žaliasai,	A green one in the garden grew,
Po tuo klevu,	Under the maple,
po žaliuoju,	under the green one,
Gul bernelis jaunasai.	Lay a young man sleeping.
(Last 2 lines twice)	

Refrain:
Viens, du, graži Lietuva,	One, two, beautiful Lithuania,
Kaip gėlelė žydi visada.	Like a flower, always in bloom.

- Nepapūski, vėjeli,	"Do not blow, o wind,
Nepapūski, šiaurusai,	Do not blow, o northern one,
Nepajudink klevo šaką,	Do not move the maple branch
Nepabudink bernelio.	Do not waken the young man."

Ir papūtė vėjelis,	But the wind did blow,
Ir papūtė šiaurusai,	But the northern one did blow,
Pajudino klevo šaką,	And it moved the maple branch,
Pabudino bernelį.	And it woke the young man up.

- Kelkis, kelkis, berneli,	"Get up, get up, o young man,
Gana ilgai miegoti:	You've been sleeping long enough.
Laikas stoti tau į kovą,	It's time for you to go to battle,
Ginti laisvę Lietuvos.	To defend the freedom of Lithuania."

LITHUANIAN

Going Out

What's there to do in the evenings?

    kur gah-*leh*-tu-ma ish-*ay*-ti vah-kah-*rais*?   *Kur galėtume išeiti vakarais?*

Are there any discos?

    ahr ee-*rah* dis-ko-*tak*-oo?   *Ar yra diskotekų?*

Are there places where you can hear local folk music?

    ahr ee-*rah veah*-too kur boo-too gah-li-mah ish-*girs*-ti lyow-deahs *mu*-zi-kaws?   *Ar yra vietų kur būtų galima išgirsti liaudies muzikos?*

How much is it to get in?

    keahk kai-*nu-aw*-yah i-eh-*yi*-mahs?   *Kiek kainuoja įėjimas?*

cinema	***ki*-nahs**	*kinas*
concert	***kon*-tser-tahs**	*koncertas*
disco	**dis-ko-*tak*-ahs**	*diskotekas*
jazz	***jyah*-zahs**	*džiazas*
nightclub	**nahk-*ti*-nis *klub*-ahs**	*naktinis klubas*
rock	***rok*-ahs**	*rokas*
theatre	**teh-*aht*-rahs**	*teatras*

PAPERWORK

name	*vahr*-dahs	*vardas*
address	*ahd*-ras-ahs	*adresas*
age	*mat*-ai	*metai*
border	*seah*-nah	*siena*
business trip	ko-mahn-di-*ru-aw*-teh	*komandiruotė*
citizenship	pil-eah-*tee*-beh	*pilietybė*
customs	*mwi*-ti-neh	*muitinė*
customs	*mwi*-ti-nehs	*muitinės*
declaration	dak-lah-*rah*-tsi-yah	*deklaracija*
date of birth	gi-*mi*-maw dah-*tah*	*gimimo data*
driving licence	vai-*ru-aw*-taw-yaw	*vairuotojo*
	pah-zhee-*meh*-yi-mahs	*pažymėjimas*
extension of visa	*viz*-aws	*vizos*
	prah-tas-*i*-mahs	*pratęsimas*
identification	ahs-*mans*	*asmens*
	loo-di-yi-mahs	*liudijimas*
immigration	i-mi-*grah*-tsi-yah	*imigracija*
length of stay	bu-*vim*-aw *lai*-kahs	*buvimo laikas*
marital status	*sahn*-tu-aw-kin-is	*santuokinis*
	stah-tu-sahs	*statusas*
nationality	tow-*tee*-beh	*tautybė*
next of kin	ahr-tim-*yow*-sas	*artimiausias*
	shay-*maws* nah-*rees*	*šeimos narys*
passport number	*pahs*-aw *nu*-ma-ris	*paso numeris*
passport	*pahs*-ahs	*pasas*
place of birth	gi-*mi*-maw veah-*tah*	*gimimo vieta*
profession	pro-*fas*-i-yah	*profesija*
purpose of trip	kal-*yaw*-nehs *tiks*-lahs	*kelionės tikslas*
religion	re-*lig*-i-yah	*religija*
sex	lee-*tis*	*lytis*
tourist trip	tu-*ris*-ti-neh kal-*yaw*-neh	*turistinė kelionė*
visa	*viz*-ah	*viza*

LITHUANIAN

I have only my personal possessions,
nothing dutiable.

> **ahsh tik tur-yu ahs-*man*-ish-kus**   *Aš tik turiu asmeniškus*
> ***daik*-tus *neah*-kaw ahp-*mwi*-ti-**   *daiktus, nieko*
> **nah-maw**   *apmuitinamo.*

What duty must I pay?

> **kaw-ki *mwi*-tah ahsh tur-yu**   *Kokį muitą aš turiu*
> **maw-*keh*-ti?**   *mokėti?*

I have an export
licence for these things.

> **ahsh tur-yu lay-*di*-mah**   *Aš turiu leidimą*
> **ish-*vash*-ti**   *išvežti.*

Are these things dutiable?

> **ahr sheah daik-*tai***   *Ar šie daiktai*
> **ahp-*mwi*-tin-ah-mi?**   *apmuitinami?*

I have paid the duty.

> **ahsh su-maw-*keh*-yow**   *Aš sumokėjau*
> ***mwi*-tah**   *muitą.*

SONG TO FREEDOM

On 3 June 1988, a huge rally of Lithuanian demonstrators gathered to support a newly-formed citizens' movement, *Sąjūdis*, in its bid to persuade the next Communist Party Conference to grant Lithuania greater national autonomy. That demonstration resulted in the old national flag, banned for 50 years, being reinstated and hoisted on the tower of Gediminas Castle. Further passionate but peaceful demonstrations followed, where people sang the old folk songs which gave them a feeling of unity of purpose. However, the Soviets continued to show a reluctance to grant too many freedoms. After a human chain pro-independence demonstration by nearly two million singing Baltic people on 23 August 1989, President Gorbachev still warned that a split from the Soviet Union would not be tolerated.

Finally on 11 March 1990, in defiance of the Soviets, the Lithuanian Parliament itself declared the restoration of Lithuania's independence.

This was too much for the Soviets and tanks were sent in to intimidate the people. Helicopters scattered leaflets urging them to continue to obey the Soviet Constitution. In a further effort to break the people's will, the Soviets imposed a devastating economic blockade. On the night of Sunday, 13 January 1991, as people held hands and sang while trying to bar the way of Soviet tanks rolling in to capture the TV tower in Vilnius, 14 defenceless Lithuanians were crushed by the tanks. Eventually, by 1993, a complete withdrawal of Soviet troops was achieved as the last Russian soldier left Lithuania.

LITHUANIAN

IN THE COUNTRY

The Lithuanian countryside is spectacular in summer. There's no dangerous wildlife, apart from the possibility of ticks. You may come across the occasional feral pig in some areas. The country is dotted with sights of historic significance and beauty. As always, a knowledgeable guide of the local area adds great value to any outing.

Weather

What's the weather forecast for today/tomorrow?

kaw-*kyah* aw-raw prog-*no*-zeh shan-*deah*-nai/reet-*deah*-nai?

Kokia oro prognozė šiandienai/rytdienai?

It's going to (be) ...	bus ...	*Bus ...*
cloudy	dab-as-*u*-aw-tah	*debesuota*
cold	*shahl*-tah	*šalta*
cool	veh-*su*	*vėsu*
drizzly	dulks-*naw*-tah	*dulksnota*
foggy	*tirsh*-taw *roo*-kaw	*tiršto rūko*
hail	*krush*-ah	*kruša*
hot	*kahrsh*-tah	*karšta*
icy	lad-*in*-gahs aw-rahs	*ledingas oras*
rain	leah-*tows*	*lietaus*
snow	*sneah*-gaw	*sniego*
sunny	sow-*leh*-tah	*saulėta*
warm	*shil*-tah	*šilta*
windy	veh-*yu*-aw-tah	*vėjuota*

Directions

Is it far?	ahr taw-*li*?	*Ar toli?*
Can I get there on ...?	ahr veah-*taw*-veh pri-*ay*-nah-mah ...?	*Ar vietovė prieinama ...?*
bike	*dvi*-rah-chu	*dviračiu*
foot	pehs-*chaw*-mis	*pėsčiomis*
horseback	ahrk-*lays*	*arkliais*

north	show-*reh*	*šiaurė*
south	*peah*-toos	*pietūs*
east	ree-*tai*	*rytai*
west	vah-kah-*rai*	*vakarai*

Animals, Birds & Insects

bird	*powksh*-tis	*paukštis*
boar	*shar*-nahs	*šernas*
butterfly	dru-*gal*-is	*drugelis*
cat	kah-*teh*	*katė*
chicken (hen)	vish-*tah*	*višta*
cow	*kahr*-veh	*karvė*
deer	*stir*-nah	*stirna*
dog	shu-aw	*šuo*
domestic animal	nah-*mi*-nis gee-vu-*lees*	*naminis gyvulys*
duck	*ahn*-tis	*antis*
elk	*breah*-dis	*briedis*
fish	zhu-*vis*	*žuvis*
fox	*lah*-peh	*lapė*
frog	vahr-*leh*	*varlė*
goat	awzh-*kah*	*ožka*
hare	*kish*-kis	*kiškis*
horse	ahrk-*lees*	*arklys*
insect	vahbz-*dees*	*vabzdys*
lynx	*loo*-shis	*lūšis*
midges	mah-shah-*lai*	*mašalai*
mosquito	*u*-aw-das	*uodas*
otter	ood-*rah*	*ūdra*
pigeon	bah-*lahn*-dis	*balandis*
pig	*kyow*-leh	*kiaulė*
seagull	zhuv-*ehd*-rah	*žuvėdra*
sheep	ah-*vis*	*avis*
snake	gee-*vah*-teh	*gyvatė*
spider	*vaw*-rahs	*voras*
squirrel	*vaw*-va-reh	*voverė*
stork	*gahn*-drahs	*gandras*
swan	*gul*-beh	*gulbė*
tick	*ar*-keh	*erkė*
wild animal	zhveh-*ris*	*žvėris*

Plants

(edible) berry	(*vahl*-gaw-mah)	(*valgoma*)
	u-*aw*-gah	*uoga*
blossom	*zheah*-dahs	*žiedas*
bush (shrub)	*kroo*-mahs	*krūmas*
fir	pu-*shis*	*pušis*
flower	geh-*leh*	*gėlė*
grass	zhaw-*leh*	*žolė*
leaf	*lah*-pahs	*lapas*
mushroom	*gree*-bahs	*grybas*
oak	ah-zhu-*aw*-lahs	*ąžuolas*
plant	*ow*-gah-lahs	*augalas*
rue	*roo*-ta	*rūta*
spruce	*ag*-leh	*eglė*
tree	*mad*-is	*medis*
woods/forest	*mish*-kahs	*miškas*

WE LOVE RUE, YES IT'S TRUE

If Lithuania has a national plant, it's the rue, an aromatic shrub with small, yellow flowers. The evergreen leaf of the rue has enough tradition and folk symbolism associated with it to fill this whole book. It plays a major role in many aspects of life, including weddings, celebrations, songs and poetry.

Camping

We'd like to go hiking/camping.
mas naw-*reh*-tu-ma	*Mes norėtume iškylauti/*
ish-kee-*low*-ti/staw-veek-*low*-ti	*stovyklauti.*

Where would you suggest?
kur yoos pah-*tahr*-tu-met?	*Kur jūs patartumėt?*

Are we allowed to camp here?
ahr *gah*-li-mah cha	*Ar galima čia*
staw-veek-*low*-ti?	*stovyklauti?*

Am I allowed to light a fire?
    ahr _gah_-li-mah uzh-_kur_-ti _ug_-ni?   _Ar galima užkurti ugnį?_
Can we fish here?
    ahr _gah_-li-mah cha zhu-_vow_-ti?   _Ar galima čia žuvauti?_
Where can I buy a fishing rod?
    kur _gah_-li-mah _pirk_-ti   _Kur galima pirkti_
    mash-ka-ra   _meškerę?_

camping	_kam_-pin-gahs	_kempingas_
axe	_kir_-vis	_kirvis_
backpack	kup-_rin_-eh	_kuprinė_
bottle opener	ah-ti-dah-ree-_tu_-vahs	_atidarytuvas_
	_bu_-tal-yui	_buteliui_
can opener	kon-_sar_-voo deh-zhu-tehs	_konservų dėžutės_
	ah-ti-dah-ree-_tu_-vahs	_atidarytuvas_
compass	_kom_-pah-sahs	_kompasas_
firewood	_mahl_-kaws _low_-zhwi	_malkos laužui_
gas cylinder	_du_-yoo bon-_kal_-eh	_dujų bonkelė_
insect repellent	vahbz-_jus_ aht-_bai_-dahn-ti	_vabzdžius_
	preah-maw-neh	_atbaidanti_
		priemonė
matches	dak-_tu_-kai	_degtukai_
penknife	pay-_lyu_-kahs	_peiliukas_
rope	_vir_-veh	_virvė_
sleeping bag	_meahg_-mai-shis	_miegmaišis_
stove	kraws-_nal_-eh	_krosnelė_
tent	pah-lah-_pin_-eh	_palapinė_
tent pegs	kawl-_yu_-kai	_kuoliukai_
	pah-lah-_pin_-ay	_palapinei_
water bottle	vahn-_dans bu_-tal-is	_vandens butelis_

LITHUANIAN

Useful Words

beach	*plazh*-ahs	*pliažas*
bridge	*til*-tahs	*tiltas*
castle mound	pil-*yah*-kahl-nis	*piliakalnis*
cemetery	*kah*-pin-ehs	*kapinės*
farm	*oo*-kis	*ūkis*
forest	*mish*-kahs	*miškas*
harbour	u-*aws*-tahs	*uostas*
hill	*kahl*-nahs	*kalnas*
lake	*azh*-a-rahs	*ežeras*
map	zham-*eh*-lah-pis	*žemėlapis*
national park	nah-tsyon-*ah*-li-nis	*nacionalinis*
	pahr-kahs	*parkas*
river	u-*peh*	*upė*
road	*kal*-yahs	*kelias*
sand dune	*kaw*-pah	*kopa*
scenery	*vaiz*-dahs	*vaizdas*
sea	*yoo*-rah	*jūra*
town	*meahs*-tahs	*miestas*
track	*tah*-kahs	*takas*
valley	sleh-*nees*	*slėnys*
village	*kai*-mahs	*kaimas*
waterfall	krawk-*lees*	*krioklys*

CREEPY CRAWLIES

There's not much in the way of insect repellents to be found in Vilnius pharmacies or shops dealing in hygiene products. Travellers are advised to carry their own roll-on repellent, as midges are prevalent and these annoying little creatures can spoil your summer holiday.

LITHUANIAN

FOOD

Traditional Lithuanian food consists of simple dishes based on potato, milk, pork or poultry and fresh fish, often served with black rye bread. Meat was often smoked as a common means of preservation. Modern Lithuanian cuisine has developed out of these traditions. Much of the especially tasty and exotic fare is reserved for festive occasions and events. These delectable dishes are not generally available in the cities where the more familiar, inexpensive, easier to prepare food of Western cafes greets the tourist. This picture is changing slowly, however, with some restaurants offering style, service and fine traditional food.

The staple food is dark brown rye bread, which is eaten practically at every meal. For breakfast Lithuanians traditionally prefer pickled herring (*silkė*) with black rye bread. Breakfast cereals are still something of a novelty to many. After bread, salted or smoked pork dishes are second in importance. An essential dairy food is a hard cottage cheese with caraway. There are lots of traditional potato dishes, of which *cepelinai* ('zeppelins') take top place and *kugelis* ('cannon ball') takes second. Pancakes, fresh fish, pickled herrings, smoked eels, mushrooms, beetroot and cabbage are the other traditional staples.

Where's the nearest ...?	kur ahr-tim-*yow*-sa/as ...?	*Kur artim-iausia/as ...?* (f/m)
cafe	kah-*vi*-neh	*kavinė* (f)
dining room	vahl-*geek*-lah	*valgykla* (f)
fast-food outlet	uzh-kahn-*din*-eh	*užkandinė* (f)
restaurant	ras-to-*rah*-nahs	*restoranas* (m)
Let's have lunch!	*ay*-kim pah-peah-*tow*-ti!	*Eikim papietauti!*

LITHUANIAN

At the Restaurant

A table for ..., please.
stah-lah ... prah-*show* — *Stalą ..., prašau.*

May I see the menu, please?
ahr gah-*leh*-chow *gow*-ti — *Ar galėčiau gauti*
man-*yew* prah-*show?* — *meniu prašau?*

I'd like the set lunch.
ahsh naw-*reh*-chow — *Aš norėčiau*
nu-stah-*tee*-tah *lan*-chah — *nustatytą lenčą.*

Do you have the menu in English?
ahr yoos *tu*-ri-ta man-*yew* — *Ar jūs turite meniu*
ahn-glish-kai? — *angliškai?*

I'd like to try that.
ahsh naw-*reh*-chow — *Aš norėčiau*
ish-bahn-*dee*-ti taw — *išbandyti to.*

This isn't my order.
ahsh taw na-uzh-sah-*kyow* — *Aš to neužsakiau.*

Is service included in the bill?
ahr pah-tahr-*nah*-vi-mahs — *Ar patarnavimas*
i-*skai*-taw-mahs *sah*-skai-taw-ya? — *įskaitomas sąskaitoje?*

Useful Words

bill	sah-skai-*tah*	*sąskaita*
bottle	*bu*-tal-is	*butelis*
butter	*sveahs*-tahs	*sviestas*
coffeepot	kah-vi-*nu*-kahs	*kavinukas*
cup	pu-aw-*du*-kahs	*puodukas*
drinks/beverages	*geh*-ri-mai	*gėrimai*
fork	shah-*kut*-eh	*šakutė*
glass	stik-*lin*-eh	*stiklinė*
knife	*pay*-lis	*peilis*
meal/dish	*vahl*-gis	*valgis*
menu	man-*yew*	*meniu*
napkin	sar-*vat*-eh	*servetė*
pepper	pip-*i*-rai	*pipirai*
plate	lehksh-*teh*	*lėkštė*

salt	*drus*-kah	*druska*
serviette	sar-vat-*eh*-leh	*servetėlė*
spoon	*showksh*-tahs	*šaukštas*
Waiter!	pah-dah-*veh*-yah!	*Padavėja!* (f)
	pah-dah-*veh*-yow!	*Padavėjau!* (m)

Vegetarian Meals

I don't eat ...	ahsh na-*vahl*-gow ...	*Aš nevalgau ...*
meat	*meh*-sish-kaw	*mėsiško*
dairy products	*peah*-nish-kaw	*pieniško*

Breakfast & Lunch

bacon	bak-*on*-ahs	*bekonas*
boiled eggs	*vir*-tahs kyow-*shin*-is	*virtas kiaušinis*
bread	*du*-aw-nah	*duona*
butter	*sveahs*-tahs	*sviestas*
cheese	*soo*-ris	*sūris*
coffee	kah-*vah*	*kava*
cottage cheese	*vahrsh*-keh	*varškė*
eggs	kyow-*shin*-ay	*kiaušiniai*
fried eggs	*kap*-ti kyow-*shin*-ay	*kepti kiaušiniai*
kefir (a kind of low-fat natural yoghurt)	ka-*fee*-rahs	*kefyras*
milk	*peah*-nahs	*pienas*
oatmeal porridge	ah-vi-zhoo *kaw*-sheh	*avižų košė*
omelette	om-*lat*-ahs	*omletas*
pancakes	blee-*nal*-ay/*sklin*-jay	*blyneliai/ sklindžiai*
sandwiches	su-mush-*tin*-ay	*sumuštiniai*
sausages	dash-*ral*-ehs	*dešrelės*
scrambled eggs	kyow-shin-*eah*-neh	*kiaušinienė*
semolina porridge	mah-noo *kaw*-sheh	*manų košė*
tea	ahr-bah-*tah*	*arbata*

LITHUANIAN

MENU DECODER

Soup

kopūstų sriuba	kaw-*poos*-too sru-*bah*	cabbage soup
lietuviški barščiai su grybais	leah-*tu*-vish-ki *bahrsh*-chay su *gree*-bais	Lithuanian borscht with mushrooms
šaltibarščiai	shahl-*ti*-barsh-chay	beetroot and sour cream soup (cold)
žirnelių sriuba	zhir-*na*-lew sru-*bah*	green pea soup

Meat

jautiena su svogūnais	yow-*teah*-nah su svaw-*goo*-nais	beef with onions
mėsos asorti	meh-*saws* ah-sor-*tee*	meat assortment
bifšteksas	bif-*shtak*-ahs	beefsteak
liežuvis drebučiuose	leah-*zhu*-vis drab-*uch*-aw-sa	jellied ox tongue
kotlietai	*kot*-leah-tai	rissoles
kiaulienos muštinis su lietuvišku įdaru	kyow-*leah*-naws mush-*ti*-nis su leah-*tu*-vish-ku *i*-dah-ru	stuffed pork
karbonadas veršiena su morkomis	kahr-bon-*ah*-dahs var-*sheah*-nah su *mor*-kaw-mis	breaded pork chop
arba su grybais	ahr-bah su *gree*-bais	veal with carrots or mushrooms
cepelinai	tsap-al-*in*-ai	boiled potato dumplings stuffed with meat and covered with bacon, cream and butter sauce
kaldūnai	kahl-*doo*-nai	Lithuanian dim sims
skilandis	ski-*lahn*-dis	pork sausage

MENU DECODER

Seafood

juodi/raudoni ikrai	yu-aw-*di*/ row-daw-*ni ik*-rai	black/ red caviar
žuvies asorti	zhu-*veahs* ah-sor-*tee*	fish assortment
silkė lietuviškai/ rusiškai	*sil*-keh leah-*tu*-vish-kai/ *rus*-ish-kai	herring Lithuanian/ Russian style
rūkytas ungurys	roo-*kee*-tahs un-gu-*rees*	smoked eel
rūkytas eršketas	roo-*kee*-tahs arsh-*kat*-ahs	smoked white sturgeon
kalmarai tešloje	kahl-*mah*-rai *tash*-law-ya	calamari (in dough)
midijos su ryžiais	*mi*-di-yaws su *ree*-zhays	mussels with rice

Poultry & Game

vištos kojelė	*vish*-taws kaw-*yal*-eh	chicken leg
vištienos kotletas su razinomis	vish-*teah*-naws *kot*-lat-ahssu rah-*zi*-naw-mis	chicken cutlet with raisins
įdarytas vištienos kotletas	i-dah-*ree*-tahs vish-*teah*-naws *kot*-lat-ahs	stuffed chicken cutlet
vištienos sultinys	vish-*teah*-naws sul-ti-*nees*	chicken bouillon

MENU DECODER

Salads

burokėlių salotos	bu-raw-*keh*-lew sah-*law*-taws	baby beetroot salad
pupelių salotos	pu-*pal*-yew sah-*law*-taws	bean salad
morkų salotos su slyvomis	*mor*-koo sah-*law*-taws su *slee*-vaw-mis	carrot and plum salad
lietuviškos salotos su kumpiu	leah-*tu*-vish-kaws sah-*law*-taws su *kum*-pyu	ham salad
apelsinų salotos su alyvuogemis	ah-pal-*si*-noo sah-*law*-taws su ah-*leev*-u-aw-geh-mis	orange and olive salad
krevečių salotos	krav-*ach*-ew sah-*law*-taws	shrimp salad
pomidorų salotos	po-mi-*daw*-roo sah-*law*-taws	tomato salad

LITHUANIAN

Meat

beef	yow-*teah*-nah	*jautiena*
ham	*kum*-pis	*kumpis*
lamb	a-*reah*-nah	*ėriena*
mutton	ah-*veah*-nah	*aviena*
pork	kyow-*leah*-nah	*kiauliena*
veal	var-*sheah*-nah	*veršiena*

Seafood

cod	*man*-keh	*menkė*
crab	*krah*-bahs	*krabas*
crawfish/crayfish	*yoo*-raws veh-*zhay*	*jūros vėžiai*
eel	un-gu-*rees*	*ungurys*
herring	*sil*-keh	*silkė*
lobster	*aw*-mah-rahs	*omaras*
shellfish	maw-*lyus*-kai	*moliuskai*
mussels	dvi-*gal*-dehs *kryowk*-lehs	*dvigeldės kriauklės*
oysters	*ows*-trehs	*austrės*
perch	*star*-kahs	*sterkas*
pike	lee-dak-*ah*	*lydeka*
plaice	*plaksh*-neh	*plekšnė*
salmon	lah-shi-*shah*	*lašiša*
shrimp	vehzh-*lyu*-kahs	*vėžiukas*
sturgeon	arsh-*kat*-ahs	*eršketas*
trout	u-*peh*-tah-kis	*upėtakis*

Poultry & Game

chicken	vish-*teah*-nah	*vištiena*
duck	ahn-*teah*-nah	*antiena*
goose	zha-*seah*-nah	*žąsiena*
hare	*kish*-kis	*kiškis*
rabbit	*zwi*-kis	*zuikis*
turkey	kah-lah-*ku*-tahs	*kalakutas*
wild pig	*shar*-nahs	*šernas*

Vegetables

beans	*pu*-paws	*pupos*
beetroot	bu-raw-*keh*-lay	*burokėliai*
cabbage	ko-*poos*-tai	*kopūstai*
carrots	*mor*-kaws	*morkos*
cauliflower	kah-lahf-*yaw*-rai	*kalafiorai*
celery	sah-*leah*-rahs	*salieras*
cucumbers	ah-*gur*-kai	*agurkai*
green beans	*pu*-paws	*pupos*
lentils	*la*-shay	*lęšiai*
lettuce	sah-*law*-taws	*salotos*
mushrooms	*gree*-bai	*grybai*
onions	svo-*goo*-nai	*svogūnai*
peas	zhir-*nal*-ay	*žirneliai*
pepper	pi-*pi*-rai	*pipirai*
potatoes	*bul*-vehs	*bulvės*
radishes	ri-di-*keh*-lay/ri-*di*-kai	*ridikėliai/ridikai*
spinach	shpi-*nah*-tai	*špinatai*
tomatoes	po-mi-*daw*-rai	*pomidorai*
vegetables	dahr-*zhaw*-vehs	*daržovės*

EGGSTRAVAGANZA!

Šakotis (**shah-*kaw*-tis**) is a special celebration cake that looks like a yellow tree trunk with lopped branches (similar to German *Baumkuchen*). It's made with 60 eggs and is very popular for special occasions, such as weddings.

Fruit

apple	aw-baw-*lees*	*obuolys*
apricot	ahb-ri-*ko*-sahs	*abrikosas*
banana	bah-*nah*-nahs	*bananas*
bilberries	meh-*lee*-nehs	*mėlynės*
blackberries	*garv*-u-aw-gehs	*gervuogės*
cherries	*veesh*-nyaws	*vyšnios*
cranberries	*spahn*-gu-ah-lehs	*spanguolės*
fruit	*vai*-say	*vaisiai*
gooseberries	*ahg*-rahs-tai	*agrastai*
grapes	*veen*-u-aw-gehs	*vynuogės*
lemon	tsit-*ri*-nah	*citrina*
mulberries	*shilk*-maj-aw u-*aw*-gaws	*šilkmedžio uogos*
orange	ah-pal-*si*-nahs	*apelsinas*
peach	*par*-si-kahs	*persikas*
pear	*krow*-sheh	*kriaušė*
pineapple	ah-nah-*nah*-sahs	*ananasas*
plum	*slee*-vah	*slyva*
prune	jaw-*vin*-tah *slee*-vah	*džiovinta slyva*
raisins/sultanas	rah-*zi*-naws	*razinos*
raspberries	ah-*veah*-tehs	*avietės*
strawberries	*brahsh*-kehs	*braškės*

Desserts

fruit compote	*kom*-pot-ahs	*kompotas*
honey cake	mad-*ow*-nin-kahs	*medauninkas*
hot fudge	*karsh*-tahs	*karštas*
	sho-ko-*lah*-dahs	*šokoladas*
ice cream	lad-*ai*	*ledai*
chocolate	sho-ko-*lah*-dahs	*šokoladas*
fruit	*vai*-say	*vaisiai*
mousse	pu-*teh*-say	*putėsiai*
pastries	pee-rah-*gai*-chay	*pyragaičiai*
pastry with jelly	pee-rah-*gai*-tis	*pyragaitis*
	su zhal-*eh*	*su želė*
… with nuts	… reah-shu-*tais*	*… riešutais*

LITHUANIAN

AT THE MARKET

Basics

bread	*du*-aw-nah	*duona*
butter	*sveahs*-tahs	*sviestas*
cereal	yah-*vai*-nyay	*javainiai*
cheese	*soo*-ris	*sūris*
chocolate	sho-ko-*lah*-dahs	*šokoladas*
eggs	kyow-*shin*-ay	*kiaušiniai*
flour	*mil*-tai	*miltai*
margarine	mahr-gah-*ri*-nahs	*margarinas*
marmalade	u-ah-*geah*-nah	*uogienė*
milk	*peah*-nahs	*pienas*
olive oil	praw-*vahn*-si-nis	*provansinis*
	ah-*leah*-yus	*aliejus*
pasta	*pahs*-tah	*pasta*
rice	*ree*-zhay	*ryžiai*
sugar	*tsuk*-rus	*cukrus*
water	van-*du-aw*	*vanduo*
yogurt	*yaw*-gur-tahs	*jogurtas*

Meat & Poultry

beef	yow-*teah*-nah	*jautiena*
chicken	vish-*teah*-nah	*vištiena*
ham	*kum*-pis	*kumpis*
lamb	a-*reah*-nah	*ėriena*
mutton	a-*veah*-nah	*aviena*
pork	kyow-*leah*-nah	*kiauliena*
turkey	kah-lah-*ku*-tahs	*kalakutas*
veal	var-*sheah*-nah	*veršiena*

Vegetables

(green) beans	*pu*-paws	*pupos*
beetroot	bu-raw-*keh*-lay	*burokėliai*
cabbage	ko-*poos*-tai	*kopūstai*
carrots	*mor*-kaws	*morkos*
cauliflower	kah-lahf-*yaw*-rai	*kalafiorai*
celery	sah-*leah*-rahs	*salieras*
cucumbers	ah-*gur*-kai	*agurkai*
lettuce	sah-*law*-taws	*salotos*
mushrooms	*gree*-bai	*grybai*

AT THE MARKET

onions	svo-*goo*-nai	*svogūnai*
peas	zhir-*nal*-ay	*žirneliai*
potatoes	*bul*-vehs	*bulvės*
radishes	ri-di-*keh*-lay/ri-*di*-kai	*ridikėliai/ridikai*
spinach	shpi-*nah*-tai	*špinatai*
tomatoes	po-mi-*daw*-rai	*pomidorai*
vegetables	dahr-*zhaw*-vehs	*daržovės*

Seafood

cod	*man*-keh	*menkė*
crayfish	*yoo*-raws veh-*zhay*	*jūros vėžiai*
crab	*krah*-bas	*krabas*
fish	*kah*-lah	*kala*
herring	*sil*-keh	*silkė*
lobster	*aw*-mah-rahs	*omaras*
mussels	dvi-*gal*-dehs	*dvigeldės*
	kryowk-lehs	*kriauklės*
plaice	*plaksh*-neh	*plekšnė*
salmon	lah-shi-*shah*	*lašiša*
trout	u-*peh*-tah-kis	*upėtakis*

Fruit

apple	aw-baw-*lees*	*obuolys*
apricot	ahb-ri-*ko*-sahs	*abrikosas*
banana	bah-*nah*-nahs	*bananas*
blackberries	*garv*-u-aw-gehs	*gervuogės*
cherries	*veesh*-nyaws	*vyšnios*
fruit	*vai*-say	*vaisiai*
grapes	*veen*-u-aw-gehs	*vynuogės*
lemon	tsit-*ri*-nah	*citrina*
mulberries	*shilk*-maj-aw u-*aw*-gaws	*šilkmedžio uogos*
orange	ah-pal-*si*-nahs	*apelsinas*
peach	*par*-si-kahs	*persikas*
pear	*krow*-sheh	*kriaušė*
plum	*slee*-veh	*slyva*
raspberries	ah-*veah*-tehs	*avietės*
strawberries	*brahsh*-kehs	*braškės*

LITHUANIAN

Condiments, Herbs & Spices

caraway	*kmee*-nai	*kmynai*
chives	tsi-bul-*yu*-kai	*cibuliukai*
cinnamon	tsi-nah-*maw*-nahs	*cinamonas*
cloves	gvahz-*dik*-ai	*gvazdikai*
garlic	chas-*nah*-kahs	*česnakas*
gherkin	roogsh-*tus* ah-*gur*-kahs	*rūgštus agurkas*
ginger	*im*-bi-rahs	*imbieras*
gravy	meh-*saws sul*-tees	*mėsos sultys*
horseradish	*kreah*-nai	*krienai*
nutmeg	mush-*kah*-tahs	*muškatas*
olive oil	praw-*vahn*-si-nis	*provansinis*
	ah-*leah*-yus	*aliejus*
parsley	pat-*rush*-kaws	*petruškos*
salt	*drus*-kah	*druska*
sugar	*tsuk*-rus	*cukrus*
vinegar	*ahts*-tahs	*actas*

Cooking Methods

baked/fried	*kap*-tahs	*keptas*
boiled	*vir*-tahs	*virtas*
rare	na vi-*sai* ish-kap-tah	*ne visai iškepta*
smoked	roo-*kee*-tah	*rūkyta*
steamed	*gah*-rin-tah	*garinta*
stewed	trawsh-*kin*-tah	*troškinta*
well done	lah-*bai* ga-*rai*	*labai gerai*
	ish-kap-tah	*iškepta*

Non-Alcoholic Drinks

Very strong black coffee seems to be the preferred daily drink
these days, although various herb or fruit teas are also popular.
Country people use all kinds of home grown products to make
beverages: camomile, beetroot and honey, sour milk, berry or fruit
marmalades, mint, birch or maple sap, acorns, rhubarb, cucumbers
and honey, vegetable juices and more.

Alcoholic drinks are also often home made from items such as
honey, fruits, vegetables, grains, bread, milk, and even horseradish.

cocoa	kah-*kah*-vah	*kakava*
coffee	kah-*vah*	*kava*
black coffee	yu-aw-*dah* kah-*vah*	*juoda kava*
coffee with cream	kah-*vah* su greah-tin-*eh*-la	*kava su grietinėlė*
coffee with ice cream topping	kah-*vah* su lad-*ais*	*kava su ledais*
fruit juice	*vais*-yew *sul*-tees	*vaisių sultys*
orange juice	ah-pal-*si*-noo *sul*-tees	*apelsinų sultys*
tomato juice	po-mi-*daw*-roo *sul*-tees	*pomidorų sultys*
soft drinks	gai-*vi*-nah-meah-yi *geh*-ri-mai	*gaivinamieji gėrimai*
tea	ahr-bah-*tah*	*arbata*
black tea	yu-aw-*daw*-yi ahr-bah-*tah*	*juodoji arbata*
tea with lemon	ahr-bah-*tah* su tsit-*ri*-nah	*arbata su citrina*
tea with milk	ahr-bah-*tah* su *peah*-nu	*arbata su pienu*
water	vahn-*du*-aw	*vanduo*
mineral water	mi-ner-*ah*-li-nis vahn-*du*-aw	*mineralinis vanduo*
soda water	gah-zu-*aw*-tahs vahn-*du*-aw	*gazuotas vanduo*

Alcoholic Drinks

beer	ah-*lus*	*alus*
local beer	*veah*-ti-nehs	*vietinės*
	gah-*mee*-baws ah-*lus*	*gamybos alus*
brandy/cognac	*kon*-yah-kahs	*konjakas*
champagne	shahm-*pah*-nahs	*šampanas*
cider	*sid*-rahs	*sidras*
cocktails	kok-*tay*-lay	*kokteiliai*
honey liqueur	*krup*-ni-kahs	*krupnikas*
mead	mi-*dus*	*midus*
whisky	*vis*-kis	*viskis*
vodka	dag-*tin*-eh	*degtinė*
red/white wine	row-*daw*-nahs/	*raudonas/*
	bahl-tahs vee-nahs	*baltas vynas*

From the Bar

chewing gum	*krahm*-taw-maw-yi	*kramtomoji guma*
	gu-mah	
chocolate	sho-ko-*lah*-dahs	*šokoladas*
cigarettes	tsi-gah-*rat*-ehs	*cigaretės*
cigars	tsi-*gah*-rahs	*cigaras*
crisps	trahsh-*ku*-chay	*traškučiai*
salted nuts	*soo*-roos reahshu-*tai*	*sūrūs reišutai*

SHOPPING

You'll find many craft shops in Vilnius where you can buy good quality handicrafts such as pottery, leather, cast iron, jewellery and amber as well as souvenirs. A number of shops stock Western goods but these are generally more expensive.

bakery	*du-aw-naws*	*duonos*
	pahr-daw-*tu*-veh/	*parduotuvė/*
	kap-*eek*-lah	*kepykla*
bookshop	knee-*gee*-nahs	*knygynas*
butcher	*meh*-sin-eh	*mėsinė*
camera shop	fo-to-ah-pah-*rah*-too	*fotoaparatų*
	pahr-daw-*tu*-veh	*parduotuvė*
clothing store	drah-*bu*-zyew	*drabužių*
	pahr-daw-*tu*-veh	*parduotuvė*
delicatessen	da-li-kah-*tas*-oo	*delikatesų*
	pahr-daw-*tu*-veh	*parduotuvė*
general store	*krow*-tu-veh	*krautuvė*
greengrocer	*vais*-yew ir	*vaisių ir*
	dahr-*zhaw*-view	*daržovių*
	pahr-daw-*tu*-veh	*parduotuvė*
kiosk	*kyos*-kahs	*kioskas*
market	*tur*-gus	*turgus*
newsagency	*laik*-rahsh-chew	*laikraščių*
	krow-tu-veh	*krautuvė*
pharmacy	*vais*-tin-eh	*vaistinė*
shoe shop	*bah*-too	*batų*
	pahr-daw-*tu*-veh	*parduotuvė*
souvenir shop	su-van-*ee*-roo	*suvenyrų*
	krow-tu-veh	*krautuvė*
supermarket	sah-*vi*-tahr-naws	*savitarnos*
	pahr-daw-*tu*-veh	*parduotuvė*

Making a Purchase

I want to buy ...	ahsh *naw*-ryu	*Aš noriu*
	nu-si-*pirk*-ti ...	*nusipirkti ...*
How much is it?	keahk kai-*nu-aw*-yah?	*Kiek kainuoja?*
Can I see it?	ahr gah-*leh*-chow ish	*Ar galėčiau iš*
	ahr-*chow*	*arčiau*
	pah-mah-*tee*-ti?	*pamatyti?*
It doesn't fit.	na-*tin*-kah	*Netinka.*
It's too ...	par-*dowg* ...	*Perdaug ...*
big	*did*-al-is	*didelis*
small	*mah*-zhahs	*mažas*
short	*trum*-pahs	*trumpas*
long	*il*-gahs	*ilgas*
loose	*lyu-aw*-sahs	*liuosas*
tight	*ahnksh*-tahs	*ankštas*

Essential Groceries

batteries	bah-*ta*-ri-yos	*baterijos*
bread	*du-aw*-nah	*duona*
butter	*sveahs*-tahs	*sviestas*
candles	*zhvah*-kehs	*žvakės*
cereal	yah-*vai*-nyay	*javainiai*
cheese	*soo*-ris	*sūris*
chocolate	sho-ko-*lah*-dahs	*šokoladas*
eggs	kyow-*shin*-ay	*kiaušiniai*
flour	*mil*-tai	*miltai*
gas cylinder	*du*-yoo bon-*kal*-eh	*dujų bonkelė*
ham	*kum*-pis	*kumpis*
honey	ma-*dus*	*medus*
insect repellent	vahbz-*jus*	*vabzdžius*
	aht-*bai*-dahn-ti	*atbaidanti*
	preah-maw-neh	*priemonė*
marmalade	u-ah-*geah*-neh	*uogienė*
margarine	mahr-gah-*ri*-nahs	*margarinas*
matches	dak-*tu*-kai	*degtukai*
milk	*peah*-nahs	*pienas*
pepper	pi-*pi*-rai	*pipirai*
rice	*ree*-zhay	*ryžiai*

salt	**drus-kah**	*druska*
shampoo	**shahm-*poo*-nahs**	*šampūnas*
soap	**mwi-lahs**	*muilas*
sugar	**tsuk-rus**	*cukrus*
toilet paper	**tu-ah-*lat*-aw**	*tualeto*
	paw-peah-ryus	*popierius*
toothpaste	**dahn-too *pahs*-tah**	*dantų pasta*
washing powder	**skahl-*bi*-maw mil-*ta*-lay**	*skalbimo milteliai*
yogurt	**yaw-gur-tahs**	*jogurtas*

LUCKY IN LOVE

There are many different fortune-telling games played in Lithuania at different times of the year. At Midsummer they usually involve a wreath of flowers. A girl stands with her back to a tree and throws her wreath over her head to try to hook it on a branch. The number of times she succeeds indicates the number of years before she marries. Pairs of wreaths labelled with boys' and girls' names are thrown into a stream and those which come together indicate who will become couples. A wreath which sinks foretells a person's imminent death. One which floats easily represents a happy life. Boys and girls link arms and jump over the dying bonfire embers. If they land still linked and unscathed, love and marriage will ensue.

At Christmas, the games involve straw from the Christmas table. The young people draw straws from under the table cloth and the length and shape of the straw drawn is said to give a clue as to the height and shape of their future spouse. Bunches of twigs are counted to see who will be married in the coming year – an even number indicates a wedding. Another clue to a person's future is gained when they turn their back to the door and throw a shoe over their shoulder in the direction of the door – if it lands with the toe end pointing towards the door, they'll leave the family home next year and marry someone who lives far away.

LITHUANIAN

Souvenirs

amber ...	gin-tah-*ri*-n(eh/ehs) ...	*gintarin(ėlės) ...* (f, sg/pl)
	gin-tah-*ri*-n(is/ay) ...	*gintarin(is/iai) ...* (m, sg/pl)
carving	draw-zhi-*neh*-lis	*drožinėlis*
cast iron	*kat*-ai	*ketai*
clogs	*klum*-pehs	*klumpeės*
folk art	lyow-deahs *man*-ahs	*liaudies menas*
handicrafts	*rahnk*-dahr-bay	*rankdarbiai*
jewellery	brahn-gan-*ee*-behs	*brangenybės*
necklace	kah-*rawl*-ay	*karoliai*
picture/ painting	pah-*vayks*-lahs	*paveikslas*
statuette	stah-tu-*leh*-leh	*statulėlė*
trinket	dir-bi-*neh*-lis	*dirbinėlis*

Clothing

blouse	pah-lai-di-*nu*-keh	*palaidinukė*
clothing	drah-*bu*-zhay	*drabužiai*
coat/overcoat	*pahl*-tahs	*paltas*
dress	suk-*nal*-eh	*suknelė*
jacket	*shvahr*-kahs	*švarkas*
jeans	*jin*-sai	*džinsai*
jumper/sweater	mags-*tin*-is	*megztinis*
shirt	mahrsh-kin-*ay*	*marškiniai*
shoes	*bah*-tai	*batai*
skirt	si-*yaw*-nahs	*sijonas*
trousers/pants	*kal*-nehs	*kelnės*
windcheater	*stroo*-keh	*striukė*

Materials

amber	gin-tah-*ri*-neh	*gintarinė* (f)
	gin-tah-*ri*-nis	*gintarinis* (m)
brass	zhal-vah-*ri*-neh	*žalvarinė* (f)
	zhahl-vah-*ri*-nis	*žalvarinis* (m)
cotton	*mad*-vil-neh	*medvilnė*
gold	owk-*si*-neh	*auksinė* (f)
	owk-*si*-nis	*auksinis* (m)
handmade	*rahn*-koo *dahr*-baw	*rankų darbo*
leather	*aw*-dah	*oda*
silk	*shil*-kahs	*šilkas*
silver	si-dah-*bri*-neh	*sidabrinė* (f)
	si-dah-*bri*-nis	*sidabrinis* (m)
wool	*vil*-nah	*vilna*

Toiletries

condoms	pre-zer-vah-*tee*-vai	*prezervatyvai*
deodorant	de-o-*daw*-rahs	*deodoras*
hairbrush	plow-koo shap-at-*ees*	*plaukų šepetys*
moisturiser	*aw*-dai	*odai*
	su-*shval*-ni-ni-maw	*sušvelninimo*
	kram-ahs	*kremas*
razor	sku-*ti*-maw-si	*skutimosi*
	pay-*lyu*-kahs	*peiliukas*
electric razor	al-ak-*tri*-nis	*elektrinis*
	skus-*tu*-vahs	*skustuvas*
sanitary napkins	*bin*-tai	*bintai*
shampoo	shahm-*poo*-nahs	*šampūnas*
shaving cream	sku-*ti*-maw-si *mwi*-lahs	*skutimosi muilas*
soap	*mwi*-lahs	*muilas*
sunblock cream	sow-lehs *kram*-ahs	*saulės kremas*
tampons	tahm-*pon*-ai	*tamponai*
toilet paper	tu-ah-*lat*-aw	*tualeto*
	paw-peah-ryus	*popierius*
toothbrush	dahn-too shap-at-*ees*	*dantų šepetys*
toothpaste	dahn-too *pahs*-tah	*dantų pasta*

Stationery & Publications

I want to buy (a/an) ...	ahsh *naw*-ryu nu-si-*pirk*-ti ...	*Aš noriu nusipirkti ...*
English-Lithuanian dictionary	*ahn*-gloo-leah-*tu*-view kahl-*baws* zhaw-*dee*-nah	*anglų-lietuvių kalbos žodyną*
guidebook in English	tu-*ris*-taw vah-*daw*-vah *ahn*-gloo kahl-*baw*-ya	*turisto vadovą anglų kalboje*
newspaper in English	*laik*-rahsh-ti *ahn*-gloo kahl-*baw*-ya	*laikraštį anglų kalboje*
novels in English	raw-*mah*-noo *ahn*-gloo kahl-*baw*-ya	*romanų anglų kalboje*

map	zham-*eh*-lah-pis	*žemėlapis*
newspaper	*laik*-rahsh-tis	*laikraštis*
paper	*paw*-peah-ryus	*popierius*
pen	tu-shi-*nu*-kahs	*tušinukas*

Photography

How much is it to process this film?	keahk kai-*nu*-aw-yah ish-*aish*-kin-ti shi *fil*-mah?	*Kiek kainuoja išaiškinti šį filmą?*
When will it be ready?	kah-*dah* bus *gah*-tah-vah?	*Kada bus gatava?*

I'd like a ... film for this camera.	ahsh naw-*reh*-chow ... *fil*-maw sham fo-to-ah-pah-*rah*-twi	*Aš norėčiau ... filmo šiam fotoaparatui.*
B&W	yu-*aw*-daw *bahl*-taw	*juodo balto*
colour	spahl-*vaw*-taw	*spalvoto*

Smoking

May I smoke?
ahr *gah*-li-mah roo-*kee*-ti?   *Ar galima rūkyti?*
A packet of cigarettes, please.
pah-*kal*-i tsi-gah-   *Pakelį*
rach-ew prah-*show*   *cigarečių, prašau.*

Colours

black	*yu-aw*-dah	*juoda*
blue	*meh*-lee-nah	*mėlyna*
brown	*ru*-dah	*ruda*
green	*zhahl*-yah	*žalia*
pink	*roo*-zhah-vah	*rūžava*
red	row-*daw*-nah	*raudona*
white	*bahl*-tah	*balta*
yellow	gal-*taw*-nah	*geltona*

Sizes & Comparisons

small	*mah*-zhahs	*mažas*
big	*did*-al-is	*didelis*
heavy	sun-*kus*	*sunkus*
light	*lang*-vahs	*lengvas*
more	dowg-*yow*	*daugiau*
less	mahzh-*yow*	*mažiau*
too much/many	par-*dowg*	*perdaug*
many	dowg	*daug*
enough	uzh-*tan*-kah	*užtenka*
a little bit	tru-*put*-i	*truputi*

LITHUANIAN

HEALTH

Where's the ...?	kur ee-*rah* ...?	*Kur yra ...?*
chemist	*vais*-ti-neh	*vaistinė*
dentist	*dahn*-too	*dantų*
	gee-dee-*taw*-yahs	*gydytojas*
doctor	gee-dee-*taw*-yahs	*gydytojas*
hospital	li-*gaw*-ni-neh	*ligoninė*

Ailments

I have (a/an) ...	mahn ...	*Man ...*
She/He has (a/an) ...	yay/yahm ...	*Jai/Jam ...*
ache	*skows*-mahs	*skausmas*
appendicitis	ah-pan-di-*tsi*-tahs	*apendicitas*
burn	nu-dag-*i*-mahs	*nudegimas*
cold	*slaw*-gah	*sloga*
fever	*kahrsh*-tis	*karštis*
flu	*grip*-ahs	*gripas*
food poisoning	ahp-si-*nu-aw*-di-yi-mahs	*apsinuodijimas*
	mais-*tu*	*maistu*
fracture	*loo*-zhis	*lūžis*
headache	gahl-*vaws*	*galvos*
	skows-mahs	*skausmas*
heart attack	shir-*deahs*	*širdies*
	preah-pu-aw-lis	*priepuolis*
infection	in-*fak*-tsi-yah	*infekcija*
nausea	veh-*mim*-ahs	*vėmimas*
sprain	ish-nah-*rin*-i-mahs/	*išnarinimas/*
	pah-tam-*pim*-ahs	*patempimas*
stroke	in-*sul*-tahs	*insultas*
swelling	ish-ti-*nim*-ahs	*ištinimas*
temperature	tam-pa-rah-*too*-rah	*temperatūra*
trauma	*trow*-mah	*trauma*
venereal disease	van-*a*-ri-neh li-*gah*	*venerinė liga*

At the Doctor

I'm sick.	ahsh sar-*gu*	*Aš sergu.*
Where does it hurt?	kur *skow*-dah?	*Kur skauda?*
It hurts here.	cha *skow*-dah	*Čia skauda.*
Could I see a female doctor?	ahr gah-*leh*-chow kon-sul-*tu-aw*-ti *maw*-ta-ri *gee*-dee-taw-yah?	*Ar galėčiau konsultuoti moterį gydytoją?*

Parts of the Body

My ... hurt(s).	mahn ... *skow*-dah	*Man ... skauda.*
back	*nu*-gah-rah	*nugara*
buttocks	seh-*dee*-neh	*sėdynė*
chest	kroo-*ti*-neh	*krūtinė*
ear	*ow*-sis	*ausis*
elbow	ahl-*koo*-neh	*alkūnė*
eye	ah-*kis*	*akis*
finger	*pirsh*-tahs	*pirštas*
foot	peh-*dah*	*pėda*
gums	*dahn*-tan-aws	*dantenos*
head	gahl-*vah*	*galva*
knee	*ka*-lis	*kelis*
leg	*kaw*-yah	*koja*
mouth	*bur*-nah	*burna*
shoulder	pat-*ees*	*petys*
skin	*aw*-dah	*oda*
stomach	*skrahn*-dis	*skrandis*
teeth	*dahn*-tees	*dantys*
throat	*gark*-leh	*gerklė*

TICKED OFF

Ticks occur in Lithuania, so it's wise to be on the lookout for them when you're out and about in a forrested area.

At the Chemist

I need medication for ...
    mahn *rayk*-yah **vais**-*too* ...   *Man reikia vaistų ...*
I have a prescription.
    ahsh tur-*yu* **rat**-sap-tah   *Aš turiu receptą.*

At the Dentist

I have a toothache.
    mahn *dahn*-tis *skow*-dah   *Man dantis skauda.*
I've lost a filling.
    ahsh a-su pah-*mat*-us/as   *Aš esu pametus/ęs*
    plom-bah   *plombą.*
I have broken a tooth.
    mahn *dahn*-tis *loo*-zhaw   *Man dantis lūžo.*
My gums hurt.
    mahn *dahn*-tan-aws *skow*-dah   *Man dantenos skauda.*
I don't want it extracted.
    ahsh ne-*naw*-ryu **kahd yis**   *Aš nenoriu, kad jis būtų*
    boo-too *ish*-trowk-tahs   *ištrauktas.*
Please give me an anaesthetic.
    prah-*show* **uzh-mah-***rin*-ki-ta   *Prašau užmarinkite.*

Useful Words & Phrases

I'm ...	ahsh a-*su* ...	*Aš esu ...*
diabetic	di-yah-*bat*-i-keh	*diabetikė* (f)
	di-yah-*bat*-i-kahs	*diabetikas* (m)
epileptic	api-*lap*-ti-keh	*epileptikė* (f)
	api-*lap*-ti-kahs	*epileptikas* (m)
asthmatic	ahs-*mah*-ti-keh	*asmatikė* (f)
	ahs-*mah*-ti-kahs	*asmatikas* (m)
I'm allergic to ...	ahsh ah-*lar*-gish-k	*Aš alergišk*
	(ah/ahs) ...	*(a/as) ...* (f/m)
antibiotics	ahn-ti-bi-*yaw*-ti-kahms	*antibiotikams*
penicillin	pan-it-si-*lin*-wi	*penicilinui*

I feel ...	yow-*chu* kahd mahn ...	*Jaučiu, kad man ...*
weak	*silp*-nah	*silpna*
dizzy	*svaigs*-tah *gahl*-vah	*svaigsta galva*

I'm pregnant.
    ahsh nehssh-*cha* — *Aš nėščia.*
I haven't had my
period for ... months.
    ahsh yow na-tur-*yu* — *Aš jau neturiu*
    meh-nas-*in*-yaw ... — *mėnesinio ...*
    meh-nas-yus — *mėnesius.*
I have my own syringe.
    ahsh tur-*yu* *sah*-vaw — *Aš turiu savo*
    shvirksh-tah — *švirkštą.*
I have a tick bite.
    mahn i-*kahn*-daw *ar*-keh — *Man įkando erkė.*

accident	na-lai-*min*-gahs	*nelaimingas*
	aht-si-ti-*kim*-ahs	*atsitikimas*
road accident	ah-*vah*-ri-yah	*avarija*
addiction	zhah-*lin*-gahs i-*praw*-tis	*žalingas įprotis*
antiseptic	daz-in-fak-*wah*-yah-	*dezinfekuojamoji*
	maw-yi maj-ah-*gah*	*medžiaga*
bandage	*tvahrs*-tis	*tvarstis*
blood pressure	*krow*-yaw	*kraujo*
	spow-*di*-mahs	*spaudimas*
blood test	*krow*-yaw	*kraujo*
	pah-*tik*-ri-ni-mahs	*patikrinimas*
injection	i-shvirksh-*tim*-ahs	*išvirkštimas*
pharmacy on duty	*bu*-din-ti *vais*-ti-neh	*budinti vaistinė*

SPECIFIC NEEDS
Disabled Travellers

I'm disabled/handicapped.
    ahsh in-vah-*li*-d(eh/ahs)   *Aš invalid(ė/as). (f/m)*

I need assistance.
    mahn *ray*-kyah pah-*gahl*-baws   *Man reikia pagalbos.*

What services do you have
for disabled people?
    kaw-*kew* pah-slow-goo joos   *Kokių paslaugų jūs teikiate*
    tay-kyah-ta in-vah-*li*-dahms?   *invalidams?*

Is there wheelchair access?
    ahr ee-*rah* pri-vah-*zhah*-vi-mahs   *Ar yra privažiavimas*
    in-vah-*li*-doo va-zhi-*meh*-lams?   *invalidų vežimėliams?*

I'm deaf. Speak more
loudly, please.
    ahsh *kur*-chas prah-*show*   *Aš kurčias. Prašau*
    kahl-*beh*-ki-ta gahr-*syow*   *kalbėkite garsiau.*

I have a hearing aid.
    ahsh na-*shaw*-yu klow-*saws*   *Aš nešioju klausos*
    ah-pah-rah-*teh*-li   *aparatėlį*

I'm blind.
    ahsh *ahk*-lahs   *Aš aklas.*

Are guide dogs permitted?
    ahr *lay*-jah-mah *vas*-tis   *Ar leidžiama vestis*
    ahk-*loo*-yoo shu-ni?   *aklųjų šunį?*

I'm mute.
    ahsh na-bi-*lees*   *Aš nebylys.*

Braille library
    brai-lyaw *shrif*-taw *knee*-goo   *Brailio šrifto knygų*
    bib-*lyaw*-ta-kah   *biblioteka*

disabled person
    in-vah-*li*-d(eh/ahs)   *invalid(ė/as) (f/m)*

guide dog
    ahk-*loo*-yoo shu-ah   *aklųjų šuo*

wheelchair
    in-vah-*li*-daw va-zhi-*meh*-lis   *invalido vežimėlis*

TIME & DATES

What time is it?	keahk dah-bahr *lai*-kaw?	*Kiek dabar laiko?*

It's ... (o'clock).	dah-*bahr* ...	*Dabar* ...
	(vah-lahn-*dah*)	*(valanda).*
2.00	ahn-*trah*	*antra*
5.30	pu-seh shash-*yew*	*pusė šešių*
11.45	ba pank-*yaw*-li-kaws	*be penkiolikos*
	dvee-lik-tah	*dvylikta*

in the morning	*ree*-taw	*ryto*
in the afternoon	paw *peah*-too	*po pietų*
in the evening	*vah*-kah-raw	*vakaro*

Days of the Week

Monday	pir-*mah*-deah-nis	*pirmadienis*
Tuesday	ahn-*trah*-deah-nis	*antradienis*
Wednesday	trach-*ah*-deah-nis	*trečiadienis*
Thursday	kat-vir-*tah*-deah-nis	*ketvirtadienis*
Friday	pank-*tah*-deah-nis	*penktadienis*
Saturday	shash-*tah*-deah-nis	*šeštadienis*
Sunday	sak-*mah*-deah-nis	*sekmadienis*

Months

January	*sow*-sis	*sausis*
February	vah-*sah*-ris	*vasaris*
March	*kaw*-vahs	*kovas*
April	bah-*lahn*-dis	*balandis*
May	gag-*uzh*-is	*gegužis*
June	bir-*zhal*-is	*birželis*
July	*leah*-pah	*liepa*
August	rug-*pew*-tis	*rugpiūtis*
September	rug-*seh*-yis	*rugsėjis*
October	*spah*-lis	*spalis*
November	*lahp*-krit-is	*lapkritis*
December	*gru*-*aw*-dis	*gruodis*

Seasons

summer	*vah*-sah-rah	*vasara*
autumn	ru-*du*-aw	*ruduo*
winter	zheah-*mah*	*žiema*
spring	pah-*vah*-sah-ris	*pavasaris*

Present

today	shan-*deahn*	*šiandien*
this morning	shi *ree*-tah	*šį rytą*
tonight	shi *vah*-kah-rah	*šį vakarą*
this week	shah sah-*vai*-ta	*sią savaitę*
this year	shays *mat*-ais	*šiais metais*
now	dah-*bahr*	*dabar*

Past

yesterday	*vah*-kahr	*vakar*
day before yesterday	uzh-vah-kahr	*užvakar*
yesterday morning	*vah*-kahr *ree*-tah	*vakar rytą*
last night	*vah*-kahr vah-kah-ra	*vakar vakare*
last week	*par*-ay-tah sah-*vai*-ta	*pereitą savaitę*
last year	*par*-ay-tais *mat*-ais	*pereitais metais*

Future

tomorrow	ree-*toy*	*rytoj*
day after tomorrow	paw-*reet*	*poryt*
tomorrow ...	ree-*toy* ...	*rytoj* ...
morning	*ree*-tah	*rytą*
afternoon	paw-*peah*-too	*popietų*
evening	vah-kah-ra	*vakare*
next week	ah-*tay*-nahn-cha sah-*vai*-ta	*ateinančią savaitę*
next year	ah-*tay*-nahn-chays *mat*-ais	*ateinančiais metais*

Dates

What date is it today?	kawk-*yah* shan-*deahn* dah-*tah*?	*Kokia šiandien data?*
It's 1 April.	shan-*deahn* pir-*mah* bah-*lahn*-jaw	*Šiandien pirma balandžio.*

During the Day

afternoon	*paw*-peah-teh	*popietė*
dawn	owsh-*rah*	*aušra*
day	deah-*nah*	*diena*
early	ahnks-*ti*	*anksti*
midnight	vi-*dur*-nahk-tis	*vidurnaktis*
morning	*ree*-tahs	*rytas*
night	nahk-*tis*	*naktis*
noon	vi-*dur*-deah-nis	*vidurdienis*
sunset	sow-*leh*-lee-dis	*saulėlydis*

Useful Words

a year ago	preahsh mat-*us*	*prieš metus*
always	vi-sah-*dah*	*visada*
at the moment	shyaw *mo*-man-tu	*šiuo momentu*
early	ahnks-*ti*	*anksti*
every day	kahs-*deahn*	*kasdien*
forever	ahm-zhin-*ai*	*amžinai*
late	veh-*lai*	*vėlai*
later on	vehl-*yow*	*vėliau*
never	neah-kah-*dah*	*niekada*
not yet	dahr na	*dar ne*
now	dah-*bahr*	*dabar*
since	nu-*aw*	*nuo*
sometimes	*kahr*-tais	*kartais*
soon	grayt	*greit*
still	dahr	*dar*
straight away	toy-*ows*	*tuojaus*

LITHUANIAN

FESTIVALS & HOLIDAYS
National Holidays

Naujų Metų Diena
  now-*yoo* mat-oo deah-*nah*
  New Years Day (1 January)

Nepriklausomybės Šventė
  nap-rik-low-saw-*mee*-behs *shvan*-teh
  Independence Day (16 February)

Velykos
  veh-*lee*-kaws
  Easter (March/April)

Valstybės Diena
  vahl-*stee*-behs deah-*nah*
  Statehood Day (6 July)

Visų Šventujų Šventė
  vi-*soo* shvan-*too*-yoo *shvan*-teh
  All Saints Day (1 November)

Kalėdos
  kah-*leh*-daws
  Christmas (25 & 26 December)

For greetings used on various holidays, see the Special Occasions section on page 199.

Festivals

National Song Festival   *Dainų šventė*

Every five years hundreds of choirs and folk dance groups from all over Lithuania and Lithuanian communities overseas converge on Vilnius to perform. You'll see many different regional folk costume styles worn by participants in this massive outdoor spectacular.

Folk music has always formed a vital part of the Lithuanian soul. During the Soviet regime a certain amount of the content of the Song Festival had to reflect a devotion to communism, but today the event has become an outpouring of the true spirit of the people.

Midsummer Night   *Joninés*

Midsummer Night was originally a pagan festival. For Christians the night of 23 June became the feast of St John the Baptist, '*Joninés*', and also the name day of all men named John ('*Jonas*').

Since pagan times, when people believed that fires would scare off witches and evil spirits which were lurking about seeking to damage their crops and livestock, bonfires were lit on hilltops on midsummer night. Sometimes burning cartwheels are hoisted on poles decorated with wreaths of herbs and flowers. The wheels symbolise the sun and the wreaths symbolise growth. Girls wear floral wreaths, which are also used in fortune-telling games.

There's a myth that the fern will produce a magic blossom on this night, and that whoever finds it will gain amazing magical powers, including the ability to understand all human and animal languages and read people's thoughts, know where treasures lie buried and foresee who will live and who will die. So at midnight everyone goes on a fern blossom hunt. Finally, those who stay around to see the sunrise will enjoy health and happiness throughout the year.

St Casimir's Fair   *Kaziuko mugé*

Lithuania has the distinction of being the last European country to accept Christianity, which was not fully established there until the 16th century. There's only one Lithuanian saint, the popular St Casimir (*Šventas Kazimieras*). He was Lithuanian by birth, a royal prince who rejected the trappings of royalty to don sack cloth and live a life of prayer and good works. He died of tuberculosis on 4 March 1483, aged 25. His best known miracle was his apparition to a small force of Lithuanian soldiers, whom he led to victory in a battle against a large Russian army in 1518. Because pilgrims used to flock to his burial place in Vilnius on St Casimir's Day, outdoor stalls were set up to cater for them. Hence the '*Kaziuko mugé*' ('Casi's' Fair) which survives to this day and is held on the Sunday closest to 4 March.

LITHUANIAN

Summer Music Festival
This happens in the historic setting of the Old Town sector of
Vilnius in July, with music, dance, street theatre, masked parades
and craft stalls for your enjoyment.

Vilnius City Days
A three-day festival in mid-September, Vilnius City Days is filled
with an amazing diversity of entertainment including folk and
international music such as country, gipsy, French, African and
jazz. There's also modern ballet and dance, circus acts, bands, a
carnival parade, children's theatre, pantomime, puppets, comedy,
satire, art exhibitions, films, disco, cabaret, ethnic food tastings,
air balloons and more!

All Souls Day *Vėlinės*
Lithuanian cemeteries are always lovingly tended and on All Souls
Day, 2 November, they're at their most beautiful.

LITHUANIAN

HORSING AROUND

Lithuania's biggest horse races take place on the
first Saturday in February at Lake Sartai in Dusetos,
near Utena.

Christmas Eve *Kūčios*

For Lithuanians the main family event of the year is Christmas Eve. The celebration centres mostly on the table which is laid with a fresh white cloth and a handful of hay, representing the hay in the manger where Jesus lay, is spread over it. The places of deceased or absent family members are marked by a fir twig and a burning candle. There are at least twelve different dishes on the table to symbolise both the twelve apostles at the Last Supper and the twelve months of the year, but no meat or alcohol. *Šližikai* (dice-sized plain biscuit cubes) with poppy-seed milk are a must.

The meal begins when the first star appears in the sky. After the head of the family says grace, a Christmas Eve holy wafer is passed around the table to be broken and shared together with everybody's good wishes to each other. It's not proper to talk or joke too loudly during this meal, which is a sacred occasion. Ancient lore says that you should try some of every dish on the table or you won't survive until next Christmas Eve.

The table is left uncleared that night, so that the souls of ancestors can come down and partake of the remaining food.

After the meal, young people play traditional fortune-telling games aimed at determining their future marriage prospects. Then it's time to gather around the decorated Christmas tree for each person to recite or sing before receiving their Christmas present.

At midnight it's customary for families to attend a midnight mass.

CROSS MY HEART

In the village of Jurgaičiai stands *Kryžių kalnas*, the Hill of Crosses. Crosses were first planted here in the middle of the 14th century. During the Soviet era, the crosses came to symbolise not only Christianity, but nationalism. The hill was bulldozed at least three times and the Red Army destroyed all the crosses, sealed off all access to the hill and dug ditches around its base, but still crosses appeared. Today the hill is covered with over 20,000 crosses of all descriptions.

LITHUANIAN

NUMBERS & AMOUNTS
Cardinal Numbers

0	*nul*-is	*nulis*
1	*veah*-nahs	*vienas*
2	du	*du*
3	trees	*trys*
4	kat-u-*ri*	*keturi*
5	pan-*ki*	*penki*
6	shash-*i*	*šeši*
7	sap-tee-*ni*	*septyni*
8	ahsh-tu-aw-*ni*	*aštuoni*
9	dav-ee-*ni*	*devyni*
10	*dash*-imt	*dešimt*
11	veah-*naw*-lik-ah	*vienuolika*
12	*dvee*-lik-ah	*dvylika*
13	*tree*-lik-ah	*trylika*
14	kat-u-*raw*-lik-ah	*keturiolika*
15	pank-*yaw*-lik-ah	*penkiolika*
16	shash-*yaw*-lik-ah	*šešiolika*
17	sap-teen-*yaw*-lik-ah	*septyniolika*
18	ahsh-tawn-*yaw*-lik-ah	*aštuoniolika*
19	dav-een-*yaw*-lik-ah	*devyniolika*
20	*dvi*-dash-imt	*dvidešimt*
21	*dvi*-dash-imt *veah*-nahs	*dvidešimt vienas*
30	*tris*-dash-imt	*trisdešimt*
40	*kat*-ur-as-dash-imt	*keturiasdešimt*
50	*pank*-as-dash-imt	*penkiasdešimt*
60	*shash*-as-dash-imt	*šešiasdešimt*
70	sap-*teen*-as-dash-imt	*septyniasdešimt*
80	ahsh-*tu*-aw-nas-dash-imt	*aštuoniasdešimt*
90	dav-*een*-as-dash-imt	*devyniasdešimt*
100	*shim*-tahs	*šimtas*
101	*shim*-tahs *veah*-nahs	*šimtas vienas*
500	pan-*ki* shim-*tai*	*penki šimtai*
1000	*tooks*-tahn-tis	*tūkstantis*
100,000	*shim*-tahs *tooks*-tahn-chew	*šimtas tūkstančių*
one million	mi-li-*yaw*-nahs	*milijonas*

Ordinal Numbers

1st	pir-*mah*/*pir*-mahs	*pirm(a/as)* (f/m)
2nd	ahn-*trah*/*ahn*-trahs	*antr(a/as)* (f/m)
3rd	trach-*ah*/*trach*-ahs	*treči(a/as)* (f/m)
4th	kat-vir-*tah*/kat-*vir*-tahs	*ketvirt(a/as)* (f/m)
5th	pank-*tah*/*pank*-tahs	*penkt(a/as)* (f/m)
6th	shash-*tah*/*shash*-tahs	*šešt(a/as)* (f/m)
7th	sap-tin-*tah*/sap-*tin*-tahs	*septint(a/as)* (f/m)
8th	ahsh-tun-*tah*/ahsh-*tun*-tahs	*aštunt(a/as)* (f/m)
9th	dav-in-*tah*/dav-*in*-tahs	*devint(a/as)* (f/m)
10th	dash-im-*tah*/dash-*im*-tahs	*dešimt(a/as)* (f/m)
11th	veah-nu-aw-lik-*tah*/ veah-*nu*-aw-lik-tahs	*vienuolikt(a/as)* (f/m)
12th	dvee-lik-*tah*/*dvee*-lik-tahs	*dvylikt(a/as)* (f/m)

Fractions

1/4	kat-vir-*tah*-dah-lis	*ketvirtadalis*
1/3	*trach*-dah-lis	*trečdalis*
1/2	*pu*-seh	*pusė*
3/4	trees kat-vir-*chay*	*trys ketvirčiai*

Useful Words

calculate	ahp-skai-*chu*-aw-ti	*apskaičiuoti*
a little (amount)	*tru*-pu-ti	*truputi*
double	dvi-gu-*bah*/ *dvi*-gu-bahs	*dvigub(a/as)* (f/m)
a dozen	*tu*-zin-ahs	*tuzinas*
few	na-*dowg*	*nedaug*
less	mahzh-*yow*	*mažiau*
many	dowg	*daug*
more	dowg-*yow*	*daugiau*
once	*veah*-nah *see*-ki	*vieną sykį*
pair	*paw*-rah	*pora*
percent	*nu*-aw-shim-tis	*nuošimtis*
some	*kal*-at-ahs	*keletas*
too much	par-*dowg*	*perdaug*
twice	du *seek*-yus	*du sykius*

ABBREVIATIONS

ež.	*ežeras*	lake
g.	*gatvė*	street
ir t.t.	*ir taip toliau*	and so on/etc
kl.	*kalnas*	mountain/hill
LAL	*Lietuvos Avialinijos*	Lithuanian Airlines
mst./m.	*miestas*	town/city
pvz.	*pavyzdžiui*	for example

EMERGENCIES

| Help! | *gal*-beh-ki-te! | *Gelbėkite!* |

It's an emergency.
   krit-ish-kah pah-deh-*tis*   *Kritiška padėtis.*
There's been an accident.
   i-*vee*-kaw na-*lai*-meh   *Įvyko nelaimė.*

Call ...!	ish-*show*-ki-ta ...!	*Išsaukite ...!*
a doctor	*gee*-dee-taw-yah	*gydytoją*
an ambulance	*gray*-tah-yah	*greitąją*
	pah-*gahl*-bah	*pagalbą*
the police	paw-*lit*-si-yah	*policiją*

Stop it!	nu-*stawk*!	*Nustok!*
Go away!	ayk shah-*lin*!	*Eik šalin!*
Watch out!	*sow*-gaw-kis!	*Saugokis!*
Thief!	vah-*gis*!	*Vagis!*
Fire!	*gais*-rahs!	*Gaisras!*

I've been raped.
   mah-*na* ish-preah-vahr-   *Mane išprievartavo.*
   tah-vaw
I've been robbed.
   mah-*na* ahp-vaw-geh   *Mane apvogė.*
I'm ill.
   ahsh sar-*gu*   *Aš sergu.*
I'm lost.
   ahsh pah-*klee*-d(usi/as)   *Aš paklyd(usi/ęs).*
I'll get the police.
   ahsh pah-*showk*-syu   *Aš pašauksiu*
   paw-*lit*-si-yah   *policiją.*
Where's the police station?
   kur paw-*lit*-si-yaws   *Kur policijos*
   nu-*aw*-vah-dah?   *nuovada?*
Where are the toilets?
   kur tu-ah-*lat*-ai?   *Kur tualetai?*
Could you help me please?
   ahr gah-*leh*-tu-met mahn   *Ar galėtumėt man*
   pah-*deh*-ti?   *padėti?*

LITHUANIAN

Could I please use the telephone?
  ahr gah-*leh*-chow pah-now-*daw*-ti *Ar galėčiau panaudoti*
  te-le-*fo*-nah?   *telefoną?*
I want to contact my
embassy/consulate.
  ahsh *naw*-ryu su-si-*seahk*-ti su   *Aš noriu susisiekti su savo*
  sah-vaw ahm-bah-*sah*-dah/   *ambasada/konsulatu.*
  kon-su-*lah*-tu
I speak English.
  ahsh kahl-*bu* ahn-glish-kai   *Aš kalbu angliškai.*
I didn't realise I was doing
anything wrong.
  ahsh na-*su*-vawk-yow kahd ahsh   *Aš nesuvokiau,*
  kah-nors *blaw*-gaw dahr-*yow*   *kad aš kąnors blogo dariau.*
I didn't do it.
  ahsh taw na-pah-dahr-*yow*   *Aš to nepadariau.*
I'm sorry.
  ahsh aht-si-prah-*show*   *Aš atsiprašau.*
My blood group is (A, B, O, AB)
positive/negative.
  mah-naw *krow*-yaw   *Mano kraujo*
  gru-*pu-aw*-teh   *grupuotė*
  ee-*rah* (ah beh aw ah-beh)   *yra (A, B, O, AB)*
  po-zi-tee-*vus*/*nay*-gyah-mahs   *pozityvus/neigiamas.*

I've lost my ...   ahsh *pah*-mach-ow   *Aš pamačiau*
                    sah-*vaw* ...   *savo ...*
  bags   lah-gah-*min*-us   *lagaminus*
  money   *pi*-ni-gus   *pinigus*
  passport *pah*-sah   *pasą*

INDEX

NOTES

Phrasebooks

L onely Planet phrasebooks are packed with essential words and phrases to help travellers communicate with the locals. With colour tabs for quick reference, an extensive vocabulary and use of script, these handy pocket-sized language guides cover day-to-day travel situations.

- handy pocket-sized books
- easy to understand Pronunciation chapter
- clear & comprehensive Grammar chapter
- romanisation alongside script to allow ease of pronunciation
- script throughout so users can point to phrases for every situation
- full of cultural information and tips for the traveller

'...vital for a real DIY spirit and attitude in language learning'
– *Backpacker*
'the phrasebooks have good cultural backgrounders and offer solid advice for challenging situations in remote locations'
– *San Francisco Examiner*

Arabic (Egyptian) • Arabic (Moroccan) • Australian *(Australian English, Aboriginal and Torres Strait languages)* • Baltic States *(Estonian, Latvian, Lithuanian)* • Bengali • Brazilian • Burmese • British *(English, dialects, Scottish Gaelic, Welsh)* • Cantonese • Central Asia *(Kazakh, Kyrgyz, Pashto, Tajik, Tashkorghani, Turkmen, Uyghur, Uzbek & others)* • Central Europe *(Czech, German, Hungarian, Polish, Slovak, Slovene)* • Costa Rica Spanish • Eastern Europe *(Albanian, Bulgarian, Croatian, Czech, Hungarian, Macedonian, Polish, Romanian, Serbian, Slovak, Slovene)* • East Timor *(Tetun, Portuguese)* • Egyptian Arabic • Ethiopian *(Amharic)* • Europe *(Basque, Catalan, Dutch, French, German, Greek, Irish, Italian, Maltese, Portuguese, Scottish Gaelic, Spanish, Turkish, Welsh)* • Farsi *(Persian)* • Fijian • French • German • Greek • Hebrew • Hill Tribes *(Lahu, Akha, Lisu, Mong, Mien & others)* • Hindi/Urdu • Indonesian • Italian • Japanese • Korean • Lao • Latin American Spanish • Malay • Mandarin • Mongolian • Moroccan Arabic • Nepali • Papua New Guinea • Pidgin • Pilipino (Tagalog) • Polish • Portuguese • Quechua • Russian • Scandinavian *(Danish, Faroese, Finnish, Icelandic, Norwegian, Swedish)* • South-East Asia *(Burmese, Indonesian, Khmer, Lao, Malay, Tagalog Pilipino, Thai, Vietnamese)* • South Pacific *(Fijian, Hawaiian, Kanak languages, Maori, Niuean, Rapanui, Rarotongan Maori, Samoan, Tahitian, Tongan & others)* • Spanish *(Castilian, also includes Catalan, Galician & Basque)* • Sri Lanka • Swahili • Thai • Tibetan • Turkish • Ukrainian • USA *(US English, vernacular, Native American, Hawaiian)* • Vietnamese

COMPLETE LIST OF LONELY PLANET BOOKS

AFRICA Africa on a shoestring • Cairo • Cape Town • East Africa • Egypt • Ethiopia, Eritrea & Djibouti • The Gambia & Senegal • Healthy Travel Africa • Kenya • Malawi • Morocco • Mozambique • Read This First: Africa • South Africa, Lesotho & Swaziland • Southern Africa • Southern Africa Road Atlas • Tanzania, Zanzibar & Pemba • Trekking in East Africa • Tunisia • Watching Wildlife East Africa • Watching Wildlife Southern Africa • West Africa • World Food Morocco • Zimbabwe, Botswana & Namibia

AUSTRALIA & THE PACIFIC Aboriginal Australia & the Torres Strait Islands • Auckland • Australia • Australia Road Atlas • Bushwalking in Australia • Cycling Australia • Cycling New Zealand • Fiji • Healthy Travel Australia, NZ and the Pacific • Islands of Australia's Great Barrier Reef • Melbourne • Micronesia • New Caledonia • New South Wales & the ACT • New Zealand • Northern Territory • Outback Australia • Out to Eat – Melbourne • Papua New Guinea • Queensland • Rarotonga & the Cook Islands • Samoa • Solomon Islands • South Australia • South Pacific • Sydney • Sydney Condensed • Tahiti & French Polynesia • Tasmania • Tonga • Tramping in New Zealand • Vanuatu • Victoria • Walking in Australia • Watching Wildlife Australia • Western Australia

CENTRAL AMERICA & THE CARIBBEAN Bahamas, Turks & Caicos • Baja California • Bermuda • Central America on a shoestring • Costa Rica • Cuba • Dominican Republic & Haiti • Eastern Caribbean • Guatemala • Guatemala, Belize & Yucatán: La Ruta Maya • Havana • Healthy Travel Central & South America • Jamaica • Mexico • Mexico City • Panama • Puerto Rico • Read This First: Central & South America • World Food Mexico • Yucatán

EUROPE Amsterdam • Amsterdam Condensed • Andalucía • Austria • Barcelona • Belgium & Luxembourg • Berlin • Britain • Brussels, Bruges & Antwerp • Budapest • Canary Islands • Central Europe • Copenhagen • Corfu & the Ionians • Corsica • Crete • Crete Condensed • Croatia • Cycling Britain • Cycling France • Cyprus • Czech & Slovak Republics • Denmark • Dublin • Eastern Europe • Edinburgh • England • Estonia, Latvia & Lithuania • Europe on a shoestring • Finland • Florence • France • Frankfurt Condensed • Georgia, Armenia & Azerbaijan • Germany • Greece • Greek Islands • Hungary • Iceland, Greenland & the Faroe Islands • Ireland • Istanbul • Italy • Krakow • Lisbon • The Loire • London • London Condensed • Madrid • Malta • Mediterranean Europe • Milan, Turin & Genoa • Moscow • Mozambique • Munich • The Netherlands • Normandy • Norway • Out to Eat – London • Paris • Paris Condensed • Poland • Portugal • Prague • Provence & the Côte d'Azur • Read This First: Europe • Rhodes & the Dodecanese • Romania & Moldova • Rome • Rome Condensed • Russia, Ukraine & Belarus • Scandinavian & Baltic Europe • Scotland • Sicily • Slovenia • South-West France • Spain • St Petersburg • Sweden • Switzerland • Trekking in Spain • Tuscany • Venice • Vienna • Walking in Britain • Walking in France • Walking in Ireland • Walking in Italy • Walking in Spain • Walking in Switzerland • Western Europe • World Food France • World Food Ireland • World Food Italy • World Food Spain

COMPLETE LIST OF LONELY PLANET BOOKS

INDIAN SUBCONTINENT Bangladesh • Bhutan • Delhi • Goa • Healthy Travel Asia & India • India • Indian Himalaya • Karakoram Highway • Kerala • Mumbai (Bombay) • Nepal • Pakistan • Rajasthan • Read This First: Asia & India • South India • Sri Lanka • Tibet • Trekking in the Indian Himalaya • Trekking in the Karakoram & Hindukush • Trekking in the Nepal Himalaya

ISLANDS OF THE INDIAN OCEAN Madagascar &Comoros • Maldives • Mauritius, Réunion & Seychelles

MIDDLE EAST & CENTRAL ASIA Bahrain, Kuwait & Qatar • Central Asia • Dubai • Iran • Israel & the Palestinian Territories • Istanbul • Istanbul to Cairo on a Shoestring • Istanbul to Kathmandu • Jerusalem • Jordan • Lebanon • Middle East • Oman & the United Arab Emirates • Syria • Turkey • World Food Turkey • Yemen

NORTH AMERICA Alaska • Boston • Boston Condensed • British Colombia • California & Nevada • California Condensed • Canada • Chicago • Deep South • Florida • Great Lakes • Hawaii • Hiking in Alaska • Hiking in the USA • Honolulu • Las Vegas • Los Angeles • Louisiana & The Deep South • Miami • Montreal • New England • New Orleans • New York City • New York City Condensed • New York, New Jersey & Pennsylvania • Oahu • Out to Eat – San Francisco • Pacific Northwest • Puerto Rico • Rocky Mountains • San Francisco • San Francisco Map • Seattle • Southwest • Texas • Toronto • USA • Vancouver • Virginia & the Capital Region • Washington DC • World Food Deep South, USA • World Food New Orleans

NORTH-EAST ASIA Beijing • China • Hiking in Japan • Hong Kong • Hong Kong Condensed • Hong Kong, Macau & Guangzhou • Japan • Korea • Kyoto • Mongolia • Seoul • Shanghai • South-West China • Taiwan • Tokyo • World Food – Hong Kong

SOUTH AMERICA Argentina, Uruguay & Paraguay • Bolivia • Brazil • Buenos Aires • Chile & Easter Island • Colombia • Ecuador & the Galapagos Islands • Healthy Travel Central & South America • Peru • Read This First: Central & South America • Rio de Janeiro • Santiago • South America on a shoestring • Santiago • Trekking in the Patagonian Andes • Venezuela

SOUTH-EAST ASIA Bali & Lombok • Bangkok • Cambodia • Hanoi • Healthy Travel Asia & India • Ho Chi Minh City • Indonesia • Indonesia's Eastern Islands • Jakarta • Java • Laos • Malaysia, Singapore & Brunei • Myanmar (Burma) • Philippines • Read This First: Asia & India • Singapore • South-East Asia on a shoestring • Thailand • Thailand's Islands & Beaches • Thailand, Vietnam, Laos & Cambodia Road Atlas • Vietnam • World Food Thailand • World Food Vietnam

Also available; Journeys travel literature, illustrated pictorials, calendars, diaries, Lonely Planet maps and videos. For more information on these series and for the complete range of Lonely Planet products and services, visit our website at **www.lonelyplanet.com**.